T0174268

Developing Creative Content for Games

Developing Creative Content for Games

Greg Johnson

CRC Press
Taylor & Francis Group
Boca Raton London New York

CRC Press is an imprint of the
Taylor & Francis Group, an **informa** business

AN A K PETERS BOOK

CRC Press
Taylor & Francis Group
6000 Broken Sound Parkway NW, Suite 300
Boca Raton, FL 33487-2742

Printed on acid-free paper

International Standard Book Number-13: 978-0-367-13788-5 (Hardback)
978-1-4987-7766-7 (Paperback)

Library of Congress Cataloging-in-Publication Data

Names: Johnson, Greg, 1969- author.
Title: Developing creative content for games / Greg Johnson.
Description: Boca Raton, FL : Taylor & Francis, 2019. | "A CRC title, part of the
Taylor & Francis imprint, a member of the Taylor & Francis Group, the academic
division of T&F Informa plc"-- Title page.
Identifiers: LCCN 2018043482| ISBN 9780367137885 (hardback : alk. paper) |
ISBN 9781498777667 (pbk. : alk. paper)
Subjects: LCSH: Electronic games--Design. | Computer games--Design. |
Computer games--Programming. | Computer graphics.
Classification: LCC GV1469.15 .J65 2019 | DDC 794.8--dc23
LC record available at https://lccn.loc.gov/2018043482

Visit the Taylor & Francis Web site at
http://www.taylorandfrancis.com

and the CRC Press Web site at
http://www.crcpress.com

Contents

Preface

This book is the direct result of the need for a non-technical method for teaching complex concepts in game design. Tasked with teaching introductory level students, game design, and development concepts to students who do not yet possess the technical skills that would allow them to execute their ideas in a video game engine, I developed the material in this book as the answer. My solution was to use table-top role-playing games as an enjoyable way to access a wide variety of game design and development topics. The resulting course was a smash success, and after polishing the material for a few years I thought it would be worthwhile to author a book on the subject for broader distribution of the approach. Nothing teaches you the material as well as having to teach it to others, and I found the act of putting my lessons into writing to be an education in itself. A wealth of practical advice was to be found inside old issues of *Dragon* Magazine and the website *Gamasutra*, plus plenty of additional books, websites, and journals. My thanks to all of those old game masters who wrote down their techniques in various advice columns, how to articles, and GMing guides; they provided the foundation upon which a lot of video games have been built.

This book answers a particular need in the teaching of games to students; how does one bridge the gap from game design theory typically taught with board games to creating hyper-real first-person shooter video games? There is a vast gap between these two ends of the game design and development spectrum, yet little in the way of educational material on how to span the difference between the two.

Game studies are usually taught with a variety of board games while "AAA" video games require extensive knowledge of 3-D software and a game engine just to get started. Students are expected to manage the jump from working on board games to building high-end video games largely on their own. For many years I have utilized a retro-clone of the *Dungeons & Dragons* role-playing game to introduce students to some of the more complicated aspects of game development, mechanics, narrative, reward systems, and character development without resort to any of the advanced technical knowledge working with a 3-D game engine requires. The results in my classes to date have been outstanding. As one of my colleagues with many years as a producer of video games under his belt has commented, "every designer I've ever known played some form of D&D." Hopefully, this book will share that process with you.

Thanks are due to my children who had to put up with me while I wrote this book. A very special thank you is due my long suffering wife for putting her life on hold and editing it into a digestible form. More thanks should be shared amongst all of my students who enjoyed the lectures that went into the formation of this work. I hope you find the material herein enjoyable and useful.

Greg Johnson

Author

Greg Johnson is a Professor of Game Development & Computer Art. For more 20 years Greg has had the privilege of teaching thousands of students a diverse array of courses including game design, character development, digital sculpture, texturing, programming, 3D modeling, rigging, and 3D animation. This book is a compilation of material developed from Greg's introduction to game development lectures, as well as some of the good advice regarding game development that Greg has managed to garner in that time. He is the proud game designer and author of the ENnie-nominated TOONZY!, the cartoon role-playing game (www.ToonzyTheGame.com), as well as a member of the Guild of Natural Science Illustrators and the Association of Science Fiction Illustrators. In addition Greg has worked as a 3D artist, consultant, and freelancers for decades. Greg's work is available online at www.gregtheartist.com.

Chapter **1**

Introduction

Overview

This book provides aspiring game designers the chance to develop playable game settings, characters, and narratives without getting bogged down by digital production details. All you need is a notebook and a pen or a user-friendly text editor for your computer or tablet. Making a full 3-D video game is too complicated a task for one person to do by themselves any more. It takes a massive team of people a year or more to put together a professional looking title. The sheer amount of information required to teach one person the entire process would take up a small library. The expensive and difficult to use software needed to create a professional 3-D video game such as Autodesk Maya, Adobe Photoshop, Pixologic's ZBrush, and the Unreal game engine to name a few, are NOT required to utilize this book. This book will teach you about game design and the complicated process of game development as far as being a designer is concerned. We are going to use a tabletop role-playing game, an RPG in geek speak, for our rules and system mechanics and develop a playable scenario or adventure that will utilize all of the traditional elements found in a full-fledged game development document. What you will end up with is a comprehensive guidebook to your own game that you can playtest with your friends, or maybe even sell as a viable product, without having to hire an entire company's worth of professionals to see your vision come to fruition. Along the way you will learn about game design, narrative, mechanics, setting and character development; all things a good game designer has to know to get a job.

Why This Book

This book fills an essential need in teaching game design—namely a way of teaching a lot of very complicated concepts such as character development, world creation, narrative production, gameplay development, and game balance without getting absorbed by the HUGE overhead involved in creating a digital video game. Trying to teach all of these design elements while simultaneously engaged in producing a proper video game usually fails terribly. Students either get so caught up in developing (and fixing) the digital side of things that they severely neglect the design aspects of their game, or their inability to manage the technical aspects of their project prevent them from ever seeing things through to fruition. Then there are the added challenges of working in large groups, asset management, and setting realistic goals and production schedules that can hinder digital video game production or even cause it to come to a screeching halt. While a group of students can produce a professional looking video game, it is a challenging task indeed and only suitable for students who have previously gone through a lot of digital and non-digital training. The flip side of teaching game design is that most introductory classes focus on relatively simple board or card games. While these examples cover plenty of ground, issues such as setting development, characterization, plot, and narrative typically get short shrift if included at all in board game centered introductory classes. A way of introducing all of the wide variety of design topics and issues without getting bogged down by technical production issues was needed. Something was needed that would allow an individual or small group of people to learn about all of the problematic design issues involved in producing a game without requiring a year or two of digital production and programming expertise first. This book solves these dilemmas.

What This Book Teaches

This book teaches you how to create the complicated storylines, settings, characters, plots, and narratives found in modern video games by using a pen and paper role-playing game as a stand-in for a 3-D video game engine. It isn't as crazy as it first might seem. The video game industry owes an enormous amount to these role-playing game systems (Bartle, 1990b; Cross, 2015a,b; Harris, 2009, 1; Radoff, 2012). Indeed, many of the massively multiplayer online role-playing games or MMORPGs popular today are the spiritual relations of tabletop role-playing games and bear a strong family resemblance to these earlier rule sets (Bartle, 1990b; Pepe, 2014; Radoff, 2012). This approach allows us to cover ground that a standard introduction to game design book or course would typically gloss over or miss entirely with their focus on board games and other more philosophical stuff.

Learn by Doing Approach

I am a firm believer in a learn by doing method. With that in mind, you will be creating a playable game world, characters, and the story to go with it using this book. The adventure and setting you will create will be something that you can play through and test to see how well your ideas, story and setting hold up as a game. Each one of these different design elements will be covered in depth by a separate chapter, and I will provide examples of this material, how it should be written up, constructed, played, and relevant examples from professional games. Using the material and examples provided, you will create your adventure, plot, narrative, characters, setting, and story. Afterward, you can playtest your work with your friends and family and even publish it yourself or start to turn it into a real video game!

A Little Job Advice

Game design is a small field with not a whole lot of people in it. It helps to know people if you want a job in this industry. One of the best ways to accomplish this is to go to the "Game Developers Conference" held each year in San Francisco. It is a fun event, and practically everyone from the entire video game industry shows up. If you'd rather focus on table-top role-playing games, then the conference to go to is the "GenCon" convention in Indianapolis. You can find info about these events by going directly to their websites at www.gdconf.com and www.gencon.com. If you are serious about game design or tabletop RPGs, I strongly suggest that you visit these conferences.

Getting Started

Start thinking about the sort of game adventure you want to build. Chapter 5 will go through the process of ideation and creativity thoroughly, but it is never too soon to begin writing down some ideas. Go out and buy a small notebook and keep it with you all the time. Whenever you see or hear something interesting—write it down—and see if it inspires you to develop an idea you wish to pursue further. Once you've started having a few game ideas, it is time to learn how to play tabletop role-playing games so you can start adding some substance to your proposals.

Assignment

Read over the Table of Contents and skim through this book. Make sure that you visit the website for this book at: http://gregtheartist.com/dccfg.htm.

Familiarize yourself with this book and download the relevant materials from the website that you will need.

Chapter 2

A Few Definitions, Systems, Mechanics and Dynamics

What Is a Tabletop Role-Playing Game?

A tabletop role-playing game (RPG) is a type of game where each player assumes the persona of a specific imaginary character (Kim, 2009). Unlike the make-believe games played by children, each character in these games is defined by a definitive set of rules and the game is narrated and moderated by a judge usually referred to as a game master (Gygax and Arneson, 1981, B3–B4). The players verbally describe or act out what their characters do in the face of the challenges and situations the game master places them in. Each participant decides and describes what their character does and says. The game master determines the adventure beforehand, describes the game world and its inhabitants to the players and helps decide the result of each player's actions during gameplay (Kim, 2009). The players then react to this information by choosing new actions to do or dialogue to say, and then the cycle of play continues with each participant taking their actions in turn. Action resolution is determined with the help of various types of dice which are used to randomly decide the success or failure of each action (Gygax, 1979a, 9–10).

What Is an MMORPG?

A massively multiplayer online role-playing game, frequently abbreviated as MMORPG, is a video game in which the player controls a fictional character and gets to play with an enormous number of other players all at the same time in a large and vibrant game world. The player can interact, cooperate or compete with a vast assortment of other players from across the globe. The settings of this sort of video game are persistent and tend to evolve and change over time as their inhabitants continue to play them. MMORPGs are a billion dollar per year industry (Tassi, 2014).

What Do Tabletop Role-Playing Games and MMORPGs Have in Common?

Tabletop role-playing games, or TTRPG, and MMORPGs have an enormous amount of material in common (Jon, 2010, 97). MMORPGs evolved out of text-based multiuser domains or MUDs in the 1990s (Castronova, 2006, 10, 291; Jon, 2010, 98). Combining elements of computer role-playing games also known as CRPGs and their MUD predecessors MMORPGs provides the player with control over a graphical character in a fictional multi-user world setting (Van Eck, 2010). All of these types of computer games, MMORPGs, CRPGs, and MUDs, owe a lot to their relative, the tabletop RPG, whose influence can be felt in the elements of character progression, advancement, story, game world, terminology and game mechanics they all possess (Church, 2012; Harris, 2009, 1; Indvik, 2012; Thoman, 2014). MMORPGs, MUDs, and TTRPGs also share a level of social interaction within the game and have their own group identity, culture, and lingo (Jon, 2010, 97; Scott, 2012). All of this makes complete sense when you realize that MMORPGs grew out of CRPGs and MUDs which in turn were often adaptations of TTRPGs (Indvik, 2012). This shared lineage and influence makes understanding traditional table-top RPGs immensely useful in the task of designing the various elements that make up modern MMORPGs and CRPGs (Jon, 2010, 97–98).

Regarding System Design, Game Mechanics, and Dynamics

System design is the act of designing various mechanics and rules to manage all of the in-game actions desired for the game (Hiwiller, 2011). Game systems create game mechanics and rules that in turn generate gameplay dynamics that players experience (Hunicke et al., 2004). The mechanics and rules that make up a game should be easy to understand, consistent, well balanced and extensible. Game systems include systems of money used to purchase in-game items, magic, combat and character generation to name a few. These game systems, in turn, require rules and mechanics to describe how each of these systems works. Most of the content of a typical table-top role-playing game, or TTRPG, consists of these rules which for some games can run to the dozens of books and thousands of pages. A gigantic set of rules doesn't necessarily make for a very good game though. System design is an extraordinarily complicated task. It is practically impossible to design a game system that doesn't break under some circumstances or contain some flaw or limitation in its mechanics. Fortunately, there is a vibrant array of existing role-playing games that have already been thoroughly playtested. These existing systems are perfectly suitable for allowing us to craft our narrative, create a setting, and pursue character development for our project. Reading through and understanding these existing games also does wonders for improving your skill at game design, creating new game systems, and crafting new game mechanics. Once you know how these games work you can begin to expand upon them, build your own unique game mechanics, and eventually design your own fully functional pen and paper role-playing game. While we don't need to go over every aspect of system design, game mechanics, and dynamics for this book, we do need to understand the tools used to build them.

What Do System Design and Game Mechanics Mean?

System design is the set of tools used to design, create and manage game content. Proper system design helps you create solid game mechanics which in turn builds enjoyable game dynamics as each player interacts with the game (Hunicke et al., 2004). Game mechanics are the rules that govern your game (Sicart, 2008). These rules provide a means for players to enact and interact with the various systems the game designer(s) have included in the game. As Achterman explains on the website Gamasutra in his article "The Craft of Game Systems: General Guidelines", proper system design requires that your rules be comprehensible, consistent, predictable, extensible, and elegant. The rules need to be understandable, so you know how to adjust, tweak and modify them to get the results you want. Understandable rules also help your players be able to design their characters in ways that provide the type of experience that they are looking for. An elegant rule is one which has a logical and aesthetic sense of appeal to it. The third edition of *Dungeons & Dragons*, for example, used a simple twenty-sided dice roll, a d20, for almost every mechanic in the game and thereby created an excellent and appealing system (Wizards RPG Team, 2012). Achterman reminds us that systems should provide a substantial level of consistency and predictability in the game world you create (Acterman, 2011). Once you decide that magic works a certain way or that level progression occurs in a particular manner, this pattern should be maintained. If the damage done by your wizard's magical zap attack does one four-sided dice worth of damage at first level, then at second level it should do two dice of damage or some different sort of progression just so long as the rules don't feel arbitrary to the player. There should always be a natural feeling to the cause and effect relationships between your various game elements so that the player never feels out of sorts or cheated by the game. Developing this sort of regular process to your rules and mechanics will have the added benefit of making it much more extensible. For example, having established the rules of magic already in the game means that extending it a bit further won't present any serious problem.

System Goals

Achterman explains system goals as the rules and systems required for your game. You must know what your goals are (Achterman, 2011). What is the point of your game? What sort of game experience are you trying to create for your players? Don't worry about fiddly details. Focus on the larger picture of what your game is going to be like. Think about the types of decisions the players will make and what the overall appeal of your game is. After you have decided upon the broad strokes that will compose your masterpiece you can move on to filling in the details. Each task the player will be asked to complete must be set out and described as well as the consequences of success and failure. The risk to reward ratio always needs to be considered. Each aspect of the game must be rewarding to the player in some mechanical, emotional, or story form. While doing this, you must never forget the big picture and become lost in the details.

System Components

A game system consists of parameters, rules, and content (Achterman, 2011). These are defined as:

> Parameters: Parameters are the values that your game systems use to simulate your game, such as health, movement speed, weight, mana cost, critical hit chance, and other values that the game must track.
>
> Rules: Rules are the functions and formulas that determine the results of actions and events in your game. Rules include things like how combat damage gets calculated, how character statistics change when they level up, and how random loot is determined.
>
> Content: Content is all things in your game, including characters, items, monsters, spells, talents, and everything else. Each type of content has parameters that define it, like damage for a weapon, or attributes for a character.

Achterman (2011)

The first step in designing your system's components is to choose what parameters your game will use (Achterman, 2011). Once you have decided what parameters the game will use you can determine if and how these parameters will change over time. In a simple game like *Pac-Man*, the parameters that control the main character, the Pac-man, don't change at all. The speed parameter varies for the ghosts that chase him as do the mazes where gameplay occurs. In a more complex game like *D&D*, the character's health, abilities, spells, and power level increase steadily over time as the character continues to gather experience (Gygax, 1978a, 18–32; Wizards RPG Team, 2012). The content of the game changes as a result of the character's power progression, so the player remains engaged (Gygax, 1979a, 177–179; Wizards RPG Team, 2003, 48–50). Chasing goblins around a field next to the home base doesn't challenge a twentieth level warrior. Powerful characters need powerful enemies to maintain the thrill of playing the game (Wizards RPG Team, 2003, 48). The story, monsters, treasures, spells, and abilities in the game should be as exciting and in-depth as you can make them (Achterman, 2011, 43–48).

Arcs and Loops

The arc and loop model for understanding complex game mechanics is a useful tool for designing game systems initially described by Daniel Cook in his Lostgarden blog. An arc begins with the player's idea on how to accomplish a task in the game. That idea is implemented as an action, which is then fed into the game system for resolution. The player then receives feedback on the result of their action as interpreted through the rules of the game. The player can now reflect upon the feedback they have received and choose what to try and do next. A loop functions precisely like an arc except that after receiving the feedback the player provides more input into the loop and the cycle repeats. An arc can feed into a loop or another arc, just as a loop can feed into itself, another loop, or an arc. All events in the game can be deconstructed into their component arcs and loops. Some arcs and loops are quite large and describe overarching elements of the game while others precisely model finite events. Large arcs and loops can be composed of numerous smaller arcs and loops. Breaking down complex interactions into quantifiable and discreet segments makes designing complex systems much more straightforward to understand.

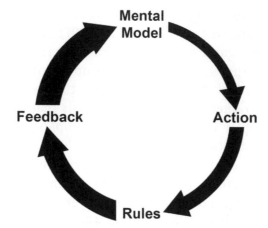

Basic loop structure; Idea > Action > Rules > Feedback > Mental model

An arc functions just like a loop except that after receiving the feedback the cycle ends.

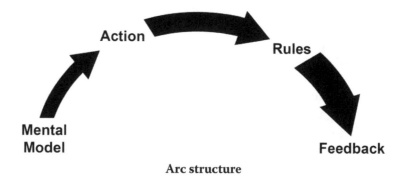

Arc structure

Both of these structures can link into either a new loop or arc (Cook, 2012).

How Arcs and Loops Apply to RPGs

The arc and loops model can be used to understand table-top role-playing game mechanics as well as video games. The primary loop of an RPG consists of the game master, or GM, describing a situation. The players then tell the GM how they respond to that situation. The GM then describes the result of the player's actions and the loop continues until some stopping point occurs. This cycle of play is the fundamental loop of a role-playing game and contains within itself many smaller, more specific loops which are used to describe the various actions in the game.

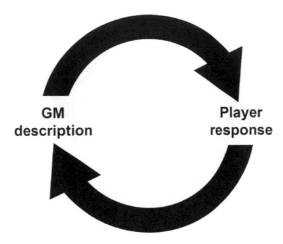

Role-playing game basic loop

How Combat Loops Work (D20)

As described in Chapter 8 of the *Dungeons & Dragons 3.5 Player's Handbook*, arcs and loops are used to resolve combat between different opponents. At the core of the combat resolution system is how to determine whether or not the attacker manages to hit the defender and deal damage to that opponent during combat.

→Begin loop

1. The attacker rolls one twenty-sided dice (the standard notation for this is 1d20) and adds in any modifiers due to strength, size, and experience. This action is an attack roll.
2. Compare the result to the defender's defense value, in d20 this is called the defender's armor class. Calculate the armor class by adding together any modifiers from armor, size, and ability modifiers plus a default value of ten. The ten gets added in to make the mechanics work—otherwise, attacks would be too powerful and hit too frequently in this game system.
3. If the attack roll meets or exceeds the defender's armor class, then the attack succeeds, and we can then calculate how much damage was done to the defender. If the attack roll isn't equal to or greater than the defender's armor class, it was a miss, and there is no result.
4. Repeat this loop until combat ends.

→End of loop

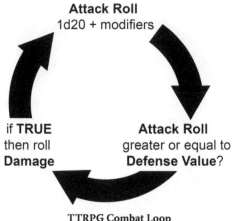

Attack Roll
1d20 + modifiers

if **TRUE**
then roll
Damage

Attack Roll
greater or equal to
Defense Value?

TTRPG Combat Loop

Once the attack is resolved the loop starts over again, except this time, the roles are reversed. The previous attacker now defends while the former defender is now on the attack. This loop continues with the combatants taking turns attacking and defending until one of the combatants is killed, knocked out, or disengages from combat. A combat round is a full cycle that includes a turn for each participant in the battle. Note the circular or loop connotations in the name! An attack loop such as this can be found in practically every role-playing game ever made although the particular method of calculating the attack varies considerably between systems.

Surprise and Initiative Arc

There is more to combat in an RPG than just hitting things of course! First, you have to determine surprise, an arc itself, then decide who goes first using another arc, and only then can the combatants move in and engage each other and begin the combat loop (Wizards RPG Team, 2012, 133–160; Gygax, 1979a, 61–72; St. Andre and Steve, 1981, 36; Norvelle, 2016, 75–79; Siembieda, 1983, 43–48).

1. Arc: check for surprise
   a. If one side is surprised, and the other is not, then only the unsurprised group gets to go in the first round of combat (Gygax, 1979a, 61). The surprised side suffers penalties to their defense during the first round of the fight (Wizards RPG Team, 2003, 21–24, 2012, 137).
2. Arc: determine initiative
   a. Both sides now roll dice with the party that gets the higher roll going first each round (Siembieda, 1983, 43).
3. Begin the combat loop described earlier.

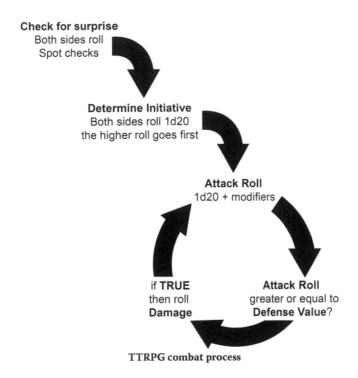

Check for surprise
Both sides roll
Spot checks

Determine Initiative
Both sides roll 1d20
the higher roll goes first

Attack Roll
1d20 + modifiers

if **TRUE**
then roll
Damage

Attack Roll
greater or equal to
Defense Value?

TTRPG combat process

This type of combat process is at the heart of many table-top role-playing games. While there is occasionally variation in the approach used for ranged combat using missile weapons, melee combat using hand-to-hand weapons, or magic use, this procedure is central to conflict resolution in TTRPGs and quite a lot of turn-based computer games as well (Gygax, 1979a, 61–72; Harris, 2009, 1, 5; Norvelle, 2016, 75–79; Siembieda, 1983, 43; SSI; St.Andre and Steve, 1981, 36; Stormfront Studios, 1991; Troika Games, 2003; Wizards RPG Team, 2003, 21–30).

How Magic Works (hint… its' another loop)

The original version *D&D* known as *Old Dungeons & Dragons*, or just OD&D for short, established how magic works in many fantasy games (DeVarque, 2009; Gygax, 1979a, 224; Gygax and Arneson, 1974, 19). Published by TSR in the early 1970's *D&D* started the entire table-top RPG craze and served as the basis for many computer RPGs (Church, 2012; Harris, 2009, 1; Indvik, 2012; Thoman, 2014). After all, you can't have a good fantasy game without magic! How do you define how magic works? The solution Gygax came up with was a fire-and-forget system known as *Vancian Magic*. The name stems from the magic described in Jack Vance's *Dying Earth* series of stories (TV Tropes, n.d.; Gygax, 1979a, 224). In this system, a wizard memorizes a set of spells each day chosen from a list of spells written in their spellbook. They can then cast these spells. Once the wizard has cast a particular spell, it fades from their list of memorized spells for that day. The mage must sleep and study their spellbook to rememorize the spell again (Gygax, 1978a, 40). The loop looks something like this:

1. Wake up then choose and memorize spells for that day.
2. Cast a spell eliminating it from your list of spells for that day.
3. Sleep.
4. Go back to step 1 and repeat.

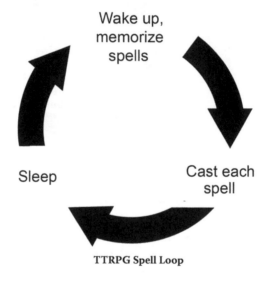

TTRPG Spell Loop

Spell memorization and use is a much more extended loop in the sense that it slowly unfolds over the course of each day of gameplay, but the principle of repeating the same process as a loop still holds true.

Performing a Skill (BRP)

The idea of using specific or generalized skills to perform various tasks in the game is a staple in many RPG systems. A classic example of a game with an extensive skill-based set of mechanics is *Basic Role Playing* by Chaosium Inc. (Stafford and Willis, 1980, 1). Chaosium is one of the very few RPG companies that have been around since the inception of the industry in the 1970s (Chaosium, n.d.). Chaosium published two very famous RPG systems, *Runequest* and *Call of Cthulhu*. During the golden age of the table-top RPG in the early 1980s, *Runequest* was one of the most popular games in the world (Livingstone, 1983, 81). Chaosium published the very first horror RPG at the same time. Based on H.P. Lovecraft's short stories, *Call of Cthulhu* set the standard for the horror genre of RPG. *Basic Role*

Playing, or just BRP, is the modern incarnation of the game mechanics used in both *Runequest* and *Call of Cthulhu*. Using a character skill in "BRP is pretty simple. Each skill has a percentage chance for the character to do the task ranging from 1% to over 100%. To see if your character succeeds at any given skill you merely roll a set of percentile dice, that's two 10-sided dice, to generate a number between 01 and 00, read as 100. To succeed at a given task, the player must roll less than the percentage chance listed on the most relevant skill. Of course, there's more to it with different rules for outstanding successes and failures, and the game master can add or subtract modifiers based on how challenging the task is, but that's the core of it. It makes for a straightforward arc.

1. Decide what skill to use.
2. The game master adds/subtracts in any modifiers based on the situation and difficulty of the task to the skill roll.
3. Roll the percentile dice commonly represented as "D%" or "D100".
4. If the result is equal to or less than the modified skill number, then that roll is a SUCCESS!

The simplicity of this system is probably one of the main reasons for the long lasting success of the Chaosium system. They use this lovely unified game mechanic for combat and most other things in the game as well. Everyone playing the game understands the mechanic and can use it to simulate almost anything (Stafford and Willis, 1980, 7–15).

How Arcs and Loops Apply to Video Games

Arcs and loops apply to video games just as in pen and paper games (Cook, 2012). In a table-top RPG, the player must understand the mechanics of the system to play the game. Video games hide most of the calculations from the player to provide more immersion into the fantasy of the game and lower the difficulty of play. When shooting a gun in a video game the player doesn't have to understand how ballistic trajectories, shot dispersion, impact angles, or any other real-world phenomenon is calculated. All of this math can be computed and used by the video game engine without the player being anything other than merely aware of whether or not his spray of bullets hurt his opponent. This sort of combat calculation is entirely different from a pen and paper system which must be heavily simplified to be playable. In a pen and paper system, if you sit down and try to make players calculate the projectile trajectory for each bullet their character's machine gun fires they'd all walk away from the table in disgust and frustration. The arcs and loops approach can still be applied to combat, magic, skills, and storylines in a video game regardless of how complex, hidden or visible they are to the player.

Video Game Combat (WoT)

Let's start off by examining what a combat loop looks like in a well-known video game. As Wargaming's World of Tanks website explains the video game is an award-winning, free to play, massive multiplayer, online video game where each player controls one out of a team of fifteen tanks that fight for dominance versus an opposing team on a vast battlefield. Capturing the enemy base or destroying all of the opposing tanks is the goal. *World of Tanks*, or *WoT* for short, has been a massively successful game which has had millions of players for several years as of this writing. Combat in this game is a reasonably straightforward affair from a player's perspective. The player puts the aiming reticle over their target using the mouse, then clicks and sends a cannon shell arcing down range toward their intended target. Providing that the player factors in the movement of the enemy tank when aiming, with a little luck the shell then hits their opponent and does damage. The player's arc looks something like this:

1. Make sure that your cannon has a cartridge loaded.
2. Place the aiming reticle over your target where you want to hit it.
3. Press the fire button on your mouse.
4. Observe the results while your cannon reloads.
5. Repeat (go back to step 1) or move on to a new target and begin the loop over again.

The arc may be pretty straightforward, but the underlying game mechanics aren't so simple. The game calculates the ballistic trajectory and shell flight time using a whole lot of beautiful physics which I won't rattle off here. Check out the Wargaming programming team's "Battle Mechanics" webpage (wiki.wargaming.net/en/Battle_Mechanics) to understand their advanced physics and programming techniques. Next, the game engine runs your shot through a random number generator to create a dispersion amount using a Gaussian distribution curve to see where the shell lands precisely. All of these calculations involve the game client and game server communicating and updating each other's information constantly. If the shot hits, then the game engine calculates whether or not the shell penetrates the other tanks armor based upon the shell type used, the impact angle, shell normalization, ricochet chance, effective armor thickness, penetration randomization, and the loss of penetration over distance. Provided that all of these calculations indicate success, the shell now does damage based upon the type of projectile used, high explosive splash distance, type of armor, and damage randomization with varying chances of critical damage to different modules or crew in the wounded tank depending upon where it got hit. That's quite a lot of calculations that take place in a split second of game time. The calculations occur so fast the player is only aware of the results and not the process. The real beauty of video games is that they can simulate a lot of very complex real-world phenomenon and calculate the effects on the fly without the player missing a beat or even noticing at all.

Magic in the World's Most Popular MMORPG World of Warcraft

In Blizzard's *World of Warcraft* massively multiplayer online role-playing game (called *WoW*), the magic system isn't a fire and forget mechanic like *Dungeons & Dragons* (Blizzard, WoW; Gygax, 1978a, 40). In *WoW*, the number of times you can cast a spell is limited only by how long it takes to cycle through a cool down or recharge period. This approach is a perfectly sensible adaptation of the *D&D* system. What player wants to spend an hour of gameplay memorizing spells that can be cast only once per day? No one of course! The arc for casting a spell in *WoW* looks something like this:

1. Select target.
2. Click on the spell icon you'd like to cast from your list of available spells.
3. The spell flies towards your target, who might or not evade it and escape damage.
4. Wait for a brief recharge period and then you can cast the spell again.

This process is similar to most pen and paper systems such as *D&D*, but not precisely so. The spell description for a typical *WoW* spell reads almost straight out of a *D&D* rulebook:

Ice Lance
Level 5 Frost mage ability
40 yd range
1% of base mana
Instant cast
Quickly fling a shard of ice at the target, dealing (76% of spell power) Frost damage.
Ice Lance damage is tripled against frozen targets.

WoWpedia (2016)

Let's compare "Ice Lance" to its *D&D* equivalent "Scorching Ray."

Scorching Ray
Evocation [Fire]
Level: Sor/Wiz 2
Components: V, S
Casting Time: 1 standard action
Range: Close (25 ft. + 5 ft./2 levels)
Effect: One or more rays
Duration: Instantaneous
Saving Throw: None
Spell Resistance: Yes
You blast your enemies with fiery rays. You may fire one ray, plus one additional ray for every four levels beyond 3rd (to a maximum of three rays at 11th level). Each ray requires a ranged touch attack to hit and deals 4d6 points of fire damage.
The rays may be fired at the same or different targets, but all bolts must be aimed at targets within 30 feet of each other and fired simultaneously.

Wizards RPG Team (2012, 274)

As you can see, the mechanics are much more descriptive in the pen and paper D20 write up. They have to be, since the player and GM have to handle the mechanics, whereas the computer can automate that process in *WoW*. The difference in gameplay is pretty striking though since *WoW* doesn't use a turn-based system utilizing a recharge timer for each spell cast instead. If you eliminate the flavor descriptors such as ice and fire and compare the damaging properties and system mechanics of each spell, the similarities are striking. You might think that the system in *WoW* is somewhat similar to that in *D&D*—and it is, that's because *WoW* and almost all of the games like it are the descendants of *D&D* in more ways than one!

Skills and Evolution (ARK: Survival Evolved)

It is far too enormous a task to analyze all of the skills within every MMO! There have been over one hundred MMORPGs released to date! We can still cite a few examples and demonstrate how arcs and loops work within MMORPGs (Cyber Creations Inc., 2002).

Skills are one of the areas that you can see a real divergence between pen and paper RPGs and their MMO equivalents. In MMOs, a skill can be a way to craft items, provide bonuses to specific actions, or it can represent a character or class ability (WoWwiki, n.d.). Skills that are character abilities often mimic class abilities from *D&D* in fantasy-themed MMOs. The Thief's lockpicking and pickpocketing skills in *WoW*, for instance, have exact matches in the *D&D* Thief's class abilities to pick pockets and open locks (WoWwiki, n.d.; Gygax, 1978a, 27–28).

It is in the crafting skills that real differences start to show up. In most pen and paper RPGs, crafting skills were rarely used in the game. Not many players would find the time to break from adventuring to craft some item they could simply buy with treasure plundered while adventuring. The rules for creating anything significant such as a magic item were usually left deliberately vague and unfinished, adding to the overall difficulty of creation (Gygax, 1979a, 116–118). This approach changed quite a bit in the 3rd Edition of *D&D*. The *D&D* 3E rule set included clear guides on how to fabricate every magic item in the rulebooks and, if you had a lax game master, this could be abused by smart players (Wizards RPG Team, 2003, 89–93). MMORPGs took the idea of crafting items and ran with it (Ludgate, 2010). Unlike traditional RPGs, it isn't unheard of for people to be able to craft things and sell them to other players for in-game or even real money (Ludgate, 2010). One example of crafting comes from the recent MMO "*ARK: Survival Evolved*" game. In this game, you start off with just a loincloth and have to run around gathering various items such as rocks, wood, various plants, or bits of dead dinosaurs to cobble together items such as a sleeping bag, campfire, spear, clothing, and armor (ARK, 2016; Studio Wildcard, 2016). The arc for building a basic stone pick in "*ARK: Survival Evolved*" looks something like this:

1. Gather one unit each of wood, stone, and flint. These materials are just lying around where the player starts and can be quickly picked up or harvested from the character's immediate surroundings.
2. Provided the character has the right "Engram," a permanent crafting recipe for the item, they can now put the pieces together and build said item. Luckily, all characters start off with the knowledge of how to make a torch.

As the character advances in level, she can build ever more complex gear. Eventually, the hero is running around with SCUBA gear, C4 explosives, and rocket launchers! Building stuff in *ARK: Survival Evolved* is not a process from D&D, or any other pen and paper RPG for that matter, and shows just how far some modern MMORPGs have evolved away from their roots in traditional TTRPGs.

Conclusion

Arcs and loops aren't just used to define combat, magic, and skills. They form one of the basic building blocks of systems and mechanics design and are crucial to understanding how things are built up from granular in-game tasks into large overarching processes. The concept applies to storytelling and plot as well. You can visualize an entire storyline as a set of arcs and loops or break down a side quest into its constituent components. In fact, the arcs and loops framework can be used at any level of granularity in the game design process from defining individual actions to the overarching plot or themes that can link together a whole series of games (Cook, 2012). The idea of arcs and loops can also be applied to other aspects of gameplay such as interface design, how MMORPG players load and save games, play through an adventure or complete a quest. We will revisit the concept of arcs and loops once we start talking about plot, story, and narrative but for now, it is enough to have examined the idea as it applies to systems and mechanics.

Assignment

Analyze a few of your favorite games and see if you can determine where and how arcs and loops get used in those games. Write up a description of what you have found.

Chapter **3**

A Brief History
of Table-Top
Role-Playing Games

Introduction to Chapter 3

To understand how video games and table-top role-playing games are related we'll need to learn some history. Don't worry, it is relatively painless and we will expand on the information we glean throughout this book. Knowing the relationships between these various genres of games will strengthen your game design skills.

Wargames

The roots of modern role-playing games can be traced back over 1300 years to India with a game called chaturanga which migrated westward into Europe and evolved into the game of chess between the fifteenth and nineteenth centuries (Parlett, 1999; Vego, 2012, 108). Chess, in turn, led to the creation of the first war games (Vego, 2012, 108).

In 1664 a merchant in the city of Ulm named Christoph Weickhmann published *Newerfundenes grosses Koenigsspiel*, also known as the king's game, one of the earliest attempts at creating what we now call a war game. Over a century later, Professor Johann Christian Hellwig, Master of Pages at Brunswick, improved upon this idea and created the first version of *kriegsspiel* (German for "war game") in 1780. The initial version of the game resembled a much more sophisticated version of chess (Wintjes, 2015).

In 1812 a new version of *kriegsspiel* was created in Prussia by Georg Leopold Baron von Reisswitz. His son Georg Heinrich von Reisswitz further refined this game by adding dice and a referee, thus forming the classic version of *kriegsspiel* in 1824. This version of *kriegsspiel* helped Prussian military strategists defeat the French in the Franco-Prussian war of 1870–1871. The results of this war generated much interest in *kriegsspiel*, and pretty soon military planners all over the world were playing versions of the game (Vego, 2012, 108–110; Wintjes, 2015).

H.G. Wells created the first simplified wargame for hobbyists called "Little Wars" in 1913 (Rundle, 2013). In doing so, the renowned author of *The War of the Worlds*, *The Time Machine*, *The Invisible Man*, and many other books began a whole new genre of popular war games. After World War 2, lots of other war games followed from publishers like Avalon Hill and SPI as the hobby took hold (Shapiro, 2004).

Pen and Paper RPGs

Fast forward to the late 1960s and the wargaming scene in the Minnesota and Wisconsin area. In 1969 college student Dave Wesely ran a Napoleonic wargaming session set in a fictional town named Braunstein. He took some ideas from a late 19th century U.S. Army military manual called *Strategos: The American Game of War* by Charles A. L. Totten and applied them to his game while adding various roles for the multiple players who showed up to participate. Though Braunstein and its successors never were published, one of the players, Dave Arneson, began working on a fantasy setting to use the ideas it had generated. Two members of a local wargaming society group, Gary Gygax, and Jeff Perren, created a medieval miniatures game called *Chainmail*. The group began to add fantasy elements such as wizards and dragons to their game. Dave Arneson took his fantasy setting of "Blackmoor" plus the idea of role-playing and added it to *Chainmail*. Arneson then presented these ideas to Gyagx who hammered out a draft of the very first tabletop role-playing game known as *Dungeons & Dragons* (Ewalt, 2013, 59–70; Tresca, 2010, 60–61).

D&D is Born!

Created by Gary Gygax and Dave Arneson, *D&D* was first published as a small boxed set of three booklets in 1974. Tactical Studies Rules, later abbreviated to just TSR, was the company Gygax and friends formed to publish it (Ewalt, 2013, 71–72). Production quality and the artwork were somewhat lacking but TSR sold out of the game regardless, and more printings followed (Ewalt, 2013, 91–93). Other games soon followed in *D&D*'s footsteps. M.A.R. Barker's *Empire of the Petal Throne* game possessed what was perhaps the first rich and truly unique game setting for an RPG. The first sci-fi RPG was the quirky *Metamorphosis Alpha* which quickly morphed into the enduring post-apocalyptic *Gamma World* RPG (Ewalt, 2013, 99, 109; TV Tropes, n.d.). Published around the same time, *Boot Hill* was the first western RPG. Other companies aside from TSR were formed and published their own rule sets such as the sci-fi game *Traveller,* the fantasy RPG *Runequest,* and the superhero game *Villains & Vigilantes* (Ewalt, 2013, 135; Perrin and Turney, 1978; Dee and Herman, 1979). By the end of the 1970s, role-playing games were firmly established, and TSR rolled out two different versions of their game (Ewalt, 2013, 133–134). There was a boxed set for introducing people to the game called the *Dungeons & Dragons Basic Set* and a set of three hardcover core rulebooks for the new *Advanced Dungeons & Dragons* or *AD&D* game (Ewalt, 2013, 133, 138–148). The *Monster Manual*, *Player's Handbook*, and *Dungeon Master's Guide* served as the rather complex foundation for the *AD&D* set of supplements, adventures, settings, novels, and even a Saturday morning cartoon (Ewalt, 2013, 143–144, 163). The *Basic D&D* boxed set continued to be published and grew into a series of products that ran parallel to the *AD&D* system (Ewalt, 2013, 161, 233). Then a strange twist of fate propelled the game into the public limelight.

Satanism and Success

As described by David Ewalt, in his history of D&D, *Of Dice and Men: The Story of Dungeons & Dragons and The People Who Play It,* in 1979 a student at Michigan State University named James Dallas Egbert III wrote a suicide note, left his dorm room, and vanished for several weeks. Egbert's family hired a private investigator to investigate their son's disappearance. This investigator started a news media fervor by suggesting that the *Dungeons & Dragons* game found in the student's dorm room was to blame. While it seems ridiculous now, the United States was in a Satanic panic at the time and this allegation fed into the media generated paranoia (deYoung, 1994; Ewalt, 2013, 155–160; Stackpole, 1990). Egbert remained in hiding for several weeks while a news media circus developed around various ill-founded theories. These events provided a massive amount of publicity to what had previously been a rather obscure game. After several weeks, Egbert turned up several states away, and the real reasons for his disappearance were revealed (Ewalt, 2013, 157). Depression, drug use, and serious mental health problems don't make for a good news story though, and the moral panic over *D&D* had already set in. Advocacy groups such as Bothered About *D&D* and other anti-occult forces joined in to proclaim *D&D* to be the work of the devil (Ewalt, 2013, 157–160; Stackpole, 1990). Throughout the 1980s, a wide variety of charges against *D&D* were leveled, including that playing the game led to Satanism, insanity, and teen suicide (Ewalt, 2013, 157–160; Stackpole, 1990). Playing up these allegations were various news outlets and TV shows such as the 1982 movie *Mazes and Monsters*. The side effect of all of this negative publicity was that it made *D&D* a household name across America. Since nothing sells better than a scandal, this publicity helped propel table-top role-playing games into their golden age as millions of new customers bought these games and began playing (Ewalt, 2013, 158–161).

The RPG Golden Age

As *D&D* grew and expanded during the 1980s, a multitude of other role-playing games and rule systems were published. This swarm of new games included the *Call of Cthulhu* horror RPG, the *Champions* superhero RPG, the humorous *Paranoia* RPG, and Steve Jackson's *Generic Universal RolePlaying System* or "GURPS" (Costikyan et al., 1984; Jackson, 1986; MacDonald et al., 1981; Petersen, 1981). Finishing off the golden age of TTRPGs in the early nineties were the magic-tech *Shadowrun* game, *Rifts*, and *Vampire: The Masquerade* (Rein-Hagen, 1991; Siembieda, 1990; Weisman et al., 1990).

During this time things changed dramatically at TSR. By the mid 1980s, the company had forced founder Gary Gygax out. TSR then subjected Gygax to an endless set of legal maneuvers to shut him out of the industry in general (Ewalt, 2013, 171–172; Peterson, 2014). TSR proceeded to publish a rewritten version of *AD&D* as its 2nd edition in 1989 and took Gygax's name off of it (Ewalt, 2013, 173).

The Decline of the *D&D* Empire

During the 1990s TSR released an inordinate number of campaign settings for *D&D* including *Greyhawk, Spelljammer, Planescape, Forgotten Realms, Dragonlance, Ravenloft, Maztica, Dark Sun, Al-Qadim, Jakandor, Mystara*, and others. With each setting release, TSR fractured its player base into smaller and smaller factions who would buy products for that setting but not for others. The result was that they didn't have a couple of million players of *D&D* anymore but many splinter groups who purchased smaller amounts of a narrower range of products (Rausch, 2004c, 1–2). By the late 1990s, the TTRPG fad was over, the industry as a whole was in trouble, and TSR was going out of business (Ewalt, 2013, 173; Perrin, 2011; Raush, 2004c, 2–4).

Wizards and Salvation

Into this crisis stepped *Wizards of the Coast* (Raush, 2004c, 4). Originally a small game company, WotC found fame and fortune with its innovative

Magic: The Gathering trading card game. WotC saved TSR from extinction by purchasing the nearly bankrupt company in 1997. It then became a subsidiary of Hasbro in late 1999 (Appelcline, 2006). Three years after acquiring *D&D*, *Wizards of the Coast* released a completely revised version of the game in 2000 (Appelcline, 2006; Raush, 2004e, 4). The third edition of *D&D* utilized a unified rule set called the D20 system and marked a significant departure from earlier editions of the game (Raush, 2004d, 3). This edition was a resounding success, and sales dutifully went up as the new system inspired a whole new generation of role-players (Raush, 2004e, 4). WotC/Hasbro proceeded to publish over twenty rulebooks for the new game. While they managed to avoid the setting fragmentation that plagued TSR's efforts, publishing dozens of new rulebooks every year created a different dilemma. The game became so bizarrely complicated and rules-laden that playing it often required the use of helper apps and insanely powerful characters could result (Perrin, 2011; Realmshelp, 2016; McRoberts et al., 2016). To fix this and other flaws, Hasbro had the Wizards RPG Team rewrite the game slightly and republished everything as the 3.5 edition in 2003 (Raush, 2004e, 4). Unfortunately, republishing the same material with only minimal changes created the same problems as before. It didn't help matters that there were even more rulebooks in the 3.5 edition.

During this process, Hasbro took the unusual decision to publish the core of their new D20 System under an Open Game License as Open Game Content (Raush, 2004d, 3). This move had several important repercussions. The first was to eliminate many competing RPG systems (Raush, 2004d, 3). Rare was the small RPG publisher who could afford not to jump on the expanded customer market potentially offered by migrating to the D20 System (Perrin, 2011; Raush, 2004d, 3). A flurry of small RPG publishers sprang up to take advantage of this license and published an array of new games which were compatible with the third edition of *D&D* (Kim, 2016). Some of these products were better than those from *Wizards of the Coast* while some were woefully worse (Perrin, 2011).

The complexity of the new rules combined with the availability of the Open Game License (OGL) produced other problems for Hasbro. Many older gamers longed for the more straightforward rule set that was the hallmark of the Orginal *D&D* game or the flavor of the first edition of *Advanced D&D* that marked the heyday of the game (Perrin, 2011). Using the OGL, they formed companies and released remakes of these old rule sets which have become known as retro-clones (Perrin, 2011; Varney, 2009). These retro-clone games include *OSRIC*, *Glory of Yore*, *Labyrinth Lord*, *Basic Fantasy RPG*, *Swords & Wizardry* and many more (Norvelle, 2016; Varney, 2009). The retro-clones weren't the only problem the OGL generated.

Problems in RPG Paradise

In 2008 Hasbro decided to restart the whole process again by publishing a significantly changed 4th edition of *D&D*. They put out a more restrictive game license and began releasing a new flood of game products but all did not go as planned (Perrin, 2011). The company had recently ended its relationship with Paizo who had been producing official *D&D* content for its *Dungeon* and *Dragon* magazines (Stevens, 2012). Paizo then began publishing *Pathfinder*, an update of the 3.5 edition under the Open Game License (Perrin, 2011; Ohannessian, 2012). Many players considered *Pathfinder* a superior product to the official 4th edition of the game and sales for *D&D* began to slacken (Perrin, 2011). Combined with the availability of other versions of the game things were on a downward swing. Hasbro canceled the remaining unpublished rulebooks for 4e and announced in 2012 a new and improved 5th edition of *D&D* (Perrin, 2011; Ohannessian, 2012).

New and Improved

The new 5th edition of *D&D* introduced new mechanics and brought back some more traditional features of the game (Ohannessian, 2012). Revelations that a few notable celebrities play the game plus some decent marketing boosted 5e *D&D*'s sales making Hasbro much happier (Adducci, 2015; Amirault, 2015; Jones, 2015). As of this writing, the tabletop RPG community is split between the players of 5th edition *D&D*, *Pathfinder*, the various retro-clones, and a smattering of other systems thrown in for variety (Jones, 2015). The 5th edition of *D&D* has proven to be quite popular with sales of this edition being better than that of the 4e, 3.5e, or 3e according to the co-creator of the 5th edition Mike Mearls on his @mikemearls Twitter feed.

Video Games Are Born

Video games got off to a slow start with a variety of checkers, chess, and other simple game simulators in the 1950s (Hunter, 2000a; Smith, 2014c; Winter, 2013). At this stage, most computers didn't have much in the way of visual displays or means to interface with the computer systems and these games were limited to a few research scientists and public demonstrations. *Spacewar!* became the first popular video game, at least popular among programmers, in the early 1960s (Hunter, 2000a; Smith, 2014b). Designed at MIT by Steve Russell the simple game involved two geometric spaceships shooting each other as they maneuver around a star.

By the 1970s, a true video game industry emerged. Based upon the pioneering work done by Ralph Baer, Bill Harrison, and Bill Rusch for the very first video game console the Magnavox Odyssey (Hunter, 2000a; Kent, 1997; Smith, 2014a). While the Magnavox Odyssey didn't succeed, it inspired an entire industry to follow in its footsteps. Nolan Bushnell and Ted Dabney founded Atari and released *Pong*, the first truly successful arcade game and launched the video game arcade phenomenon of the 1970s and early 1980s (Gemperlein and Scheinman, 2000; Hunter, 2000b). Games such as *Asteroids*, *Space Invaders*, *Pac-Man*, and *Donkey Kong* had became cultural icons and huge successes (Glancey, 1996, 8–9, 14–16). The release of the Atari 2600 set off the home console craze that saw many arcade games ported over and a wave of new games as well (Barton and Loguidice, 2013; Glancey, 1996, 8–23; Sullivan, 1982, 9).

The First CRPGs

Meanwhile, games were being made for mainframe computers by college students. *Colossal Cave Adventure* was an early text adventure game. Created in 1976 by Will Crowther *Adventure* was based on a combination of *D&D* and cave exploration (Jerz, 2007; Hunter, 2000d). Originally called "DND," the role-playing dungeon crawl *Telengard* became one of the first commercially distributed computer video games released in 1982 (Lawrence, n.d.). The *Zork* trilogy was another popular early text-based game ported over from the DEC PDP-10 computer (Anderson, 1985; Hunter, 2000d). The dungeon crawl game *Rogue* was important because of the way it procedurally generated content providing a fresh experience every time the game was played (Wichman, 1997). Created by Michael Toy and Glenn Wichman and released in 1980 *Rogue* was based on *D&D* and inspired a whole class of similar video games called "roguelikes" (Craddock, 2015; Wichman, 1997). Possessing only crude graphics at best these text-based game were somewhat limited in the play experience they offered but they still found popularity among players.

Crash and Burn

The video game industry took an enormous hit with the North American video game crash of 1983 (Hunter, 2000c). Triggered by a flood of home consoles and video games of dubious quality the entire industry crashed and burned that year. It ended the glory days of classic arcade games and stagnated video game development for years. During this period home computer systems such as the Apple II, IBM PC, Commodore 64 and the Amiga provided a safe space for video games (Glancey, 1996, 30–31; Hunter, 2000c). Games for personal computers now began to slowly come to the fore.

Getting Better

Published in 1985 the video game *Xanadu: Dragon Slayer II* was a pioneering action role-playing game where the player controlled the game character in real time combat along with elements of dungeon crawls and platform style play (Harris, 2009, 13). Yuji Horii's *Dragon Quest* from 1986 was another early role-playing video game notable for its use of anime style graphics (Harris, 2009, 12). The break out video game for this genre was undoubtedly Shigeru Miyamoto's *The Legend of Zelda* published in 1986. *Zelda* contained several notable innovations for its genre such as non-linear gameplay, open world exploration, puzzles, and other role-playing elements (Gerstmann, 2006; Superplay Magazine, 2003). Published a bit later in 1986 the hit game *Metroid* combined elements from *Zelda*, platform jumping, with darker themes and started a very successful franchise for its publisher Nintendo (Gamespot, 2013; Nutt, 2010).

MUD Slinging

Roy Trubshaw developed the game *Multi-User Dungeon* or *MUD* as a multi-user tribute to *Zork* while at Essex University in the UK (Bartle, 1990a; Tedman and Tedman, 2007, 121–122). The popularity of this and similar games such as *SHADES* and *Federation II* led to these MUD style games getting licensed by early internet providers such as CompuServe, AOL, and others (Bartle, 1999, 2003; Smith et al., 2003). Technical innovations like being able to change the game while it was running appeared with Rich Skrenta's *MONSTER* which eventually spawned *TinyMUD* by James Aspnes (Tedman and Tedman, 2007, 122). The wide use and social interaction focus of *TinyMUD* helped popularize MUDs (Stewart, 2000). A landmark game in MUD development was *Avalon: The Legend Lives* which marked the introduction of a continuous game world lacking the resets of other MUDs, along with in-game economies, professions, and skill systems. The game was noted for having the first virtual real estate deal (Bartle, 1999). By the 1990s a plethora of MUDs were up and running such as MONSTER, TinyMUD, UberMUD, MOO, and more (Tedman and Tedman, 2007, 122).

CRPGs to the Fore

Successful video games such as the *Ultima* and *Wizardry* series of games helped kick off the computer RPG genre in the early 1980s. Following these popular games were the *Might and Magic* and *Bard's Tale* series of games in the mid-80s. Strategic Simulations, Inc. published thirty video game titles under an *AD&D* license with TSR including the *Pool of Radiance* and *Dragonlance* series (Harris, 2009, 2–7, 22).

Blizzard Entertainment leveraged the latest advances in computer graphics and processor speed to release *Diablo* in late 1996. This roguelike dark fantasy game featured improved graphics, real-time action, and online play. "*Diablo*" began a line of successful products that continues today (Blizzard, 2016). The video game *Fallout* featured an expansive post-apocalyptic open game world, non-linear gameplay, and a distinctive aesthetic. The *AD&D* game licenses continued with *Baldur's Gate*, *Icewind Dale*, and *Planescape: Torment* games at the very end of the 1990s (Barton, 2007). *Planescape: Torment* and *Fallout* rank consistently as some of the best CRPGs ever made (Boyer and Cifaldi, 2006).

FPS Beginnings

While CRPGs were evolving, essential developments were happening elsewhere in the video game field. FPS or first-person shooters are video games where the player sees things from the viewpoint of the character holding the weapon. The progenitors of this genre were *Maze War* and *Spasim*. Both games were released in 1974 and used simple wire-frame graphics. *Maze War* was the originator of numerous features found in later FPS games including the use of the first-person perspective, avatars, and network play (Bowery, 2001; Colley, 1998). The innovations found in *Maze War* inspired many imitations and variants such as *MIDI Maze* and *Battlezone* (Dunn, 2008, 3). The most influential games in the FPS genre are undoubtedly id Software's *Wolfenstein 3D* and *DOOM* games (Dunn, 2008, 5–6; News Team, 2014). *Wolfenstein 3D* featured great graphics, a fast pace, and a seamless experience that was amazing for the time. The id Software quickly followed *Wolfenstein 3D* with the even more successful and influential *DOOM*.

MMORPGs Arrive

MUDs slowly transmogrified into MMORPGs. *Habitat* by Lucasfilm was a very early graphical online community active in the 1980s (Rossney, 1996). *Neverwinter Nights* was a licensed version of *AD&D* that ran on AOL from 1991 to 1997 (Harris, 2009, 5; Raush and Lopez, 2004). Using the same game engine as *Pool of Radiance* and other titles from SSI, *Neverwinter Nights* was the first MMORPG with graphics (Harris, 2009, 5; Raush and Lopez, 2004). *Ultima Online* followed in 1997 and marked a rise in the popularity of MMORPGs (Indvik, 2012; Olivetti, 2010). Launched in 1999, *Everquest* was another enormously popular MMORPG for several years (Indvik, 2012). Released in 2004 the *World of Warcraft* MMORPG became massively successful with millions of player accounts (Machin, 2001). Though other MMORPGs have followed, none have yet achieved the success that *World of Warcraft* has for Blizzard Entertainment (Tassi, 2014).

Conclusion

Many different types of games such as MMORPGs, CRPGs, and FPSs have been cross-fertilizing each other and evolving while leveraging tabletop role-playing games for systems and themes. Examples of this process include the so-called *SPECIAL* game system the video game *Fallout* used as a substitute for the GURPS RPG (Indvik, 2012; Pitts, 2012). There are an enormous number of games based off of *D&D* such as *Dark Ages of Camelot, Everquest, World of Warcraft, Guild Wars*, and *Dungeons & Dragons Online* to name a few. The best way to see the relationship between these video games and TTRPGs is to play a wide variety of them and observe the connections and similarities yourself. While you do so, try to note how the systems of advancement, terminology, and themes are similar or dissimilar to each other.

Assignment: Let the Games Begin!

As the benchmark of the genre, *World of Warcraft* is the essential game to play to understand MMORPGs. The current versions of *EverQuest* and *Ultima Online* are still available and active as well. Other popular modern MMORPGs include the *Final Fantasy* series, *Guild Wars 2*, and *Elder Scrolls Online*. Download and play as many of these games as you can. Afterward, you should have enough experience to begin learning how to design material for this type of product. When playing through these MMORPGs take the time to observe how the classes, power progressions, spells, equipment, and abilities work mechanically as a system. Later, you can use the results of your observations to draw connections between the MMORPGs you are playing and the table-top RPG systems in the next chapter.

Chapter 4

Choosing the Right Game

Choosing a Game System

We are going to learn about complex design issues for video games by leveraging an existing tabletop role-playing game. Doing so will let us focus on design issues rather than spending time creating new game systems and mechanics. Not only does developing a good game system require many weeks of playtesting, but we don't have room in one book to do it! We will take a shortcut around this problem by using a retro-clone RPG and the Open Game License (www. wizards.com/default.asp?x=d20/article/srdarchive).

Leveraging the OGL

In 2000 the Open Gaming License or OGL was published by *Wizards of the Coast*. The OGL allowed individuals and other companies to publish supplementary material for the 3rd edition of *Dungeons & Dragons*. The open-ended wording of the license permitted the publication of many retro-clones and other d20 based games as well (Perrin, 2011; Raush, 2004d, 3). The practical meaning of this is that you can create something compatible with one of the many d20 OGL games or retro-clones and publish your work under the OGL if you so choose. Using an existing OGL based retro-clone is a handy way of keeping everything safely legal while providing us with a rules framework we can use to develop our adventure.

Picking the Right RPG to Use

Before you can start working on your adventure, you will need to choose which rule set to use. There are many retro-clones to choose from, and I will briefly highlight a few of the pros and cons of each one. By the end of this chapter, I will reveal the choice that I will be using for the remainder of this book. While you are free to use any game system you like, the examples in this book will be done using just the one RPG system specified.

A D&D of Many Flavors

System resource documentation and open gaming licenses exist for the 3rd, 3.5, and 5th editions of the *Dungeons & Dragons* game (Jury, 2015; Wizards of the Coast, 2016). The 4th edition of the game has the similar but more restrictive Game System License (GSL), and since that particular version was not nearly as popular as either 3rd or 5th, we'll just politely ignore it (Jury, 2015). The 3rd and 3.5 editions have been out of publication for at least seven years so we can eliminate these from the contention easily. The 5th edition is much more tempting. It has a large number of players and is widely recognized. 5th edition has 992 pages of rules in just the core three gamebooks. That isn't even counting the rules included in the various supplemental rulebooks. This set of books is a bit too much to digest for someone just getting started in tabletop role-playing. *Pathfinder*, also known as the 3.75 edition, could also be used but it has even more rules than the 5th edition. We'll have to keep looking.

Meet the Retro-Clones

Fortunately, there is a wealth of D&D retro-clones currently available. Each of these games has a small but devoted following of players. These books tend to be a lot smaller, more manageable, and more affordable than mainstream products, plus these publishers tend to encourage player developed content. Let's examine a few of these.

OSRIC

First up is the *OSRIC* retro-clone of the first edition of *Advanced Dungeons & Dragons* from the early 1980s (Marshall, 2008, xiv). This edition of *AD&D* was the most popular version ever published. It has some excellent mechanics and game balance as well. This version of *D&D* also served as the starting point for many of the video game systems now widely in use. It also has a historical appeal since anyone who plays it gets a feel for how the role-playing industry began. Unfortunately, the *OSRIC* rulebook weighs in at a massive 400+ pages of rules. We can move on.

Swords & Wizardry

This game is a retro-clone of the original white box edition of *D&D* put out in 1974 (Finch, 2008). While an excellent contender, this game follows the original rules a bit too closely and includes some of the flaws eliminated in later versions of the game. It is also rather expensive for this type of product. However, the game does possess cover art by Erol Otus who illustrated many of the original *D&D* books during the game's zenith.

Labyrinth Lord

Fairly accurate to the 1981 Basic *D&D* boxed set of rules and well supported by its publisher Goblinoid Games, this game is a strong contender. It contains a few minor tweaks to the rule set, but overall Labyrinth Lord is compatible with any of the old basic edition *D&D* supplements and adventures already published (Proctor, 2010). If you want an excellent role-playing experience as close to *Basic D&D* as possible, then this is a superb way to go. It contends with some of the same problems the original *D&D* game possessed though.

Glory of Yore

Glory of Yore is very reminiscent of *Basic D&D*. However, the game mechanics are a bit updated which alleviates some of the more confusing attributes that *D&D* was infamous for (Norvelle, 2016). The game has an intriguing King Arthur theme which we can safely ignore since it in no way impacts the game mechanics. The rules are quite easy to understand and come in a fairly slim volume. The game is also reasonably priced for the amount of content it contains.

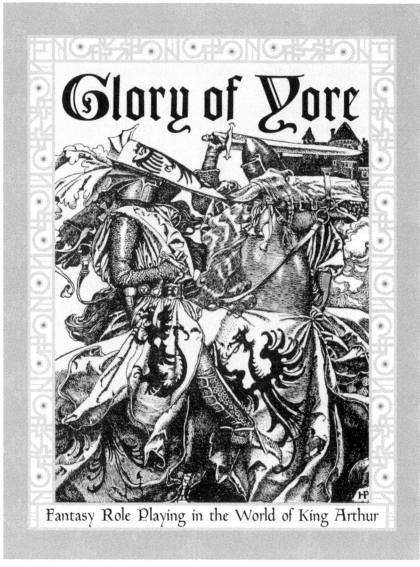

Glory of Yore, 2016, A. Norvelle

Other Open License Games: Fate, Fudge, BRP or OpenD6

There are a few other RPG systems that have equivalents of the Open Game License such as Fate, FUDGE, Basic Role-Playing, and the OpenD6 system (Kim, 2015a). All of these systems are quite good in their own right and have their devoted followings. I highly recommend downloading copies of all of these games and taking a look at their mechanics. These games do not have the history that the *D&D* or D20 systems have and don't form the basis for many MMORPGs or CRPGs the way *D&D* has. While interesting from a system design perspective, developing an adventure for any of these systems doesn't have the same level of payoff.

Off-Beat Genres: *Toonzy!*, *Call of Cthulhu*, or *GURPS*

These three games are attractive because of the wide variety of role-playing settings they represent. *Toonzy!* is one of the few cartoon RPGs ever produced. *Call of Cthulhu* is probably the most famous horror RPG ever made. *GURPs* can emulate almost any setting imaginable. Each has an interesting take on game systems and mechanics as well. None of these games have open game licenses so you wouldn't be able to publish your work for profit. This fact eliminates them from use with this book. Nevertheless, they are all marvelous case studies for game system design.

Making a Choice & Going Forward

I will be using *Glory of Yore* for the examples in this book. This system uses the Open Game License, is easy to play, relatively brief, and not so caught up in recreating an older game that it fails to fix some of the flaws in the original. It also happens to be a system I have taught successfully in several of my college courses at the Savannah College of Art and Design, so I know that it works. Since it is one of the retro-clones, this means that whatever material we develop will also be compatible with the other systems we looked at such as *OSRIC*, *Swords & Wizardry*, and *Labyrinth Lord*.

Conclusion

We have settled on what system to use, and you've learned a little about the various types of table-top role-playing games available. Now you need to start playing some of these TTRPGs so you can analyze and compare them to the MMORPGs and video games you have been playing. The results of your analysis should demonstrate the connections and differences between these video game and table-top systems. After you do that, you are ready to start designing your very own adventures, settings, characters, and quests.

Assignment: Play, Play, Play!

Get a copy of *Glory of Yore*, *Labyrinth Lord*, or *Swords & Wizardry* and learn how to play it with your friends. Reading the rulebook will familiarize you with the game system this book will be using. Take a look at popular games such as the 5th edition of *Dungeons & Dragons*, *Pathfinder*, and a few other retro-clones such *OSRIC* as well. If you are serious about learning a variety of game systems and mechanics, then peruse through a copy of *Runequest*, the *Star Wars D6* system (available used or as PDFs), or *GURPS* for alternative approaches to how RPGs should work. Some of the older versions of *D&D* are instructive as well. The first edition *AD&D* books from 1979 are readily available as used books. The 4th edition *D&D* books are interesting for the influence MMORPG, and CRPG games had on that rule set.

Additional Resources

Table-top RPGs have been around long enough for a large body of free adventures and other materials to be available. Dragonsfoot.org has quite a collection of modules available as does pandius.com, enworld.org, and rpg.net to list just a few. A number of the old netbooks for earlier editions of AD&D can be found at www.textfiles.com/rpg/ as well. The book's website has links to all of these websites and more: www.gregtheartist.com/dccfg.htm.

I strongly suggest playing through a few classic adventures such as:

B2 Keep on the Borderland (Basic D&D)
B3 Palace of the Silver Princess (Basic D&D)
Quest for the Silver Sword (Basic D&D)
C2 Ghost Tower of Inverness (AD&D 1e)
G 1-2-3 Against the Giants (AD&D 1e)
L1 Secret of Bone Hill (AD&D 1e)
L2 The Assassin's Knot (AD&D 1e)
N1 Against the Cult of the Reptile God (AD&D 1e)
T1 Village of Hommlet (AD&D 1e)
U1 Sinister Secret of Saltmarsh (AD&D 1e)
U2 Danger at Dunwater (AD&D 1e)
Dragotha's Lair (AD&D 2e)
For Duty and Deity (AD&D 2e)
Dungeon magazine's Savage Tide Adventure Path (D&D 3.5e)
Masks of Nyarlathotep (CoC)
Queen Euphoria (Shadowrun)

Some of these classic adventures are freely downloadable from various websites, or you can purchase a used copy or PDF through legitimate vendors such as DriveThruRPG.com or Amazon. These specific products represent some of the best RPG adventure modules ever published and provide examples of how we will format our adventure in the forthcoming chapters. Make sure that you read through a few of these sample adventures and play the game a few times before attempting to write any material for it. You can't write an effective module if you don't understand how the game works!

Converting Old *D&D* or *AD&D* to *Glory of Yore*

The old *Basic D&D* and *Advanced D&D* systems used a rather clunky system to calculate combat which modern RPGs have long abandoned. Fortunately, it is easy to convert these old values into the new system. To change the old To Hit Armor Class 0, or THAC0, system into new "To Hit" values subtract the THAC0 from 20. Likewise, to turn the old Armor Class or AC value into the new Armor Class value, you subtract the old AC value from 20.

New values = Old D&D/AD&D values
To Hit Bonus = 20 − THAC0
Armor Class = 20 − AC

Play and have fun with whichever system you choose. Once you are comfortable with the rules, we can start developing material for it.

Chapter 5

Ideation

Overview

Now that we have established the groundwork, it is time to get creative and do a bit of brainstorming. For our purposes, you will need to come up with adventure ideas for a role-playing game. An RPG adventure consists of a story and scenario that players of the game can interactively play through using a specific RPG system. Since we are using the *Glory of Yore* RPG our adventure will need to be compatible with a somewhat generic King Arthur based fantasy setting. Watch some episodes of *Merlin*, *Camelot*, *The Mists of Avalon* or the movies *Excalibur* and *King Arthur* to get some rough ideas about what you could do in this setting. Coming up with a great idea isn't as easy as it seems. It takes considerable effort and a whole lot of trial and error. The key is just volume. If you produce a whole bunch of ideas, then one of them is bound to be good. Now let's discuss how to generate some great ideas.

Keep an Idea Book

You're going to need inspiration. Go out and buy a small notebook that you can keep with you. Anytime you see something interesting, have a neat idea, or are just struck with a random thought, take a minute and write it down in your idea book. These little nuggets of inspiration can serve as food for thought later on when you are trying to generate fresh ideas.

Start a Dream Journal

In a similar vein to the idea book is the dream journal. Keep a notebook near you while you sleep. When you wake up, roll over, grab your journal, and write down any dreams you remember. This method of tapping into your unconscious mind is a straightforward way of generating some creative ideas. Make this a habit and you will start remembering your dreams much better as an added benefit (Sponias, 2012).

Free Writing

On a clean sheet of paper just start writing down sentences and paragraphs in a free flowing stream of ideas. Don't concern yourself about grammar, spelling, or even whether or not it makes sense. Don't stop writing until you fill a few pages. Don't inhibit yourself. Just let everything out as you write. Just keep writing for at least a half an hour and don't worry about how much paper you use.

The madness behind this method is to write so much material that it empties your head of any preconceptions about your writing topic. Your brain will naturally start to fill in the blanks as you keep writing. With any luck, some of the semi-random material your write down will contain a kernel of a great idea in it.

Once you have finished, look through all of the material that you have written and see if anything jumps out as being exceptional or provocative. You can use the ideas you come up with here as source material for further work and development. Try using the words or ideas you generate this way as a starting point for the other ideation techniques presented elsewhere in this chapter.

neutron are proton supremacy riddled rung Taco thin bovine supremacy cold institute vapor lock liquid beam sail supine the superlative blathering blundered blustery buffalo laughs.

Obsequious octopoids elevate alarmingly.

Vacuous veloci-motion miserably migrate northward to milder climes. Victims of vicious viscitudes the vimy eradicates fortunate falumphors. Pleasing plesiosaurs perambulate in passing pleasantries.

An example of free writing

Photo Journal

Keeping a photo journal is a fun and easy way to give yourself creative ideas as well as maintain a history of things you've seen. Start by keeping a camera with you at all times. Doing so isn't very difficult anymore since just about every cell phone made has a built-in camera now. Anytime you see anything interesting take a photo of it and save it for later. It might be a nifty pattern on the sidewalk, an unusual tree or bird, an old car, or just an interesting looking individual. Save all of these neat photos into a file folder on your computer and when you need some additional inspiration, go through the folder and see if anything stands out or inspires you.

Sample photo journal

Art Journal

Buy a cheap sketchbook. In it draw anything you like. Whatever strikes your interest at the moment is a suitable subject to work on. Try to use it every day. Take all of the weird and strange things that live in your imagination and put them on the pages of your art journal. Later, when you need a dose of creativity, flip through your art journal and grab an idea from it. Some folks call it a doodle book or just a sketchbook, but whatever you call it, this sort of journal is an excellent source for creative ideas.

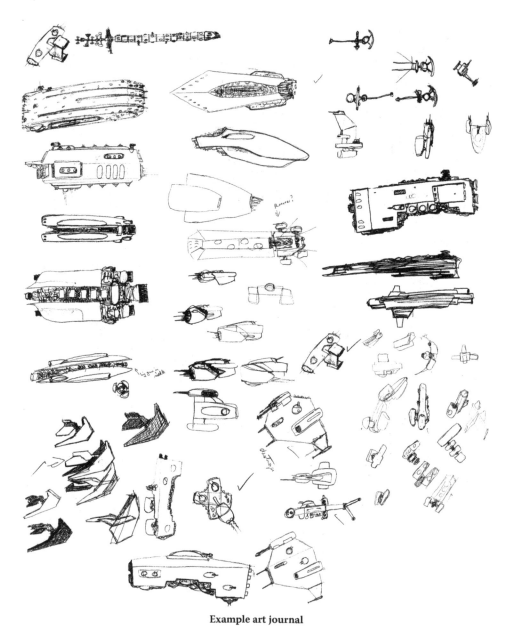

Example art journal

Create a Mind Map

In the middle of a large whiteboard, blackboard, or sheet of paper, write down a topic you'd like to explore and circle it. As quickly as you can manage, think of as many different words, pictures, or symbols that relate to your central topic and write or draw these out in a radiating circle around your starting topic. The idea is to visualize your ideation process, so the more visual you make things, the better. Make the connecting lines curved, zig-zagged, color-coded, or otherwise visually interesting or try using pictures instead of words. Once you have encircled your original topic with connected words, use each of these new terms as a starting place and repeat the process. Each line of your mind map should branch off in a different direction. Go on until you fill all of the available space (Buzan, 2011; Passuello, 2016).

Once finished, look at what you have written. Is any of it compelling or worthy of further development? If so, you can use that word you wrote as the starting place for another mind map or as the starting place for one of the other creative techniques discussed here.

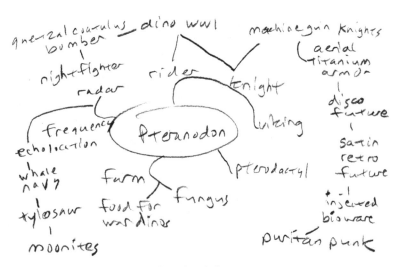

Sample mind map

What If?

One straightforward approach is to start asking "what if?" about a situation, place, or thing. Imagine a scenario and play out the results in your head. Where does it go? What situations does that scenario lead to? What if this or that event happens? What if the world worked this way? How does the princess get a dragon to fit in her boot? Take any situation that you can think of and start asking as many questions about it as you can and then see where it goes from there (Neidlinger, 2015).

Column Mixing

Choose a topic and create a list of as many things as you can describing that topic. Try to fill the whole page. Take a new page and repeat this process. Do this for several unrelated topics. Now pick two of these pages at random, place them side by side, and start combining random words from each list. Try to create exciting combinations of words that fire your imagination and are worth pursuing further. Try again using a different pair of lists that you have made and continue the process until you get something interesting (Janes, 2014, 10–11; Rosner, 2014; Venis, 2013, 54–55).

Sample column mixing exercise

Something Random

Another simple and useful technique is to find a random word and see if you can incorporate it into your idea. You could take it from anywhere, the ingredients on a soda bottle, a newscast, web page, book, or a random object lying around your house (Chua, 2016). Try to use something as unrelated to your topic as possible for the best results.

Repeat

Take one or more of the best ideas you have generated so far and use that idea as a starting point to go through one of the techniques previously mentioned again. Repeat this process cycle using these techniques until you have something worthwhile. Spend a whole afternoon trying out these various approaches until you find one that works for you then focus on that technique. The trick is to try to do a little bit every day. If you can devote half an hour to developing your creative process each day, you will start to tap into your full creative potential.

Research and Inspiration

Creativity doesn't take place in a void. The media and games you consume act as a constant influence upon you. It is imperative that you expand your mind by including novel material. Go out and gather some information on history, science, current events, politics, social sciences, anthropology, scuba diving, or anything else—just so long as it isn't from a game or other entertainment medium. Take a look at the news from a few foreign countries to gain a novel perspective. Britain, Russia, India, Singapore, Australia, Iceland, and South America all have news pages available written in English which can be used to create game plots, scenarios, or characters. There are various sites for getting exciting tidbits of science news such as iflscience.com and sciencedaily.com. The website provided below has links to all of these websites and more. Explore this wealth of material at your leisure and feed your brain. A well-fed mind is a source of original ideas.

Science and news resources link: www.gregtheartist.com/dccfg.htm.

Example

A brief perusal of today's news provides me with a conflict suitable for further development. Two nations, quite closely related culturally suffered a religious split a millennia ago and are now sworn enemies who have fought several wars with each other. These two nations have recently developed devastatingly powerful weapons, and as tensions escalate, they threaten to use them on one another. We can throw in a bit of a fantasy twist. Let's make the main participants gnomes and their arch-rivals gnomes whose religion insists that they dye themselves green and call themselves goblins. The gnomes have developed gigantic town-crushing magma powered war wheels whereas the goblins have made a titanic steam-powered wooden mecha-dragons. As various religious extremist groups within both cultures incite mutual hatred between the two countries, they totter towards declaring total war and unleashing their fiendish new weapons. I can leverage a bit of history to provide a few interesting characters. Let's base the goblin leader off of, say, Lucrezia Borgia, famed Italian Renaissance femme fatale and the gnomish leader off of the Roman Emperor Nero. Now that we've got our setting figuring out our short-term goals for the game shouldn't be any problem at all. Maybe have the characters be a crack squad of gnomish commandos out to steal the secrets of controlling the goblin mecha-dragons or a band of goblin ninjas out to sabotage the production of gnomish magma-wheels. The possibilities are as vast and wide as history itself.

Suggested Reading

In all of the wealth of material you can access online and in print, a few books and authors stand out as especially influential and worth reading. A short list of science fiction books you should read includes Robert A. Heinlein's *Starship Troopers*, Isaac Asimov's *Robot* and *Foundation* series, Arthur C. Clarke's *Childhood's End*, plus anything by H.G. Wells. These books and authors are the foundations of science fiction and what amount to required reading if you want to develop sci-fi games. If you like those books then expand your reading to include Joe Haldeman's *The Forever War*, Frank Herbert's *Dune*, Larry Niven's *Ringworld*, William Gibson's *Neuromancer* and any of the books by Ursula K. Le Guin, Andre Norton, Hal Clement, Poul Anderson, Roger Zelazny, or A.E. van Vogt.

Essential reading in fantasy literature includes J.R.R. Tolkien's *Lord of the Rings* and *Hobbit* books, Robert E. Howard's "Conan" short stories (just be sure to get the short stories written by Howard himself), Edgar Rice Burrough's *Tarzan* or *John Carter of Mars* series, and H. Rider Haggard's novel *She*. More recent fantasy literature includes works such as Fritz Leiber's *Fafhrd and the Grey Mouser* series, Michael Moorcock's *Elric* books, and Terry Pratchett's *Discworld*. Notables as Lord Dunsany, E.R. Eddison, C.L. Moore, and M.A.R. Barker have also produced works that can provide enormous amounts of fantastic inspiration. A brief foray into horror writing yields Edgar Allen Poe, H.P. Lovecraft, and Stephen King as essential reading for that genre.

Non-fiction and other titles are a bit more difficult to compile into a brief reading list. Edward Gibbon's *The History of the Decline and Fall of the Roman Empire*, with its stories of imperial conquest and treachery, is an excellent source of inspiration for political intrigues for any game. Will and Ariel Durant's eleven-volume *The Story of Civilization* provides innumerable examples of adventure, political machinations, empire building and collapse while Shirer's *The Rise and Fall of the Third Reich* provides an in-depth look at the working of political evil. *The Hero with a Thousand Faces* by Joseph Campbell provides us with the details on creating a functional heroic cycle for our story plot. Finally *The Golden Bough* by Sir James George Frazer outlines and compares numerous religions and cultures, any of which can serve as the basis for a fictional setting. Real history is replete with events more bizarre than any fiction. Many tales of adventure, intrigue, and strife can be found in the echoes of the past if you care to look for them.

Keep in mind while you read these titles that the goal here is to find interesting stories, settings, and material that you can use in your creations.

A lot of these books and stories are quite old and no longer reflect modern sensibilities, but this also means that they are freely available. There are numerous online libraries from which you can download these titles. Try looking at Google Books (books.google.com), Project Gutenberg (www. gutenberg.org), Gutenberg Australia (gutenberg.net.au), and the Internet Archive (archive.org) to find good copies of these texts. The book's website has links to all of these websites and more.

Internet book resources link: www.gregtheartist.com/dccfg.htm.

Creating a Pitch

An idea pitch is just a brief way of presenting your concept to a group of interested people. When creating an idea pitch, you will need to be as concise as you can. Invariably you will have to explain how your idea will benefit your audience and succeed in its goals, so it is critical to get used to presenting your ideas to different groups of people. Doing this sort of presentation is a crucial component of working in the game industry. Practice is vital. Make a habit of speaking to groups until you find yourself at ease presenting in front of a sizable number of people. Make a point of trying your presentation out on a few people you trust before you put your pitch to the test and see if there is anything in it you need to explain better. You need to listen to the critical feedback your audience provides. Incorporating constructive criticism is a vital ability if you intend to be successful in this field (Davis, 2010; Olchawska, 2015, 2–3). An idea pitch frequently contains two components: an elevator pitch and an idea pitch.

Elevator Pitch

An elevator pitch is a short one-sentence summary of your concept. This one sentence should neatly summarize your idea in as brief a time as possible. Write down your idea using as many phrases as needed to describe everything. Now start removing words and combining things until you whittle it down to just the fundamental essence of the idea. In an elevator pitch, you present the core element of your concept without comparing it to any other existing material. Here are a few examples of various elevator pitches for some potential *Glory of Yore* adventures:

- A series of tests based upon one or more of the seven cardinal virtues that reward players for their nobility of character or punish them for the lack thereof.
- A group of goblins pose as a bridge troll and exact a toll from all passersby.
- An evil cult targets anyone who trespasses into the local forest.

Comparison Pitch

Similar to the elevator pitch is a comparison pitch. It is a short sentence that compares your idea to existing intellectual properties. When paired with an elevator pitch, it can succinctly deliver your concept to an audience in a very brief time. We'll take the elevator pitches listed above and do the comparison pitches for them.

Like the story of "Gawain and the Green Knight" with an updated set of virtues tested.

A comedic misdirection-themed adventure that ends up like something between *Sherlock Holmes* and the *Three Stooges*.

Like being the Sheriff of Nottingham fighting an evil Robin Hood.

Conclusion

The ideation techniques presented in this chapter are useful in a broad sense. You can use them for any project that requires creativity and originality. Crafting good ideas and communicating them effectively to others is no small task. Indeed, being able to develop and present creative ideas is a critical skill for working in the game development industry. You can use these techniques, resources, and pitch methods to efficiently develop and coalesce your thoughts down into practical ideas for use in this project and many others. Hopefully, by now you have some neat and innovative ideas percolating around inside your head. You have also learned how to create a proper elevator and comparison pitch. Let's put all of these nifty ideas and knowledge together and make a few pitches that you can use.

Assignment

Create Three Adventure Pitches using Elevator and Comparison Pitches

Use the ideation techniques presented in this chapter to think up some ideas for the fantasy adventure you are going to write. Work up an elevator and comparison pitch for each concept. Taken together, the elevator and comparison pitches should create a cohesive picture of what you are trying to propose. Compare all of your proposals to each other. Start combining ideas and eliminating unworkable or weak proposals. Whittle down the number of pitches to just your three best ones. After you have finalized these three elevator and comparison pitches, present them to someone you trust such as a friend or family member. Based on their review of your three pitches, choose one of your ideas to proceed with and develop throughout the rest of this book.

Chapter **6**

Game Design Basics

This chapter goes through the most relevant game development theories that have been published to date and relates them to your tabletop role-playing game adventure. Some of these theories are well established while others are still in the formative process. All of them have a bearing on our project.

The Magic Circle and Beyond

Back in 1938, Dutch cultural historian Johan Huizinga coined the term "Magic Circle" to indicate the space containing a play-ground. This separate virtual world can be a court trial, a football match, or any game (Huizinga, 1949, 10). Huizinga's idea was elaborated upon by Katie Salen and Eric Zimmerman in their book *Rules of Play* to mean the "special place in time and space created by a game" (Salen and Zimmerman, 2004, 95).

How events within the magic circle and its game world relate to the broader sense of human culture and various models of human psychology or sociology is the subject of much writing and discussion within game design. The magic circle as created by Johan Huizinga in *Homo Ludens: A Study of the Play-Element in Culture* and refined by Salen and Zimmerman defines the space in which the game takes place and marks a useful boundary between what occurs in the game and events that occur outside of the game. The circle is permeable in the sense that the players can cross into it and enter a fantasy world or step outside of it back into reality. The world within the magic circle obeys its own rules which can be entirely different from the universe outside. The rules of the game establish how the virtual world within the magic circle operates and this supersedes the ordinary laws of reality while the players are within the magic circle. The concept of the magic circle can be applied to many different sorts of events but has come to have significant relevance regarding game design due to its utility.

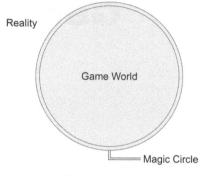

The Magic Circle

Mechanics-Dynamics-Aesthetics (MDA Theory)

Mechanics-dynamics-aesthetics, or MDA theory, is a framework used to understand the process of game design and development. MDA theory developed from a series of workshops taught at the Game Developer's Conference by Robin Hunicke, Marc LeBlanc, and Robert Zubek from 2001 to 2004. The theory visualizes how information flows from the game designer to the player. First, the designer builds the mechanics or rules of the game. This system of rules defines the runtime dynamics of the game. These game dynamics, in turn, create the emotional experience of playing the game that the player enjoys. The experience a player typically looks for when playing a game is to have "FUN." How you define what is fun is the critical question that the MDA framework tries to answer. MDA Theory provides a list of eight elements that can be used as a definition for fun within a game (Hunicke et al., 2004).

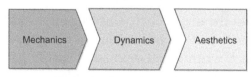

Mechanics-dynamics-aesthetics

Back in 1999, before the 3rd edition of *D&D* was rolled out, the Vice President and Brand Manager of *Wizards of the Coast (WotC)*, Ryan S. Dancey, surveyed players in an attempt to discover what its players were looking for in a role-playing game. The results of the *WotC* study showed that there are eight core values critical for a successful RPG experience to happen. Interestingly, the eight core values of RPGs defined by *WotC* line up quite naturally with the eight elements of fun defined by the MDA framework created by Robin Hunicke, Marc LeBlanc, and Robert Zubek in their *MDA: A Formal Approach to Game Design and Game Research* paper. Listed out these values and features are:

1. *Sensation*: Players must experience something new. Including new rules and abilities for things such as new magic items, spells, and monsters to more ambitious material such as a new character class, settings, and adventures. Anything new is okay just so long as it is unfamiliar to the player and doesn't break the game. Exactly what counts as a fresh experience will vary considerably from player to player.

2. *Fantasy*: The players must use their imagination. The designer must provide a setting and adventure capable of triggering the player's suspension of disbelief and immersion into the game world.

3. *Narrative*: The game must have strong characters and an exciting story. The non-player characters, villains, and storyline must have enough flavor, depth, and breadth to draw the players into it. The storyline must be strong enough that the players wish to see it finished.

4. *Challenge*: The complexity of the problems the players face must increase over time. Much like a narrative arc, you usually start off slowly and build up over time. At no point should the players be overwhelmed by the difficulties they face—unless you are writing a horror story. The players should feel a natural desire to complete the adventure.

5. *Fellowship*: The game must allow friendly competition between players. This competition is what makes the players feel a part of a community and fosters relationships with other players. The designer must make sure that he provides the opportunities within their adventure that encourage developing a sense of community and comradeship between the players.

6. *Discovery*: The game should fulfill a need to explore and reward such behavior. The players should be encouraged to use strategic thinking to make long-term plans, develop these goals, and explore the fantasy world that the designer has created. The game designer should put in place various rewards for doing so which can take the form of spectacles, new allies, treasure, knowledge or other things that benefit the players.

7. *Expression*: The game should encourage each player to express themselves and their creativity within the game. The game must have

actual role-playing. The players should be allowed to develop and define their characters, interact with other players and NPCs, and interact with the game world in which the characters exist. Engaging the players in the game world will make the players care about the game world and the goals of the game.

8. *Submission*: The player should want to come back and continue playing the game. The total level of annoyance and frustration with the game should never overwhelm the player's desire to keep playing it. The game must be mentally challenging but not frustratingly so. The game should offer enough new challenges, experiences, and rewards to keep the players coming back for more. It should never allow any technical or other elements to distract the players from the fun of playing the game.

The MDA framework and RPG core values are fantastic tools for us to use since they provide a robust framework for considering the different elements game designers must include when making a game. While your game might not hit every single one of the eight different goals listed here, it should utilize at least a few of them. If your game isn't doing so, then it is time to think of some ways to improve your game.

Semiotics

The field of semiotics is the study of signs and symbols and how they create meaning. Salen and Zimmerman connect the study of semiotics with game studies. The core concepts of semiotics can be broken down into the following four elements:

1. "A sign represents something other than itself" (Salen and Zimmerman, 2004, 57). The pieces on the game board act as stand-ins for the person playing the game, marking their spot and also denoting the current state of the game. A great example of this is a flag of any given country. The flag is a symbolic representation of the country itself and all that it stands for.

2. "Signs are interpreted" (Salen and Zimmerman, 2004, 57). People have to interpret the sign for it to have any meaning. Culture shapes that interpretation. Without a culturally agreed upon association of meaning to a specific sign, the sign would be either meaningless or have its meaning subject to change. An example of this happened to me on a trip to Taipei, Taiwan some twenty odd years ago. My group flagged down a taxi in front of our hotel. To our shock and horror, the taxicab had little Nazi flag stickers plastered all over the body of the car. We quickly dismissed this taxi and signaled another. This one too was covered with the same offensive flags, and we sent it

away. By the time the third taxi covered with red flags with swastikas showed up we were running late and had little choice but to enter it. On the drive, I asked the driver why he had these flags stuck all over his cab. "Oooh, that's double good luck!" he exclaimed. "It's the good luck color with the good luck symbol!" To him, the swastika is the traditional sun symbol and red a good luck color. The taxi driver had no idea whatsoever about the flag's association with Nazi Germany or the brutality and horror of that regime. Indeed, these flag stickers were on every taxi I saw on that trip, and I never talked to a single taxi cab driver who thought anything of them other than "double good luck."

3. "Meaning results when a sign is interpreted" (Salen and Zimmerman, 2004, 57). This statement seems an obvious corollary to number two, but it emphasizes the outcome of the process rather than the process itself.

4. "Context shapes interpretation" (Salen and Zimmerman, 2004, 57). The cultural context, immediate setting, or even the time in which the symbol occurs can influence its interpretation. The paintings of the Renaissance masters such as da Vinci, Michelangelo, Donatello, Raphael, and many others are full of symbols that conveyed great meaning to their audiences. Over time though these meanings have now become either lost or distorted to the point that it takes a significant amount of study to understand the meaning the artist initially envisioned (Gruden, n.d.).

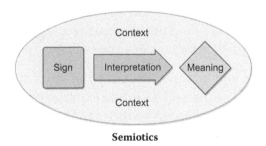

Semiotics

Meaningful Play

As a designer, you must strive to provide meaningful play to your players. Salen and Zimmerman provide a precise definition of meaningful play within games. Players must have clear choices in the game, and these choices must have a discernable impact on the outcome of the game. Players need to be able to see the connection between their decisions and the results of these choices in the game. Making sure the goal(s) of your adventure are clear will help you do this. Achieving these goals then provides the player with a more profound feeling of satisfaction and helps connect their actions to the outcome of the game (Barwood and Falstein, 2006; Salen and Zimmerman, 2004, 47–52). To design clear choices it helps to understand just what comprises a choice.

Salen and Zimmerman break down the anatomy of each choice into five events.

1. What is the context of the choice? What events preceded the decision and what is the current status of the game in which the choice occurs?
2. How is the opportunity for making a choice conveyed to the player? What lets the player know that they need to make a decision?
3. How is the player given an opportunity to make a choice? What exactly does the player have to do to make a choice? Do they roll the dice, state their action, or utilize some other process?
4. What is the outcome of the choice? How does the result of the decision affect the game? Does it change the story or affect future choices?
5. How is the player informed of the result of the choice they have made (Salen and Zimmerman, 2004, 76)? Usually, the GM describes the outcome in a TTRPG. If this isn't the case, then decide what method you are using to communicate the consequence of the choice to the player.

Flow

Enabling your players to engage in meaningful play is a key requirement in the concept of "flow." When a player is in a state of flow they operate in a timeless state of absolute focus, absorption, and enjoyment. Putting your players into a state of enjoyable flow is a fundamental goal of any game. Csikszentmihalyi and Nakamura define eight features of a state of flow.

1. Absolute focus and concentration on the current task. The player must be able to lose themselves in the experience of play.
2. Time passes quickly or seems to distort. Absorbed in the game, the player loses any sense of time.
3. The player engages in meaningful play. The goals and potential rewards of a situation must be known as the player takes action, receives feedback, and experiences the consequences of that action.
4. The gameplay is so intrinsically rewarding that the act of playing the game becomes a goal in and of itself. It becomes the hobby you can't seem to put down and look forward to doing.
5. A corollary effect of being entirely focused on the game is that players lose their sense of self. Any sense of self-consciousness recedes into the background.
6. As the player becomes ever more involved in the game playing, it becomes effortless. A seamless merger of perception, consciousness,

and actions occurs until playing the game becomes as natural as breathing.

7. The player understands how to deal with the situations occurring within the game. This understanding provides the player with a sense of control and mastery over the narrative.

8. The level of difficulty within the game syncs to the player's skill level. That is to say, that the game is not so challenging that it becomes frustrating to play, nor so easy that the game is boring. The level of tension in the game will, of course, vary from scene to scene, but in a general sense, the degree of intensity that the game provides to the player is neither overwhelming nor trivial.

Nakamura and Csikszentmihalyi note that what exactly constitutes the correct amount of flow differs from person to person. A challenge that might embody a stern challenge to a new player provides only a minor problem for an experienced participant. Finding the correct balance for the various encounters, puzzles, and hazards of your game that will appeal to different player types throughout your narrative is a truly arduous task and requires practice to perfect. Remember that you can't keep your players on edge all of the time. You will need to have alternating periods of stress-inducing intensity and other periods where you allow the players to rest their minds a bit and prepare for the next bout of high-energy gameplay. Successfully achieving the right balance between anxiety and boredom and placing your players into a state of flow will keep them playing your game.

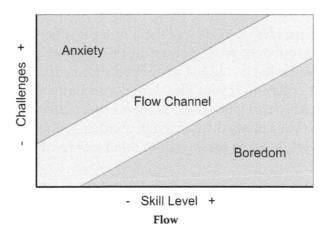

Flow

Additional Resources

Game design is a young field of scholarly inquiry and no single golden rule to making a successful game yet exists. There is, however, a lot of accumulated advice from successful game designers that has built up over the years. A fantastic collection of information is available online at Gamasutra

(gamasutra.com). This website is an online smorgasbord of game-related material which the game industry has been using for many years to post relevant articles. It is probably the largest repository of game-related documents anywhere. Make sure that you visit this website and dig through its extensive archives and game design related material. Books such as Jesse Schell's *The Art of Game Design: A Book of Lenses* or Salen and Zimmerman's *Rules of Play: Game Design Fundamentals* form a brief critical reading list about game design and theory. The video game theories and development advice found within these books and websites are useful to our task of developing a TTRPG adventure and form a sound basis for understanding game development.

Conclusion

Between the magic circle, the MDA framework, semiotics, choices, and the goals laid out by the *WotC* survey results, we can cobble together a useful philosophical guideline to steer our development efforts. As you develop your adventure idea, you will need to keep in mind the eight aesthetic goals and core values of an RPG that your game will have to include for your efforts to be successful. Juggling all of these different goals is no small task, and we will go over a few developmental methodologies and processes soon to help you do just that.

Assignment

Review your game ideas and analyze them to see if what you are proposing meets all of the different goals laid out in this chapter. Make a list of the eight core goals of role-playing and write out the elements from your concept that fulfill that criterion. If your idea does not accomplish these goals then what can you add so that it better meets these expectations? Are you offering clear choices to your players? Go through another round of brainstorming and ideation while keeping these goals in mind and see if you can develop a robust concept.

Chapter 7

The Game Development Process

Creating an adventure worthy of publication is a very challenging task. It requires skilled writing, beautiful artwork, level design, as well as good page layout, typography, and graphic design skills. Unless you have all of the required skills already, you will need to put together a team of people if you want to make an excellent product worthy of your portfolio. Having a team means that you will need to manage a team. What follows is a brief guide to several popular approaches to team management used by developers and industry professionals.

As game development evolved from the simple video games of the 1970s to the massively complex and graphically demanding current generation of games, the need for organizing the development process became very acute. In response to a variety of production problems, the game development industry discovered a variety of flexible approaches such as Agile, Scrum, XGD, and iterative design to efficiently creating games (Demachy, 2003; Dreyer, 2013; McGuire, 2006). Even though these processes evolved in large production facilities, knowledge of them is beneficial to almost any sort of group project. Organizing and prioritizing an elaborate production can be a daunting task even for the most professional group. Having a familiarity with these methodologies is useful for anyone working on group projects or who intends to go into the game development industry. Read and review the different approaches presented in this chapter. Take what you need from them for your project to help you keep things organized.

Agile

The first of these development methodologies that we will discuss is Agile. The "Agile Manifesto" was published by Martin Fowler and Jim Highsmith based upon the work done by the members of the Agile Software Development Alliance. Agile is a set of guidelines and practices to help manage a development team. While initially created for software development, the Agile methodology has been used successfully to develop many video games.

Agile can be boiled down to a set of fundamental principles to be followed by the development team for a project. Modified from the "Principles behind the Agile Manifesto" list on the original "Manifesto for Agile Software Development" website, the following principles can be applied to a TTRPG development team (Beedle et al., 2001):

- The primary goal is to satisfy the players.
- Embrace change even if it occurs late in development.
- Develop a working product as quickly as possible.
- Everyone on the project must work together every day throughout the development process.
- Enable the motivated individuals on your team to get their jobs done.
- Prioritize face-to-face communication between team members.
- A working product is the primary measure of progress.
- Everyone should be able to maintain a steady rate of development.
- Pay constant attention to delivering a quality product.
- Keep the production process simple.
- Self-organized teams are the most efficient.
- The team should regularly reflect on how to improve their operation.

Since Agile was initially conceived, there have been numerous expansions, expoundings, iterations, and offshoots of these core principles and methods. Applying Agile to a project has proven to provide a solid basis for many different types of production (Beedle et al., 2001; Keith, 2010b; Matuszek, 2003; McGuire, 2006; Meulle, 2014). In the process, Agile has become quite a buzzword among the business class, even though it does have its flaws (Miller, 2008; Rantaeskola, 2013). The most notable drawback is that it can shift the focus of development away from product results and place too much emphasis on method (Kupersmith, 2011). That being said, any technique or methodology that can enhance team collaboration, eliminate wasteful processes, encourage practical development goals, and enable product iteration has value (McGuire, 2006).

Scrum

One of the outgrowths of Agile is the Scrum development framework (Dreyer, 2013; McGuire, 2006). Designed to be lightweight and flexible, Scrum is a modified approach to Agile development (Keith, 2010a). More formal than other Agile based approaches, Scrum contains a set of clearly defined roles and events. Use this brief guide to Scrum to discover the aspects of this approach worth leveraging in your work.

Ken Schwaber and Jeff Sutherland in *The Scrum Guide* (2016) define the principal roles as the Product Owner, Scrum Master, and the Development Team. The product owner is in charge of determining the material slated for creation called the Project Backlog. Acting in large part like a film producer, the product owner keeps track of production, determines priorities, and ensures that everyone is kept informed on how production is progressing. The Scrum Master acts as a director of the project. This person manages the development team and serves as an intermediary between the other elements of the Scrum team and outside groups as well. The Development team works to meet the targets set out in the Project Backlog by the Product Owner and Scrum Master. The entire team is responsible for achieving the production goals at the end of each production period.

The Scrum development cycle is broken down into a set of five discrete events: Sprint Planning, the Sprint, Daily Scrum, the Sprint Review, and the Spring Retrospective. Taking no more than a maximum of eight hours, the sprint planning stage sets a specific goal and a fixed scope for the next sprint cycle based on the project backlog. A Sprint is a development cycle of a set time, or time-box, such as one month during which a finished product or increment gets completed. Each sprint is like a mini-project with a limited scope and timeframe. During the sprint, the goal should remain fixed to avoid delays. The daily scrum is a brief time for the entire team to create a daily work plan, held at the same time and place each day to avoid confusion. Communication and problem identification are critical components of the daily scrum. Sprint reviews happen at the end of each sprint cycle and allow the team to discuss what the sprint accomplished (Rubin, 2018). The analysis provides an opportunity to demonstrate all of the work recently done and familiarize the team members with the overall progress of the project. The sprint retrospective is a team meeting which analyzes problems and improvements for the next sprint cycle (Sutherland and Schwaber, 2016). While this is a rough overview of the sprint process, it shows how the Scrum development cycle derives and relates to the Agile methodology (Keith, 2010a).

XGD: Extreme Game Development

Thomas Demachy explains the main points of Extreme Game Development (XGD) in his Gamasutra article, *Extreme Game Development: Right on Time, Every Time*. A much looser approach than the formalism of Scrum or the guidelines of Agile, XGD forms what amounts to a production philosophy. The tenets of XGD are:

- *Simplicity*: In artistic circles this is known as the "don't make it if you aren't going to see it" principle. Summarized as only doing what needs to be done and nothing more (Demachy, 2003; Parr, 2009). Figure out the minimum required to get the job done and do that (Parr, 2009).
- *Communication*: Prioritize face to face interaction and make sure that everyone on the team is in regular contact with each other. Anything written down needs to be accessible and brief enough that everybody reads it.
- *Feedback*: At a regular interval have meetings of the whole team to provide critical feedback. Include the things that are going well and issues that need addressing. Use this to keep the entire team up to date and on track.
- *Courage*: It takes courage to admit mistakes and deal with problems. Pushing forward without already knowing the answers or even the issues that you are going to face during development takes a leap of faith for those involved.

In addition to these core principles, there are a few other elements to XGD. Use short development cycles which allows team members to provide feedback quickly. Be flexible with your schedules so you can respond to changing needs. Overlap the responsibilities of your team members so if a team member leaves, the production isn't irrevocably damaged or delayed. Keep the focus on making a working product (Demachy, 2003; Parr, 2009).

Iterative Design

Zimmerman describes iterative design as a process focused on playtesting. You produce a playable prototype of your game as quickly as possible then playtest the prototype. Decide how to evolve the game based on the experience of the playtest after each round of playtesting.

The critical steps in this process are:

1. Build a prototype
2. Playtest it
3. Analyze the results of the playtest
4. Describe the problems encountered
5. Fix issues

Now return to step 1 and repeat the cycle until you have a viable product. Zimmerman sums up the core principles of iterative design as follows.

- It is not about the concept it is about the playtesting. Don't get overly attached to your ideas. Try them out and see where the playtesting takes you instead.
- Just do it. Stop planning and thinking about the problems. You won't know what they are until you start trying things out.
- Don't be afraid of failure. Failure teaches you what you need to fix. Get on with finding out the problems and providing solutions.
- Critique! Don't be afraid to rigorously critique yourself and others during the development process. You will end up with a stronger end product by being critical.
- Experiment! Don't be afraid to experiment wildly with your ideas and approaches. Just remember that the more unusual you make it, the more you will have to test things to make sure they work.
- Simplicity! Don't worry about how it looks in your design iterations. Keep the quality of things as basic as possible until you have finalized your design, then you can worry about making it look good (Zimmerman, 2013).

One caveat is that iterative design can dilute the original vision if taken too far. Remain focused on your idea and don't weaken it (Kim, 2015b). Iterative design is a very flexible and easy to understand approach to design. It is a great way to try out many things very quickly and has been used on many big budget games.

Other Approaches

Agile, Scrum, XGD, and iterative design aren't the only approaches to game development by any means. Other methods such as test-driven design, lean software development (LSD) and Six Sigma, to name a few exist as well. The goal with all of the methods presented in this chapter is to find ways to be more productive, efficient, and make a better product. Perhaps the best approach is to try out the elements of these methods that appeal to you and determine what works best with the team of people you have.

Conclusion

For small development teams, having a formal development methodology isn't necessary. All you need is good communication within the team and a well-defined vision and set of goals. Managing larger groups requires a lot more effort, and this is where these development methodologies shine.

The purpose here is to present these approaches as a sort of development buffet. Take the parts you want and discard the rest! If you eventually end up doing professional product development, you will need to have a working familiarity with these useful development methodologies.

Assignments

Assemble a test group to discuss your ideas and iterate your designs.

Chapter 8

Creating the Game Concept Document

Game Concept Document Overview

Based on what you have learned since writing up your initial game pitches, it is time to go back, revisit, and polish your best idea into a final game concept document. The game concept document is the first concrete step in turning your idea into an actual product. It describes your concept and defines the scope of your game. A useful game concept document provides a way to solidify your ideas, review them, and make sure that your project has what it takes to succeed. Crafting a good game concept document is a fundamental requirement before you begin production of the game adventure that you will work on for the rest of this book.

The goal of the game concept document is to identify any strong or weak points in your proposal and communicate your idea to your team. For our purposes it will be used more to refine and review our ideas since we aren't relying on outside funding to finish the project. It is a good idea to get used to preparing and presenting this sort of document. Understanding how to convert a nascent idea into a finished game concept document ready for production is essential for anyone who plans on becoming a future leader in the field of game development.

When developing your concept document, one critical early step is to identify what your proposal must do, could do, and can't do. These three things form the constraints that define the core, periphery, and perimeters of your project. The core consists of all of the elements you must have for your idea to work. The periphery is composed of all of the things that would be nice to include if you have the time and capacity to do it. Anything laying outside the perimeter should be cut from your proposal immediately. When deciding where each element of your project falls in this model you need to be utterly ruthless in your judgment. If it doesn't contribute to your story or gameplay, eliminate it (Barwood and Falstein, 2006)!

Philosophy of Play

First, you must define the principles behind your game idea. Will your gameplay center on action, comedy, horror or something else? What you decide for this choice will determine much of the flavor of your game adventure.

According to Barwood and Falstein's *The 400 Project Rule List*, developing a philosophy for your concept will help you maintain a consistent vision throughout the development process. This philosophy doesn't mean that you can't change your mind later on, but if you do, then you should rewrite this section so you can maintain a coherent vision of your game. Maintaining and communicating your game's philosophy of play is critically important when you have multiple people working on your game.

In an action game, the most important thing is the action! Players will have to be quick-witted and tough to survive the fierce hordes of monsters and foes you will throw at them at every turn. They may even need to have a few crafty moves up their sleeves to survive. Action stories tend to be simple and straightforward with fundamental goals such as survival or defeating the bad guy in a straight up fight. Action elements can be an easy fix to other types of stories as well. Anytime the story gets a bit slow, throw some foes at your group of adventurers to provide a bit of excitement.

An adventure centered on comedy can be a real challenge to write. Comedic elements such as incongruity, misdirection, good humor, callbacks, appropriate repetition, and most of all the timing, can be challenging to get right. Don't be afraid to put yourself out there and take a few risks in your material. Comedy writing frequently involves jokes. A typical joke can be broken down into two or three parts: the setup, the punchline, and an optional tag. The setup provides the background the joke will need to succeed without going into excessive detail. The punchline offers the counterintuitive surprise that creates the laughs. The punchline is where you steer things sideways from the direction the setup seemed to indicate. The tag is an additional twist provided on top of the punchline to grab a few more laughs. Just so long as you can keep going in unexpected directions, you can add as many tags as you want.

Horror themes put your players up against the unstoppable. The trick in writing these sort of adventures is to keep it from becoming too oppressive. You don't want to beat your players into submission. Allow them some slight chance of hope or survival as the situation merits. You will need to provide strong clues to your players so they will know when to run away from foes that are too powerful for them to beat. A suitable description can be critical to this. If you spend a while describing the overawing nature of the foe, such as how the main villain streams black ichor from the seething mass of tentacles that comprise the mile-long unholy blight that is their body, then it might provide the hint your player characters need to run away and fight another day. The goal is to create the proper atmosphere. Pick a mood or emotion and write towards that goal (Lovecraft, 2009). Horror stories are like comedy in that they can be quite tricky to write. Nevertheless, it is a rewarding experience to try your hand at it.

Take a few minutes and write down a short list of your five most favorite games, movies, books or shows. Do they share a common theme or flavor? Which one is your favorite? Why? Figure out why you chose the stories you did. What elements in your list made you select these stories over all of the others that you have experienced? Once you have identified the features that make up your favorite stories, try to inject one or more of these elements into your adventure idea. Think of all of the possible scenarios that you can create from the ingredients you have identified here and use these in your material. These elements and features that you have described should help you craft your own game and figure out the philosophy of your own game.

Write down the goal you have for your game. What is the overall emotion you are trying to achieve in your game adventure? What is the point of its story? Answer these questions as succinctly as possible. That's the guiding philosophy to your game.

Describe the Principles behind Your Adventure

Now we need to paint in the broad outlines of your module. We will go back in later and add the details, but for now, work on defining the framework for your game. Figure out what are the central conflicts and issues that comprise your story. Are you trying to touch upon a societal or ethical dilemma or are you providing an entertaining diversion? Do questions of good and evil or murkier issues of morality play a role? Do the players act the part of heroes, villains, or both in this narrative?

A dose of ambiguity in the moral choices presented to players can be quite healthy. It makes the game more exciting and mysterious if the players don't know which way they should turn in a crisis. Taken too far, this risks making the gameplay undefined, not far enough and things become too predictable.

Moral questions shouldn't be limited to just one character. In your adventure, there will probably be a team of characters playing the game and so issues centering on only one of them would become tiresome for the other players. The trick is to put the whole group into situations that put their ethics and morality to the test and then see what the players do. The central conflict does not have to be a simple one. In fact, it doesn't even have to be about good and evil. The battle can be between law and chaos, sanity and insanity, blue versus orange or some other moral variation.

Be aware of your internal reasons for wanting to make a game. Does it stem from your internal struggles or repressed emotions and desires? If so, then you will need to make sure that these emotions resonate with your target audience enough to create a workable product. You shouldn't make your game so personal that it is incomprehensible to anyone else. It can be difficult to write about your innermost emotions and secrets. If this is what you are trying to do then at least make sure that the choice is a conscious one and that the message you are conveying is a clear one.

How big is your project? This project is probably your first attempt at creating something this ambitious. As such, you need to keep the scale of the project relatively small and manageable. Misjudging the size of your project is pretty much inevitable the first time around. The project will end up bigger than you thought. You need to begin the process with a fair bit of wiggle room in what you are trying to achieve. If there is an idea that you have had floating around your head for years that you've always wanted to get out onto paper, this isn't the time for it. That great project you've been working on for years isn't going to be a small or manageable one. Save the big plan for when you have gained some experience working on this sort of material and can do a professional job on it. Trying to create your masterpiece the first time out of the gate is a recipe for frustration and failure. Go with a fresh idea that you aren't emotionally attached to. That way, if you need to make significant cuts and edits you aren't so attached to the material that you can't trim away the excess. Failure to accurately judge the scale of a project is the single most common error unexperienced designers make. Factor that into your considerations. It won't prevent you from misjudging things, only experience will do that, but it will make things more manageable knowing that you will get the workload estimate wrong the first time you do this.

Think about whom your game appeals to and how it will do so. What are you focusing on in your product? Will your customers be attracted to your game adventure for the excellent graphics, exciting story, thrilling action or novelty of the product? What makes your product better than any similar products?

There are many questions to answer, but figuring out the answers will help you pitch your product to a board of executives, investors, or customers one day. Answering these questions will help you build a stronger product with enough depth and vision that others will recognize the value of what you have made. Don't limit yourself to just the questions I have prepared for you, but ask your own. Figure out the purpose behind the problems and goals presented here for you. If you don't have enough information on the issue at hand, then you will need to figure out how to gather more information. Consider alternative interpretations of the information you have. Spend the time you need to discover the implications and consequences of your answers.

The Game Concept Document

The core of the matter is the game concept document. This document is a set of questions that you will need to be able to answer to pitch your proposal to a group or company. The point of all of these questions is to determine the feasibility of your idea. Can your concept be completed with the resources currently available? If not, what additional resources are required? Is more equipment, personnel, software or financing needed? Does the eventual return on this investment justify the expense of the project? The game concept document is an attempt to answer all of these questions. Select your idea carefully by considering its originality, scope, target audience and difficulty. Remember to pick a proposal that you enjoy enough that you will not mind working on it for many, many days because you most certainly will. Hard work now will pay off handsome dividends later in the quality of what you create.

GAME CONCEPT DOCUMENT WORKSHEET

Name: Your name goes here. It is important to assert ownership of your ideas.

Title: What is the working title of your adventure.

Genre: Describe or list the game's genre.

Description: Provide a brief description of the core of your game or adventure.

Conflict: Describe the central conflict in your story. How does this conflict motivate your players?

Audience: Who is your target audience?

Selling points: What are the unique features of this game? What will make people want to buy this product? What is different about your product that makes it stand out against the competition?

Market information: What similar products already exist?

Ship date: What is the estimated completion date?

Cost: How much will it cost to complete this project?

Challenges: Are there any obstacles to completing this project? What are they?

Now that we've got our questions let's address them each in turn.

Name: **Your name goes here.**

You've got this one covered!

Title: **What is the title of your adventure?**

Though it might seem obvious, this is a tricky question. The title needs to be something both catchy and memorable. It also needs to be available. There shouldn't be a similar existing product that already uses that name. Do a trademark search at the "United States Patent and Trademark Office" (www.uspto.gov/trademarks-application-process/search-trademark-database) to see if there are any trademarks you might be infringing on. You do NOT want to get sued for copyright or trademark infringement! Google is your friend. Make sure that a quick search doesn't give you anything wildly popular or return millions of results. You want a name that quickly links to your product. If the name you select sends people to other websites or products instead then you haven't helped yourself at all. The availability of a suitably named website address might also be a factor depending on how you want to market your product.

Example: "Forest of the Blood Moon"

Genre: **Describe the game's genre?**

The primary genres to choose from are action, adventure, comedy, drama, horror, mystery, and romance. Your game adventure might fit into several of these categories or be something else entirely, but whatever is the defining feel of your proposal you'll need to describe it. You can combine features from multiple genres and create a hybrid, but your idea will probably have one dominating theme even so. You can always include additional topics within the broader purview of things to provide contrast or ratchet up the tension a bit. Action stories have lots of explosions, combat and physical risks. Adventure stories take the players on a journey or mission somewhere exciting and dangerous. Comedies try to get the audience laughing through jokes or humorous situations. Drama concerns itself with serious character development in one form or another. A horror tale uses suspense or shocks to frighten the players. A mystery involves solving a puzzle or conundrum. Romances have at their heart the relationship between the characters in the story. There are many genres that we could also include such as satires, political fiction, thrillers and more, but the ones listed form a pleasantly broad spectrum. We will explore the particulars of each genre later on when we discuss writing the story and plot. You only need to figure out the overall theme for now. The details we will fill in later. Write up your answer in a short paragraph.

Example: The adventure will mix aspects of the action, adventure and horror genres. The overall mood will be dark and quite grim. There will be some brutal scenes to elicit horror and fear, but unlike a traditional horror narrative where there is a feeling of helplessness in the face of overwhelming evil in this tale, the heroes should ultimately prevail. Woe to the adventurers whose bravery fails and they choose to run.

Description: Provide a brief description of the core of your game or adventure.

In one or two paragraphs, outline your game adventure's central features. The outline should match the genre you've just selected reasonably closely. Start by taking your elevator and comparison pitches and expounding upon them to fill in the rough outline of how your story will unfold. You don't need many details just enough to give the reader a coherent idea of what will be going on so be succinct and to the point.

According to Magic the Gathering's head designer Mark Rosewater a good game has a central defining goal behind it. Your idea needs to have pizzazz (Rosewater, 2011). When you write out your adventure's core idea, try to be descriptive and engaging. Your goal will help you make future decisions and aid you in designing all of the different elements that will compose your final product. Since the core of your game is so critical to its success, you should take your time and develop your thoughts until you have something exciting (Rosewater, 2011).

Example: In "Forest of the Blood Moon," the adventurers are out to discover why travellers who travel through the nearby forest are vanishing and fix the problem if at all possible. After stumbling upon a few gruesome incidents, the players will eventually uncover the vicious wolf cult of Fenris behind these disappearances and have to stop the cult from completing the terrible ritual designed to summon Fenris to Earth and bring about the end of the world as we know it.

Conflict: Describe the central conflict in your story. How does this conflict motivate the players?

A good adventure story involves a lot of conflict (Irvine, 2016). The strife can be as simple as fighting a boss monster and their minions or include solving a complex mystery or puzzle. Conflict arises from putting an obstacle in the way of the characters and forcing them to overcome it. These obstacles can take many varied forms depending on the nature of your story. Climbing a mountain, fighting a dragon, or solving a murder are all appropriate obstacles for a group of player characters. Players need a goal interesting enough to make them want to overcome the challenges you place in their path (Sutherland, 2005). That goal should reflect the core of your game, and the conflicts in your adventure should flow from that central idea (Barwood and Falstein, 2006).

What is the conflict at the heart of your adventure? Is it a quest for an item, a person, a place, or to survive? Who is the main villain in your story? Are you saving the princess from the dragon or the dragon from the princess? In literary circles, conflict breaks down into man against man, man against nature, man against self, or man against society. These conflicts broadly break down into external or internal conflicts. In a man against man conflict, it is the conflicting desires of the different characters that create the conflict. The opposition can take the form of a great villain such as Sauron from the *Lord of the Rings* trilogy or something a bit more modest such as the tribal leader of a band of goblins raiding the local trade routes. Man versus nature boils down to being a survival story. The characters might be caught in an earthquake, a blizzard, or find themselves stranded on a desert island. Man versus society tales force the character to make tough moral choices that may conflict with social norms. In this type of story, the characters might find themselves battling the institution of slavery such as in the classic "A" series of D&D modules set against the slaver pirates of the Pomarj. Man against self is trickier to pull off in a TTRPG adventure because the struggle is internal to the character. The character must choose a path or overcome their nature in some fashion. The contest could be between the character's good and evil nature, desires and virtues, or even their self-image. Since most adventures involve a group of different characters and the GM has little control over the internal dimensions of the player's characters, this one would be tough to pull off and I don't suggest trying it for your first attempt at writing game adventures! There are a few other possible types such as man versus fate or the supernatural where the struggle is against destiny, the gods, or some other force outside of nature, or even man versus machine which is a battle between the created and the creator. Like genres, you can have a bit of crossover and complexity to the struggles you place your players up against, but there's usually one central theme you can settle on to sum the game up quite nicely.

Example: The heart of the story is first to uncover who or what is behind the disappearances and then to eliminate the source of the problem. The culprits are the Cult of Fenris and their high priest who must be defeated to stave off disaster.

Audience: Who is Your Target Audience?

The critical question if there ever was one! To whom are you selling this product? You will need to do your research here. Fortunately, this has already happened. Back in 2000, the manufacturer of *D&D Wizards of the Coast* surveyed their players (Dancey, 2000). Though a bit dated, the info serves as a useful baseline for marketing our product since it was quite thoroughly executed. The target space consists of roughly 5 million people, about half of which play at least monthly. Around 20% of the target market is female. Around half of the players also play CRPGs with a quarter to a fifth also playing miniature or trading card games as well. The study goes into a lot more depth, but that is the core of it. The major caveat to this data is how dated it is. Hasbro frequently runs a current survey at their website, but the nature of the questions tends to be oriented strictly towards *D&D* rather than broader trends in the TTRPG industry (Lindsay, 2016). Spend time researching your target audience and market space. Thorough knowledge of your target market will make you a better game designer and will help you sell your product. After all, you need to know what the people want before you can sell it to them, most of the time at least.

Example: While dated, this information is still accurate enough to suffice. The target audience for these types of games hasn't changed much since this is a well-established market. Written up it reads something like this:

Our adventure targets the traditional tabletop RPG fan base. According to Dancey's survey for WotC, around 2 million people play a tabletop RPG every month (Dancey, 2000). The age range is approximately 12–50 years of age, roughly 80% male and 20% female, with most players are in the older half of this demographic (Dancey, 2000).

Selling Points: What is the Feature set of This Product?

A feature set consists of the central elements and features of the adventure you are proposing (Ryan, 1999). It forms an outline of the main events, attributes, and features of your concept.

Example: The feature set of "Forest of the Blood Moon" might look like this:

Mystery: solve the disappearances of the local villagers.

Exploration: discover where the evil cult lairs in the grim forest.

Combat: defeat the evil cultists and their minions.

Heroism: Save the world by stopping the ritual the cult is trying to complete.

Selling the Product?

Getting people to buy your product is the end goal. To sell your product, you need to list out the strengths it has as thoroughly as you can. It might be the features, pricing, distribution, ease of use, smart marketing, or an excellent story that provides your best selling point. Is there a problem your game solves or a product gap it fills? Are their aspects to the product that can be leveraged to help sell it? You can use features that are intrinsic to the project such as story and artwork, as well as external elements such as marketing to assist in selling the product. Be as thorough and persuasive here as you can be.

What Makes Your Product Better Than Other Similar Products?

To stand out in a busy market space, you will need to offer something that your competitors do not. Figure out what those essential elements are and focus on them. Maybe the competitors don't have a quality product, or you are addressing the needs of a forgotten market segment. Perhaps there is some other external opportunity your product can exploit. Take the time to study and analyze your competition carefully. Find out what has been working in your target market and what hasn't.

Mention in your feature set any unique or novel elements that you are planning to include in your game (Ryan, 1999). These form part of your selling points for your idea. In his interview with Chriss Bratt for Eurogamer. net, Sid Meier extols the rule of thirds. One-third of your feature set should be new and innovative. One-third should be standard to your genre. The last third should be an improvement upon already existing material. This balanced approach to the amount of innovation you are trying to include helps manage the amount of developmental risk your project involves. It is difficult to sell something so entirely new and original that your audience has a hard time relating to it.

Example: This particular module will serve as a demo distributed with a textbook. As such, it will likely be freely available on this book's website as a promotional tool. The goal is to make the product polished and attractive enough to serve as good promotional material and get people to buy the design book.

Market Information: What Similar Products Already Exist or Are Expected out Soon?

Time to do your research. You'll need to look at game modules and articles that are currently available. You can safely discard from consideration things that are over ten years old. You are looking for items that might impact your sales. Interestingly, pitching games that are unique is just as risky as proposing ones that are copycats. The business logic goes something like this: if no one has ever made anything like it, then there might not be any market for it at all. Remember that a typical business wants as close to a guaranteed return on its investment as it can get. Most will get gun shy about committing to something truly original. It's why you see so many bad

Hollywood remakes. The thinking is if we remake this favorite thing then everyone who liked it earlier will be sure to see it giving us a guaranteed audience base onto which we can build. On the other hand, if everyone is doing it, then you will have a more difficult time making your version good enough to see stellar sales. The key is to prove to anyone willing to listen how your idea will make them money and be competitive.

Example: Numerous similar products were once in the market such as *Against the Cult of the Reptile God* and the *Assassin's Knot* adventures. These products have been out of print now for decades and cannot be considered viable competitors. Additional research indicates that there have been only a minimal amount of adventures published for the *Glory of Yore* RPG.

Ship Date: What is the Estimated Completion Date?

It can be difficult to estimate how long your project will take if you haven't had much experience in production. Sit down and guesstimate out how long you think it will require. Now double it. If you haven't done this sort of production project before, double your estimate again. The first time you produce something, it will take you about four times as long as you initially thought. While this isn't a perfect system by any means, it is usually enough to give you a reasonable idea of how long making your project will take.

Example: We estimate the development time to be approximately six months working part-time around 8–20 hours per week. It should take three months to develop and playtest the content of the adventure and a further three months to create the artwork and do the page layout for the publication.

Cost: How Much Will it Cost to Complete This Project?

Take the guesstimate you just did for the time and repeat the whole process for cost as well. Things will end up a lot more expensive than you first imagined. The reason for this is that the first time you do something, you will make mistakes costing you money and time. These mistakes add up quickly and if you aren't careful time and cost can spiral out of control before you get finished. The good news is that the second time you do it things will go much smoother. Every time after that it gets even easier and cheaper. These rules hold true no matter what you are talking about producing. Multiplying your initial guess by only a factor of four is pretty conservative, to be quite honest. Sometimes things will take even longer.

Fortunately for us, developing a pen and paper RPG product isn't very expensive, just time-consuming. The cost is mostly only labor, otherwise known as sweat equity. If you do not have access to a computer or the appropriate software, then there are additional costs for buying the hardware and software and perhaps the time training yourself to use these systems. The monthly fee for the Adobe Creative Suite currently runs about $53/month, but there are plenty of free alternatives to this software available such as Gravit, SVG-Edit, GIMP, and Krita.

Example: Working part-time for six months results in a total of 192–480 work hours invested in the project including time spent learning how to do the process as well as any resulting problem-solving.

Challenges: **Are there any obstacles to completing this project? What are they?**

Anything else you can think of that might be an issue, or delay production goes here. Delays can range from things like setting up your business, finding a printer or a distributor, acquiring staff, and so forth. The reasons vary as much as the different types of products exist. It all depends on the situation you find yourself in, and no one else can foresee the specific problems that you are going to have.

Example: Challenges include finding a willing illustrator, setting up our business, and finding a distributor for the resulting ebook.

Conclusion

After reading this chapter, you should be ready to write your Game Concept Document. Once you have finished and polished up this document, it can serve as the starting point for actually writing up your game adventure. Materials such as this are a pretty standard part of the process of making a game. These docs will provide a framework that you can build onto to flesh out your TTRPG adventure project. Your adventure will assuredly evolve. The concept document will undoubtedly change as new features get included, and the story grows to incorporate new ideas and themes. The essential thing is never to lose sight of the core of your game.

Assignments

Fill out the Game Concept Document. Take your time and try to answer each question thoroughly. The final document should be between 1–5 pages long when finished. Show it around to people whose opinion you trust and get some feedback. Practice presenting the paper until you are comfortable speaking in front of a crowd.

Chapter **9**

The Goals of the Game

Games present a series of challenges that stimulate the interest of the player. These challenges are designed to entertain, amuse, and offer a form of escape from the everyday drudgery of life. It is crucial that you decide how your game will provide that escape. How will you convey the story to your players? How will your players progress through your game? What do you win when you complete the game? You need to provide a hook that ensnares your players" interest and then maintains that interest throughout the game.

Goals and Victory Conditions

Every game has a goal that the player is trying to reach (Rosewater, 2011). For people to keep playing your game, this goal needs to be interesting enough that the players want to pursue it. An exciting goal lets the players know what they are supposed to do and keeps the game fun (Barwood and Falstein, 2006). The nature of the purpose you provide will shape the rules of your game. A game where the goal is to use magic and swordplay to win through the dastardly monsters and rescue the king is very different from a game where the goal is to kick a ball through a basket. The trick is making the end goal interesting. You must communicate the objective in a flavorful way, not just order the players to do it. While you could just tell the characters at the beginning of the adventure that they need to rescue the king, it is a whole lot more interesting to hear about the goal from a panicked city guard who bursts into the tavern the player characters are at and desperately asks if anyone has seen the king or his abductors. When the players talk to the guard, he can inform the players that they need to speak to the king's castellan (the governor of the king's castle). The castellan can then hire the adventurers to rescue the king and provide some additional backstory about whom the kidnappers are suspected to be. These approaches differ in their use of backstory. Backstory allows you to explain to the players the reasons why the story goals exist. This approach makes the game seem more realistic and helps maintain player immersion in the game world.

Falstein reminds us that players should always have a goal provided to them. While the ultimate objective doesn't have to be apparent to the players, they should never have to search for a purpose during the game. While careful misdirection can be used to provide a sense of mystery to the game, the players should never be at a complete loss for what to do at any point. You can use smaller intermediate goals to lead the players towards your larger end goal. The use of smaller goals can help keep players interested and motivate them to pursue the primary goal you have in mind. These different goals can be used to create decision gates which take the players down one path or another and help determine which of the different endings will be the final result. To reinforce the player's desire to achieve the goal, you design in various rewards. Experience points, level ups, magic items, character wealth, and new adventure opportunities can all be used to entice players to complete your story's goal. Providing various types of rewards will help you engage the different kinds of players who play TTRPGs.

Issues in Story-Telling

Tabletop role-playing games are multi-player and social in nature. A few attempts to create solitary TTRPGs exist such as *Tunnels and Trolls* RPG and the *Fighting Fantasy* series of books, but these were the exception to the norm. Usually, the game consists of a group of characters who confront various monsters, foes, and obstacles. The game master provides the antagonist. Think about what sort of opponent you want to present to the players in your game. Will there be some snarky non-player characters in your game taunting the player characters (PCs) with sarcastic comments? Will an intelligent foe flee when it looks like he might lose a battle? Will the monsters rush in and fight mindlessly to the death? Can you write a script for what the villains will do or does the GM need to analyze and respond to the situation at hand? Do you need new rules or mechanics for you adventure to function? These questions should help you design the type of experience you are trying to create.

Steady Progress

The first step you have already taken. You have previously stated the genre for your idea in your game concept document. Now you need to flesh it out a bit more. The vast majority of game adventures center around action, adventure and mystery solving. In adventure games, the emphasis is frequently on the story. The players must overcome a series of opponents, obstacles, challenges, and puzzles to explore their environment and finish their quest. This story-telling model describes the world and a specific narrative that accompanies it. As the adventurers complete each challenge and overcome obstructions, the story builds up in each player's mind. This type of story construction is called progressive disclosure. This storytelling model presents only the minimum amount of information needed to complete the task at hand. As the game continues, the elements of the story are pieced together by the players to form a deeper understanding of the game world and plot. Frequently the adventurers must solve a progression of challenges some of which require the completion of previous quests or puzzles. This series of interdependent obstacles form the structure of the story when taken together.

Open-ended Adventure

A different approach is that of open-ended storytelling. In this sort of adventure, there is no preset sequence of events. Instead, the story consists of multiple independent or loosely connected challenges which connect in any order. An excellent example of this sort of structure is the *D&D* adventure *X1 The Isle of Dread*. In this module, the players are tasked to explore a jungle island filled with fierce monsters and hostile tribes. There are numerous different paths the player can take to complete their quest, and the module provides a broad leeway to the game master in determining how the adventure progresses. This type of free-roaming approach significantly increases the total number of hours of potential gameplay the module can provide. The challenge in writing such an experience is that you must give a significant amount of detail to a broad number of locations and encounters. There is a strong possibility that the players may never even see the majority of encounters the designer had planned. This potential encounter waste is a serious drawback to the open-ended format. The advantage is that you can provide a wide range of possibilities by treating the adventure like a sequence of short, independent stories. If you are a bit ambitious, you can run multiple plots parallel with each other thus providing the potential to cater to a variety of different players. The downside is that this can be confusing if there are too many plots going on at the same time. You can see this approach in television dramas that have multiple main characters as the show's focus shifts from one character's perspective to the next with each episode. It takes work to manage various storylines told in parallel with each other.

Time

As the game designer, you have control over many aspects of gameplay. One frequently overlooked element when designing games is the element of time. Don't forget that you control the pacing of the game. You can fast forward time to speed by the dull bits or slow things down to focus in on the important stuff. You can provide a flashback to let the player relive a previous experience or a learning montage to allow the character to progress and learn new skills or abilities rapidly. You can jump around in time skipping between various important events. You can shift your character's viewpoint providing the opportunity to experience a game event through the eyes of a secondary or minor character. Imagine letting the player experience the battle in which they defeated a demon lord through the eyes of a terrified inhabitant of the village the fight annihilated. Flashback storytelling and shifting perspective, as seen in the film *Pulp Fiction*, can be used to good effect. The viewpoint jumps around in time and space in this movie and lets the audience experience events from both the hero's and villain's viewpoint. While this sort of flashback and forward approach might be difficult to implement in a game, it still serves as an artful example of the manipulation of time. Don't be afraid to skip over some bits and fast forward time a bit. You don't need to play out every barter or financial transaction the players go through if you don't want to. Time in-game is one of the things you can manipulate to maintain player interest.

Victory

You have to decide how the players can win, or lose, your game. Victory should answer any remaining questions and tie up the remaining loose plot threads. If you want to create a sequel you can leave a few threads hanging or questions unanswered to provide the hook for the next adventure. Victory should give some emotional satisfaction. The triumph could be the thrill of beating that tough boss, saving the town from destruction, or the boon of a lot of treasure and magical goodies. Maybe the characters get to click their ruby slippers and finally go home. Whatever the answer, make sure that the victory conditions are apparent to the players. Provide the winning conditions as part of the setup to the story to achieve clarity amongst your players. If the characters are answering an advert for dragon slayers, then the adventure will likely involve killing a dragon. While it doesn't have to be so clear-cut, you will need to provide cues to the players that let them know how to win and when they"ve won. It is a fundamental principle of games that the players must understand the connections between their actions and in-game results (Salen and Zimmerman, 2004, 52).

You can provide multiple paths to victory. If the goal is to rescue the king, then the players might arrange a negotiated ransom between the kingdom and the kidnappers, or they could stage a violent rescue attempt. The players might even do something underhanded like find an impersonator for the king and provide that person to the kidnappers instead! Any of these solutions might work, and each would provide for a very different flavor for the game. Whatever you decide the victory conditions are, you must make sure that there is a path to achieving those conditions. It is enormously frustrating to players to have a goal they have no chance at achieving. The game will be dull if the victory conditions are easily met, or frustrating if the player doesn't know when they have completed their quest. You can use the minor goals you set for the players to foreshadow the nature of the greater objective and to steer players in specific directions. Good use of incremental goals will also build up a sense of anticipation in your players and provide extra motivation to complete the adventure.

Maintain Your Vision

It is critical that the designer has a clear vision for the game. Reinforce the story and mood you are creating in your adventure at every opportunity. Present a clear goal for the players and set a distinct mood or aesthetic. If you change your mind during development, you will need to go in and rewrite your material to maintain consistency. Having a clear vision and presenting it helps your players suspend their disbelief and become fully immersed in your game. Enabling this escapism is the goal of any game. Once you have achieved it, you must take steps to maintain it throughout your game.

Providing Hooks

Every adventure needs a few good hooks. Things that draw players into the game and make it real to them while they are playing. Frequently these take the form of character hooks, elements of the character's background or personality that provide an opportunity for adventure. Maybe the character lost their family to war and are now motivated by revenge against the soldiers that killed them—that's the plot to the movie *The Outlaw Josey Wales*. It could be the player has a mentor whose death or dishonor provides the motivations to adventure—pretty much the plot to any old martial arts movie. It could be anything. Some characters are in it for the money and fame, others for honor, power, or just the laughs. Whatever the motivation, you need to have aspects of the adventure there to appeal to that type of character. Decide what you want the primary motivation to be for your adventure. The defense of what is good and just against evil, revenge, destiny, envy, glory, or even just money can all serve as your primary motivation for your characters. It is a good idea to throw in a few secondary motivations to appeal to a wide array of different characters types. A noble paladin won't do anything for so base a cause as money, whereas a thief won't work for anything else. It can be tricky to provide motivations when you have no idea what type of characters will be playing your game. Fortunately, players normally fall into only a handful of categories which you can work towards (Bartle, 1996).

Player Types

Richard Bartle in his online article, *Hearts, Clubs, Diamonds, Spades: Players Who Suit Muds*, defined the four main types of players by their relationship to the game world and other players. The Bartle taxonomy of player types, or a variation thereof, were used in Darcey's WotC survey and refined in Sean K. Reynold's *Breakdown of RPG Players* webpage.

Power gamer: This type of player enjoys combat and tactics, short but intense games, and doesn't have much connection to their character as such. They enjoy creating havoc and seek to demonstrate their superiority over other players. Role-playing and character development aspects of the game are of minimal concern for this player. Their focus is on immediate concerns such as combat and tactics. They can end up causing grief to other players if you do not provide enough violence and thrills to keep them occupied.

Socializer: The socializer is there to develop relationships with other players and NPCs. Getting to know other people in and out of the game is their primary motivation. These players like to focus on immersing themselves as their character, developing their character's personality, and playing the game from the character's perspective. They enjoy acting and near-term problem solving. Developing interpersonal contacts and gaining influence is a strong motivational factor for them.

Achiever: This player focuses on the overarching plot, narrative, and the story progression of the adventure. They aren't afraid to look outside of the rules for answers and like their characters to grow as the story develops and their characters seek out in game advancement, treasure, and magical items.

Explorer: These players enjoy solving puzzles and leveraging every possible advantage out of the rule system. Strategic decision making and combat are their priorities. Explorers want to discover everything about the game there is to know. Their interest lies in the game world and game mechanics. They crave a sense of wonder and to interact with the game world.

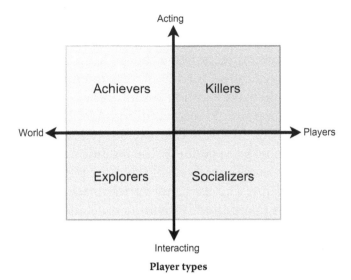

Player types

Your job as a designer is to balance out these different desires and provide something in your adventure for everyone. You must provide opportunities to advance, explore, socialize, and kill things in your adventure. Players require a mix of all of these components for a TTRPG to be considered viable though each player's preference for how much of each of the eight aspects that make a game fun might vary.

Appeal to Greed!

When the characters succeed in a quest or complete a mission, be sure to provide enough level advancement, treasure and magic items to keep your achievers happy (Bartle, 1996; Falstein). The trick is not to overdo it and break your game world or system. In other words, don't give the 3rd level paladin a +5 holy vorpal sword or enough money to buy a kingdom! The rewards should be commensurate with the level of the challenge faced, or the game will feel pointless and not challenging enough for the players who play for this sort of reward. Make them earn their rewards, and they"ll enjoy the game more. Achievers require this sort of motivation if they are to enjoy the game and the other players will likely enjoy the sense of progress and advancement this sort of positive reinforcement provides as well.

Setting Appeal

The setting itself can provide the hook that engages the players (Bartle, 1996). Doing so requires that you provide a detailed, vivid, and lively setting. It could be an ancient city steeped in corruption, politics, intrigue, and danger like the city of Sigil in *TSR*'s *Planescape* setting (Cook, 1994). A world abandoned by the gods and dominated by evil dragons such as the

AD&D Dragonlance setting or a blasted desert world filled with ruins and powerful monsters like the *Darksun* setting (Weis et al., 2003; Brown and Denning, 1991). Whatever direction you choose to go with, ensure that you provide plenty of opportunities for the players to engage with the world. These opportunities will make creating adventures easy. A great example of a very detailed setting was the old second edition *AD&D* adventure *For Duty & Deity* (Donovan, 1998). In it, the characters traveled through a demonic abyss to rescue a captured good goddess. The module was notable for having a detailed account of the realms of one of the more popular and influential demon lords in the game. The flavorful setting made it one of the better offerings from TSR in that period. Providing a detailed environment and game space for your players to reconnoiter appeals to the explorer player types and makes your job of developing an adventure all the easier.

Someone to Talk to

Try to provide settings and opportunities for players to engage with the inhabitants of your game world (Bartle, 1996). Most of the inhabitants of a standard medieval flavored fantasy world are uneducated farmers, and their conversation will reflect this. There should also be enough engrossing merchants, wizards, priests, and nobles around to provide stimulating conversation if the players choose to talk to them. A quick way of creating believable NPCs is to describe their appearance and give a couple of noteworthy details about them. These details can be their interests, problems, or personality traits. Bob, the local farmer, isn't very exciting but Humdig the local farmer who grows the only supply of wizard weed in the five counties, has a sizeable runny nose, a white shock of hair, and an overweening interest in local bee species is a much more stimulating NPC with which to interact. Compelling NPCs are the lifeblood to the socializers who play games and a critical element to any gaming experience. Developing at least a handful of these will make your adventure seem all the more real.

Danger and Excitement!

Don't let your players get bored. Boredom can kill a game faster than anything else. If you see your players looking uninterested or messing with their phones, it is time to shift gears and provide something stimulating. Create a sense of tension and danger. Even random encounters can help build your story by dispensing false leads and presenting a spark of excitement if things start to drag. The atmosphere of resulting danger that then envelops the players will only add interest to the game. That said, don't let the game devolve into a series of pointless encounters. Players need a goal to remain motivated in the long run. Further back than I care to admit I was a player in a game run by a gamemaster with severe mental health and criminal issues, though none of us knew it until long afterward. The game was deadly. There were no less than fourteen players each with two characters apiece. It made for a virtual army of player characters. Of these twenty-eight characters, only four survived the ten sessions our game lasted before the gamemaster fled town. I am proud to say two of them were mine. One of my characters survived by being smart and tough, the other by remaining unnoticed all of the time. The game was a non-stop string of deadly random encounters. I don't think we ever even got to where the proper adventure was supposed to begin. After two months of playing, the majority of characters were dead and most of the players just stopped showing up. The gamemaster then fled town on the run from the police for a litany of things the rest of us hadn't even suspected. The game was entertaining for the level of danger involved, but the overwhelming number of deadly random encounters eventually sapped the desire of everyone to keep playing. The trick is having enough of these encounters to keep your killers happy while not making the game an endless torrent of pointless battles. Make sure that each encounter has some meaning and purpose within your story then provide enough of them to keep the level of adrenaline pumping for your killers and the rest of the party as well.

Conflict Resolution

You need to provide a variety of obstacles for your players to overcome. The different types of challenges should be balanced to meet the needs of all of the different types of players who participate in the game (Falstein). Your power gamers or killers will want a good deal of violence so be sure to provide enough villainous villains and their mooks for them to hit and bludgeon. The character actors and socializers are going to want to talk to interesting non-player characters and interact with the social dimensions of the game so make sure that your NPCs and monsters are flavorful and full of personality. The explorers will desire new environments, settings, and spectacles to engage them, whereas your achievers will want generous helpings of advancement, treasure, and magical items. You can draw from real-world examples of conflict to insert material into your game. There's plenty of cases of economic strife, ideological clashes, border disputes, theft, and abuse of power that with a tweak to be more medieval and setting specific in flavor would fit quite nicely into any fantasy adventure setting. Some of these can be resolved with violence while others require entirely different approaches. The goal here is to find conflicts that fit in with the core of your game and can engage as diverse an audience as possible. Conflicts can have multiple types of resolution, and there are often several approaches to solving any given problem that can work (Falstein). For example, there might be a tribe of goblins migrating into a forest enclave of elves. The player characters could storm the goblin's village and kill them all. Alternatively, they could work to discover what is triggering the goblins migration; say a troll has taken up residence in the goblin's old cave, and fix that problem thus allowing the goblins to go home. They could just convince the goblins to go elsewhere or any number of other solutions. While you can angle your adventure primarily towards any of the player types, it is always a good idea to follow Falstein's suggestion to provide alternate routes for overcoming the foes and challenges the adventure presents. This sort of multi-path approach to completing the adventure prevents bottlenecks in your plot, provides interest for different types of players, and allows for greater flexibility when running the adventure.

Conclusion

Use the meta-rules in this chapter to make informed choices when designing your module. They are merely a set of overarching principles and goals for you to keep in mind. Pay particular attention to creating elements that will appeal to the different player types. Think about how you will be presenting the story to your players and the overall goals of your game. Make creative use of time, hooks, and establish clear victory conditions that will motivate your players to keep playing and let them get the most enjoyment from the experience you are providing.

Assignments

How does your adventure appeal to each of the four different player types? Figure out which elements of your design fit best with each player type. If you are neglecting any of the player types, decide how you will address that omission. Now revisit your concept with the knowledge of the game elements players seek out and bolster any weaknesses you perceive. You might need to rewrite quite a bit of your material if your initial game concept document was too lopsided in favor of one player type.

Chapter 10

Setting

Immersion

To lose yourself in the fantasy of the game is to become immersed in it. Immersion occurs whenever the game becomes so utterly engaging that your perception of reality subsides and is replaced by the virtuality of the game world. A primary goal of any good designer is to plunge the player so deeply into the game that they forget the outside world for a while. Your job is to craft the world, story, mechanics, and characters in such a way that the player suspends their disbelief, accepts the premise of the game, and then immerses themselves entirely into it. If the material is engaging the player will overlook any minor inconsistencies and enjoy the game.

The Three Stages of Immersion

How do you define immersion? What are the core components of an immersive experience? How can you leverage your knowledge of immersion to provide a more enjoyable game experience for your players?

Brown and Cairns (2004) delineate the three stages of immersion that a player experiences.

- engagement
- engrossment
- total Immersion

Engagement is the first level of immersion and a prerequisite for attaining the other levels. Achieving this level of involvement is all about getting the player to engage with the game by providing something that interests the player. The method used could be a superior setting, fascinating characters, new game mechanics, or just an intriguing description of an event. Engagement happens when the game reaches out and establishes a connection to the player on some level.

Engrossment is where the various elements of the game's construction combine to influence the player's emotion. It takes a well-constructed game with sufficient attention to detail to ensure that all of the disparate elements that make up the game work well enough together to get players to this level of engagement. The players have to suspend their disbelief to enter this phase. For our purposes, this means that they have to get into the mindset of the game world where dragons, magic, and other fantastical things exist.

Total immersion occurs when the player becomes cutoff from outside reality. They are now so focused on the game world that external events cease to matter. The players now feel like they are there actually fighting the dragon, being knighted by the Queen, or whatever specific scenario happens to be unfolding in the game. The story, setting and characters combine to create an alternate reality that the players submerge themselves into and leave the real world behind for a time.

Try to avoid long periods of inaction or any dull, uninspired events. Keep the players engaged with frequent short bursts of intensity, though don't overdo it and have nothing but a constant stream of action. Nonstop activity is a recipe for player fatigue. The key is to find a balance and provide a set of highs and lows in the story. The players will need time to rest and take a break from frenetic activity just as much as they will want to have periods of excitement. You have to keep your players engaged and immersed while not making the game dull or overtaxing.

Achieving Immersion

To achieve immersion, it is critical that the player accepts the game world as real. Crafting a relationship between real-world objects that the player is familiar with and fictitious in-game objects can help the game designer create that critical sense of immersion. A schema, a mental pattern of how things look and function in the real world, exists in the mind of everyone (Gard, 2010). Indeed, these mental schemas on how things work are some of the very first things everyone learns as an infant. By creating links from your game world to real-world schemas you can encourage players to suspend their disbelief and achieve a state of immersion. To do this correctly, you will need details about what you are creating. To create a believable fantasy you will need to base it in some measure off of reality.

In the adventure we are making you will need to paint mental images by creating good descriptions of what your players will see in your game world. You will have to use evocative language to paint a picture in the mind of the player of what their characters see. Do this by using descriptions your audience can relate to and try to include as many details as possible (Hausman, 2016, 47–51). Don't go overboard and make your phrasing or diction too complicated, flowery, or verbose. Keep things brief and to the point, while instilling the right "feel" for what you are describing.

An example of descriptive text can be found in the classic *AD&D* adventure module *Against the Cult of the Reptile God* by Douglas Niles. Here we have his description of a typical carpenter's shop.

> A wooden board in the shape of a saw hangs before this well-constructed building. The front part of the structure is unwalled, and inside of this breezy area the carpenter is at work. Many tools (saws, hammers, nails, pry bars, etc.) are scattered about, and some boards are mounted on sawhorses.
>
> **Niles (1982, 7)**

While not particularly florid, it manages to evoke a real sense of a typical carpenter's shop that you might find in a typical medieval fantasy village. Another example of descriptive text used in an adventure can be found in the *D&D* module *Keep on the Borderland* by Gary Gygax himself.

> For many years a solitary hermit has haunted this area of the forest, becoming progressively wilder and crazier and more dangerous. His home is in a huge hollow oak, the entrance to the hollow concealed by a thick bush. Inside is a mound of leaves and a couple of pieces of crude furniture. Even his cup and plate are handmade of wood and are of no value.
>
> **Gygax (1979b, 13)**

This brief description provides a solid feel for a hermit driven mad by his loneliness. In most adventures, the text read to the players is inside a box at the top of the encounter description. Underneath this box of descriptive text you can put the game statistics and notes for the Game Master on any of the monsters, foes, or traps that the encounter will involve. For our adventure we can write up the location like so:

> The overgrown trees parts to reveal a small clearing. At the far end of the clearing squats a large crudely hewn stone statue of a wolf. In front of this cruel visage is a dark altar of rough stone covered by many centuries worth of blood stains. The clearing is littered with the bones of previous sacrifices piled so thick that no grass can grow through it. From behind the statue come three wolfmen, human priests dressed in wolf skins, crawling on all fours like beasts towards the party of adventurers.

Wolf priests (AC 13, HD 2, HPS 12, TH +2, DMG 1d6+2, MV 12, SV 13). These powerful men wear wolf skins and act like the wolfs they worship. Unless the party initiates action to prevent it the wolfmen will run to the attack with iron clubs shaped to mimic wolf jaws.

The wolf priests are fanatics defending their sacred shrine so they will fight to the death. If the party members lose this fight, any survivors will be bound and sacrificed to their evil deity forthwith. Concealed in a small secret chamber set in the base of the statue (if the party searches the statue have them roll a Notice check with a target number of 15 to find it) is the treasure of the temple; 5,000 copper pieces and three handmade gold wolf statuettes of an evil demeanor. These small statues are worth 300 gold pieces due to their gold content but to a collector of unusual artworks the statuettes might be worth up to 1,500 gp.

So we have painted a picture of the setting and backdrop to the action, provided the game statistics for the encounter, and provided notes on possible activities and potential rewards for the players for overcoming this challenge. While a move in the right direction, there's a lot more to creating immersion than just one well-crafted encounter.

Creating a Believable Setting

Games don't happen in a vacuum. Every game has a game world in which it occurs each with its own set of laws, locations, and history. While each setting varies in detail and scope according to the nature of the game it is built for, all have in common the need to be believed. To achieve this believability, each setting requires a coherent set of natural laws, history, and environments which can engage the player. In a fantasy TTRPG like we are working with, the world needs to have captivating locales, a believable populace, and invoke a firm sense of reality even though it's all fiction. The setting will need to function as a complete environment with each different element reinforcing the sense of immersion the game is trying to create. Avoid any component in your game world that is wholly jarring or contradictory to your world or story. Such things shake the player out of their immersion and destroy the players' positive experience of the game.

Creating intricate, living, and breathing worlds is a very, very difficult task. A technique frequently used by authors and game developers is to base their creations off historical examples. It is relatively easy to access detailed accounts from archeological, paleontological, and historical examples of strange places, unusual events, and unique personalities. All of this material can be leveraged to create a fresh new setting for your adventure or game setting. It helps a lot that history is full of things more bizarre than almost anything a person could dream up. For example, a professor of ancient languages at Oxford University, J.R.R Tolkien used his extensive knowledge of medieval European languages, mythology, and culture to create the richly detailed "Middle Earth" fantasy setting in which his famous novels *The Hobbit* and *The Lord of the Rings* trilogy occur. George R.R. Martin based much of *Game of Thrones* on medieval European history. The dinner massacre, betrayals, and assassinations found in the series all have their historical equivalencies in European and Asian history (Bond, 2014). The *Assassin's Creed* series of video games base a lot of its internal mythology off of the historic hashashim group of assassins that plagued the ancient middle-east (LoPresti, 2010). Many more examples can be made here, from the ancient Egyptian themed aliens in *Stargate* to the Roman coliseums of *Gladiator* (Emmerich, 1994; Scott, 2000). History provides us with a fertile tree of knowledge to feed our imaginations.

Our brief wolf temple encounter I used earlier has its alleged historical counterparts. The Beast of Gevaudan was a gigantic wolf or beast that terrorized a French province in the eighteenth century, and there were spates of leopard man cults in central Africa reported roughly a century ago (Linnell et al., 2002; Beatty, 1915). The stories and legends generated by these events provide a wellspring of ideas for designing an engaging adventure.

Overview of the Setting

Provide a grand overview of your setting. Work from the biggest decisions to the smallest ones. You will have to decide upon the broad strokes that outline your game world first. You can go back in later and fill in the details. Are you going to use the default Arthurian England setting in *Glory of Yore* or will you go with a generic fantasy setting? Maybe you want to create your own fully detailed fantasy world. Whatever the answer, you will need to define in broad terms where your adventure will take place. First, figure out the time period of your adventure. It could happen any time from the stone age to the distant future. What happens to your story idea if you change the period it is set? Does it still work and make sense? Imagine taking Homer's *The Odyssey* and altering its time period. What elements would you have to change to make the story work?

A suitable setting can set the tone for the entire story. For example, George Lucas included a shot in *Star Wars: Episode IV - A New Hope* where the main character, Luke Skywalker, looks out towards the horizon at the twin suns of his home planet. This scene establishes the mood and emphasizes the sci-fi nature of Luke's environment. The setting suns symbolically signify the ending of Luke's life as a farm boy. Good use of color, time and lighting can create a mood for your game and add a lot of atmosphere and feeling to your story. The setting can help define the story and the characters that constitute the game. A world of endless desert will breed a different sort of characters, critters, and narrative than a water world of infinite ocean. Your setting has an enormous impact on your story and the goals that are available to your characters.

If you don't wish to get into modifying the rules extensively to match your setting, then the *Glory of Yore* rule set provides some boundaries for us. Our adventure is going to be set in a roughly medieval period somewhere between 500 AD and 1400 AD to keep the setting's Arthurian flavor intact. The rules also cover how magic works in this world, though you will have to decide precisely how routine magic is. If you make magic too commonplace that changes the setting away from the traditional Arthurian world. Based on the rules, we know that there will be a lot of physical combat, Vancian magic, and the options to play characters as clerics, fighters, thieves, and wizards.

For the wolf temple, we can use *Glory of Yore*'s default setting, Arthurian age Britain. In this world magic is a rare but potent force. Good and evil are both dynamic forces and frequently manifest in the actions of the various characters in the world. No one remains neutral for long. Characters either gravitate towards the good or fall away into evil over time. Monsters such as dragons and ogres exist and are a plague upon the peasantry. We have a wealth of historical information which we can leverage. We can go with an authentic, dark ages version of King Arthur or the more mythical, high medieval variant found in the stories. Since we want to tell a grim tale about wolves, werewolves, and evil cults, we can use the historical Arthur since the dark age of fifth–sixth century Britain was forbidding indeed and provides a flavorful backdrop for such a gruesome story.

One technique when developing a game is to work from the biggest to the smallest elements. The flow goes like this: World→Place→People→Story

Development work flow

You begin by creating the world. Defining its features, cultures, religions, and unique attributes at a very high level without much specific detail. Decide how magic, technology, religion, and society works. Once you have the world sketched out, move onto the particular places that your game will need. Describe the cities, villages, and terrains where your adventure will take place. Flesh out a few of the most important people in your game. Anyone the players will interact with needs to be detailed out to some degree. Once you have described the significant players, it is usually a pretty easy job to derive a few storylines from them. While this approach is only one way to develop your adventure, it is a sound one and relatively easy to manage. You can go different routes, for instance, coming up with the storyline first and then creating everything else to fit around that idea. There is no set process for creativity, just a bunch of helpful hints and guidelines.

World Features

What is your game world like? What significant things about this world stand out in your mind when you think about it? Consider for a moment the features that define your own real-world culture, nation or religion. How would you briefly describe these things if you were explaining them to a stranger unfamiliar with your home? What are the highlights of your home country? State or province? City? Neighborhood? What makes each of these places unique? Answer these questions regarding yourself, then answer the same questions about your fantasy world and setting.

First, you will have to decide what your world looks like overall and rough out its major features and how they relate to each other. Start by examining a few of the real world's outstanding features. The Himalayas, Sahara desert, plains of the Serengeti, Amazon rainforest, or the vast expanse of the Pacific Ocean immediately spring to mind. Any well-developed world needs a handful or two of impressive features. What features of your world stand out the most and get noticed first? For example, we can briefly describe the planet Mars.

> A cold, dry world with a unbreathably thin atmosphere. The ancient volcano, Mons Olympus, towers above its dusty windswept plains. The only water on this desert planet occurs at the frozen poles. The silent remains of strange faces and alien architecture dot the landscape as mute testimony to a dead alien civilization that flourished ages ago when the planet was lush and full of life.

OK, so maybe I'm exaggerating a bit about the dead alien civilization, but it certainly sounds more fun that way. Once you have described the significant features of your world pick out the locale you need for your game and add more detail to it. What makes this place unique from its neighbors? Is it a floodplain dominated by the large rivers flowing through it or is it a mountainous country of meadows, canyons, and small lakes? Look around for real-world examples with similar terrain and use these places as references for your make-believe setting. The more reference material you have, the more realistic your final product will be. Think about how much movement the players in your game will have. During the dark ages, most people lived their entire lives within a radius of a few miles. Travel over the rough unpaved roads was both dangerous and difficult. Few attempted journeys unarmed. People lived near rivers, lakes, and oceans to facilitate trade by ship since it was nigh impossible to transport a large quantity of goods over land. If you intend to emphasize the fantastic aspects of the game, the players might have access to flying magic carpets, ride a pegasus, or magically teleport from place to place. Magic and fantastic mounts such as these give the players access to a much more extensive array of areas, and you'd have to describe a much broader swathe of territories than if you restrict the players to foot or horseback travel. We'll be setting our game in dark ages Britain rather than Mars so we ought to describe that instead, and since the players are going to be somewhat limited in their transportation choices, we can look at Europe during the sixth century and focus on Britain in particular.

> Britain during the dark ages is a grim and unforgiving land. The old Roman civilization has fallen to waves of barbarian invaders from the mainland. Tribes of Angles, Saxons and Jutes have recently displaced the former Romans from the coast. The ancient forests to the west are still the home of the resilient Welsh. Fierce Scottish and Pictish clans live in the northlands.

Create a mental map and fill up your landscape by adding rivers, lakes, forests, plains, and mountains. Don't worry about things that won't play a role in your game. You can leave those areas of map undefined and blank for now and fill them in later if you need to. Focus on the areas where your players will spend their time adventuring. Think of your favorite real-world place. How would you describe it? Try to write up an evocative description of that place. Now try to describe a place in your game world with the same level of detail.

> The Wolf Forest is a dark and ancient place. The forest is thick and impenetrable in many places. Twisted and gnarled trees cast their shadows upon the ruins of ancient buildings that predate man's arrival in Britain. Strange and unnatural beasts stalk the depths of this forest, and only a few hardy souls dare to live on the fringes of this enormous woodland expanse.

I'm basing this description loosely on an actual place called the Puzzlewood in Gloucestershire county in south-west England which has been used for numerous movie and television backdrops and provides a suitably eerie forest to base our woodland adventure. Real-world environments offer excellent examples of different environs, geologic formations, biomes, and how these different terrain features relate to one another.

Culture

Once you have established the natural environment, you can start tailoring the local populations and cultures to fit. Consider how the world's geography has influenced your world's civilizations. How does the local culture reflect the space that it exists? Create a brief history for your local populace and define their religion(s), culture, and world outlook. Describe two of this culture's most important features or notable aspects. Keep in mind the effect that environment will play on the culture. People who live in a jungle will have a very different outlook to a group that lives in the Arctic.

Cultures can be used to provide flavor to your setting and create the illusion of depth and backstory. Every detail about your world's civilization doesn't need to be laid out. Just define the most notable features of the cultures the players will encounter. You can imply quite a bit about other cultures and achieve much the same effect as if you had fully fleshed each out. The more the players will encounter the culture the more detail you should give it. Just provide the highlights for cultures only referenced once. If the local culture is an essential component of the plot, then you will need to give a much more thorough description of it. These different cultures can be used as a source of conflict in the game setting or provide character story elements. Many ideas for how culture can create conflict and drama can be found in any news source you care to peruse. Describing the people and cultures in your setting will provide a plethora of storylines and adventure ideas to your readers.

> King Arthur's Britain is a chaotic mix of pagan Anglo-Saxon tribesmen, Christian urban Romanized British people and rugged Welsh, Pict and Scottish tribes living on the fringes of civilization. The vast majority of people are serfs and farmers with only a small percentage of the population being from the merchant or noble caste. Many petty kingdoms constitute the land of Britain, each ruled by an armored force of knights and a local king.

Places

If your world has people, then it will have cities, towns or other locales. Unique sites can add flavor to your world. Make sure that your location has a handful of fascinating things to set it apart and give it a memorable identity. A city might contain such notable features as the impossibly tall wizard's tower in the Terry Pratchett's metropolis of Ankh-Morpork or the real world example of the golden gate bridge in San Francisco (Pratchett, 1994). A place could have a unique culture or type of people like Washington DC has its politicians, Louisiana its Cajuns, or Camelot the Knights of the Round Table. Having a few real-world references to base your setting on always helps. A great example of this is Neuschwanstein Castle built by the "Fairy Tale King" Ludwig II of Bavaria. The castle was used in several films and was one of the inspirations for Disney's various fairytale castles. It epitomizes the stereotypical magical castle trope and can serve as the basis of an evocative fairy castle for our game world.

Neuschwanstein Castle (Neuschwanstein)

Consider the types of business and trade your locale conducts. If it is coastal community, then it might be a port town with a thriving trade in import and export. Precisely what the settlement is trading will depend on the rest of the setting and the size of the city. London grew rich in the middle-ages exporting raw material such as wool and importing luxury items in exchange. A smaller coastal town might have industries such as fishing, shipbuilding, or rope making for ships as its primary sources of revenue. Bigger cities will usually have more extensive trade and manufacturing of goods while a smaller locale will focus more on producing raw materials or a few specialty items. Decide the scale of your city. Is it a giant hub of population and trade or a bucolic country town? Does it have a port or essential trade route running through it? All of these questions could easily be scaled to apply to entire kingdoms or down to the smallest village. Even an entirely rural area will have a local business if people are living there. Maybe the place has sheep herders like the highlands of Scotland or is famous for its onions like Vidalia, Georgia. The choices you now make will have significant consequences later on. These choices will make the following decisions easier as you begin to add more and more detail to your setting. You may want to create maps of the land, cities, and other locations to aid in your development process. These plans can be used later to create the maps needed for our adventure. Try to detail out as much as you can, but remember that you only need to provide a setting for your module. You won't need to write up a description of medieval Madagascar if you are setting your tale in England! Be as descriptive as possible of the elements you need for your game the most. You can paint the rest of the world in broad strokes.

Let's develop a location for our adventure as an example.

The town of Wulfesheafod, or Wolfshead, is a small town located on the Black River downstream of the Wolf Forest. Wolfshead sends lumber from the forest downstream to the larger cities on the coast, but the amount of lumber produced shrank in the last few decades when the lumberjacks began vanishing into the woods never to be seen again. Now the town subsists as a little trading post exporting a small amount of produce and fish downstream. Many families have fled the place as more unsavory types have moved in. Smugglers and criminals infest the port using the dark paths of the forest to conduct their trade then shipping it by barge or boat downstream to the big cities. The local mayor and constabulary are corrupt and take bribes to look the other way. For all practical purposes, the local thieves' guild runs the town. There is a fair amount of street crime and woe to any unwary traveler out after dark or down in the dock area. The remains of an old stone wall circling the city date back several hundred years. The wall is in deplorable shape since the locals have been using it as a source of stone for building materials for a few centuries now. One benefit of all of the criminal activity is the thriving market where one can buy almost any stolen good imaginable for the right price. The low prices of this black market help keep the locals from complaining too much about the criminal elements in the town.

So now we have a description to work off of and a few exotic locations within the town. The docks are full of seedy bars, danger, and criminal types. The old city wall might have abandoned guard towers or other secret rooms to explore. Given all of the criminal activity in town, there are probably more than a few secret storerooms of stolen goods stashed in places along the old wall. The bustling black market in the central city square provides an opportunity to purchase almost anything and could spark adventures in and of itself. Maybe a character needs to go to this market to recover a specific stolen good, or the character might get robbed before or after making a purchase. Perhaps the hero is held up by brigands in a nearby alleyway or suffers the depredations of a local pickpocket. Once you have the outlines decided upon, filling in the rest of the details becomes a lot easier.

Every place needs a history. You will need to figure out the why and how of things as well. Adding a sense of history to the elements of your story is a crucial component in making your narrative feel real. Tolkien's *Lord of the Rings* trilogy is believable because of the enormous effort he devoted to developing the backstory and history of everything in Middle-Earth. Tolkien even created fake languages for each of the different races that occurred in his setting! You may have noticed the Old English word Wulfesheafod as the town's name. That was done to add a little bit of flavor and realism to things.

While we don't need to use Old English for everything, a little touch here and there helps provide that sense of history and authenticity that we desire. The core issue is why is our town of Wolfshead a criminal haven now? We'll use the Wolf Forest we mentioned early to help fill in this detail.

> Deep in the wild tangle of the Wolf Forest is an ancient temple dedicated to Fenris the Norse wolf-god. The evil priests of Fenris discovered the ruins of this temple a dozen years ago and moved in. After consecrating their new temple, they began abducting the lumberjacks who came into the forest and using them as sacrifices to their dark god. The priests also brought in and bred wolves which added even more danger to those venturing into the woods. With access to a ready lumber supply gone, the lumber industry in neighboring Wulfesheafod dried up. As the jobs deserted the town, many people left, and the ones that remained grew desperate and turned to banditry. As a midpoint on the river trade route, this proved quite lucrative, and a thriving criminal enterprise has developed in and around Wulfesheafod now.

Try to write evocative descriptions of each aspect of your game setting. It isn't just the Wolf Forest; it is the wild tangle of the Wolf Forest. Just a few choice words can lend enormous flavor to your setting. Think about what emotions you are trying to convey and how these translate into visual terms. If you want to create tension, then describe things in a way that alludes to this. If you want a lively scene, then write up the environment as bright and festive. Emotive descriptions of the setting can help clue your players to how they should be feeling at any given point of the adventure. Analyze your favorite movies or books and note how the lighting, colors, and setting are all used to set the mood of each scene. Try to write the descriptions of your adventure locations in such a way that it drives the emotions of your players.

Now we've got an evil temple in the forest and a town to go with it. This setting will provide the basis for building the rest of the adventure around it. Though I started with the locale first, you can just as easily begin by creating a unique antagonist, storyline, or even start by creating the end reward. Whatever triggers your imagination can work—you merely need that initial trigger to get your imagination started.

Conclusion

While you work on the setting for your adventure, always bear in mind the three stages of immersion and be sure to create an environment that is interesting, unique, and flavorful. Work from the biggest to the smallest elements, adding detail as you get ever closer to the things that your players will experience firsthand. You can keep the outlines of your world a bit vague but when it comes down to the things the players interact with you will need to be exceedingly detailed in your descriptions and background information.

It might seem tedious at times, but creating a robust and engaging setting will help you write the non-player characters and plots that you will need for the next few stages of development.

Assignments

Start with an outline of your world and then work down layer by layer from there, describing things in increasing amounts of detail. Since the rule set we are using defaults to an Arthurian setting, this will simplify our world development process quite a bit. Use this worksheet and fill it out for your game. You can then use the results as a basis for further development in future chapters.

Setting Worksheet

1. What period is your adventure taking place? The earliest King Arthur stories date from the sixth century while the latest a traditional Arthurian tale could reasonably take place is the fourteenth century.
2. Decide how magical a place your Arthurian England is. Does it have fairies under every hill and magic in the very air or is magic in the hands of a just few powerful wizards?
3. Where in Britain are you setting your story? Scotland, Wales, Cornwall, the Isle of Man, the Midlands or any number of other locations work. You could set your account in London or Camelot itself or go for a more exotic locale such as Ireland, Brittany or even Avalon.
4. What is the climate and geography of the specific location that the adventure occurs? What season is it? Describe the local rivers, lakes, grasslands, hills, caves, and forests? Describe any buildings or ruins the adventure needs.
5. Describe the culture and belief system of the local populace.
6. Describe how people make a living in your location. What jobs and industry exist in your adventure setting?
7. Create at least three unique places within your overall location. These can be natural or human-made.
8. Describe each of these individual locations and write down in detail what makes them unique.
9. How did each location become the way it is? Write it out and see if you can weave these details into your adventure.
10. Go through what you have developed so far and make sure it is evocative and triggers the appropriate emotions in your players.

Chapter 11

Narrative and Plot

Introduction

As explained by the esteemed E. M. Forster in his *Aspects of the Novel* book, a narrative is merely a story or a series of connected events. The plot consists of the significant events that move a story along. While related, the plot and the narrative are not the same things. The elements of the plot relate to one another and serve to advance the action of the story. We are crafting a plot for the adventure we are writing. The steps our players take while they follow our adventure's plot will create the narrative of the game.

A good plot often involves resolving a need. This need can be anything from finding true love, completing a quest, protecting the innocent, seeking vengeance, or just surviving in the face of difficulty. In your adventure, you will throw many challenges at your players. The process of finding the resolution to these challenges will create our gameplay. The problem in a game is in its inherently non-linear nature. If we were writing a book, it would be a pretty straightforward matter. You'd have complete control over the characters in the story. In a game, it is your players who control the characters and whose actions create the narrative. Predicting what players will want to do can be difficult. You will have to motivate your players to follow the plot and finish the adventure that you are designing for them. You will have to create challenges that your players must overcome to advance the plot. The problems you include should create enough tension and drama to maintain your players' interest.

These challenges will naturally form a set of decision gates that create a branching plot structure for your adventure. Luckily for us, there's a wealth of material on plot and story from which we can draw to help create our adventure. Blogs such as Carlton Reeve's fabulous play with learning, Ian Schreiber's Game Design Concepts, online articles Ben McIntosh and friend's Nonlinear Narrative in Games: Theory and Practice, as well as Chris Bateman's speech at the 2007 Austin Game Developers Conference provide ample resources to help outline the primary narrative and plot structures used in modern games.

Linear or Nonlinear Adventure

Games fall somewhere on the spectrum between being wholly linear or non-linear in their structure. A linear game is one where you start at point "A," proceed to point "B" to accomplish a specific task, then move on to point "C" to complete the next task, and so on until all the required tasks or done. Since the order of events is predetermined, linear adventures are easier to write, and the player will get to experience all of the different story elements that you have prepared for them (Reeve, 2010a; Schreiber, 2009). The challenge with a linear approach is that it can be difficult to keep players on such a direct path and a bit dull if the players figure out that they can't affect how the story ends. To make a linear story work you have to provide the player with a strong motivation to keep going until the end and make sure that they don't get distracted and veer off course. A non-linear game is one where events flow down two or more narrative paths decided by the player. The exact form a non-linear game takes can vary wildly, but the critical element is that the player's choices affect how the story ends.

Traditional Linear Narrative

In a completely linear way of doing traditional storytelling, there aren't any actual narrative choices to be made. The players go down a specified path. They either complete each plot point and proceed to the next one, or they don't. This approach allows you to shift the focus onto other elements of gameplay such as combat, characterization, or puzzle solving which occur in the lead up to each major plot point. Indeed, there can be a great amount of latitude offered to the player in each section of the game, but they must still complete each section in sequence to finish the game. Linear narratives are grand for movies and books, but they aren't always the best solution for a game. Nevertheless, linear stories are widespread in games due to the ease of writing them. Since the players are forced to play through each section, little of the game gets wasted.

Linear narrative

Branching Narrative

The branching approach to narrative presents the players with a set of decisions, each with different consequences. Each decision provides two or more solutions and takes the players down a different path which then leads them to another unique decision point. This new decision point, in turn, provides two or more paths down which the players can follow, and so forth. Each solution opens up only one of many possible futures. Divergent narrative structures like this quickly become overwhelmingly complex as the number of possible outcomes grows exponentially for each decision point. Of these possible outcomes, the players only experience one path, meaning that most of the work put into making the game gets wasted. You can structure things so that some branches end quickly or the results merge with other paths, but this doesn't adequately address the complexity inherent in this approach (McIntosh et al., 2010; Reeve, 2010b; Schreiber, 2009).

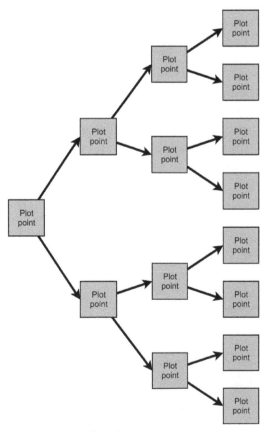

Branching narrative

Parallel Paths

The parallel paths narrative structure attempts to combine a branching narrative with a linear one. In essence, you allow the players multiple opportunities for minor choices that lead down several different paths, but all of these branches eventually merge back together leading the player to the next major plot point. This approach offers a fair compromise between the branching and linear approach. Parallel path narratives require careful management and planning, or they can still end up feeling like a forced narrative in much the same way of a purely linear plot (McIntosh et al., 2010; Reeve, 2010c; Schreiber, 2009).

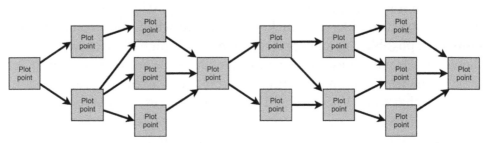

Parallel paths narrative

Linear Plot with Detours

A variation on a linear path that provides a series of stopping or decision points along the otherwise linear plot where the players can choose to go on a side quest or pursue an ancillary goal for a while. The detours provide the illusion of choice since the players are effectively deciding at each decision gate whether to continue on their current storyline or pursue something else for a time. Despite this illusion, all paths inexorably lead back to the main plot (Hartzog, 2003; Zucker-Scharf, 2011).

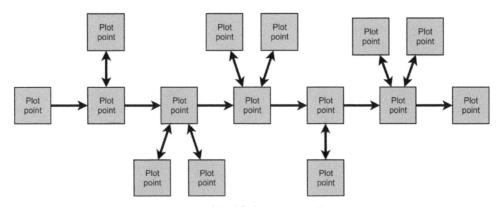

Linear plot with detours narrative

Non-Linear

A non-linear approach consists of pre-set plot points, but the order in which they occur is entirely up to the player. Since the order of events doesn't matter, each segment of the adventure must be self-contained by necessity. Only once the players have completed all of the portions does the ending unfold (McIntosh et al., 2010; Reeve, 2010d).

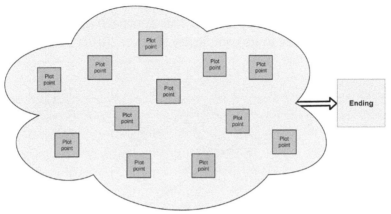

Non-linear narrative

Threaded

In a threaded approach, there are several small plot arcs that the players can choose to follow, each of which may or may not intersect. The players can follow whichever of these plot arcs they wish in whatever order they want to. While this approach eliminates any feelings of being forced, it creates problems with its complexity. This sort of plot structure is challenging to develop and may be hard for players to keep track of (Nutt, 2007; Schreiber, 2009).

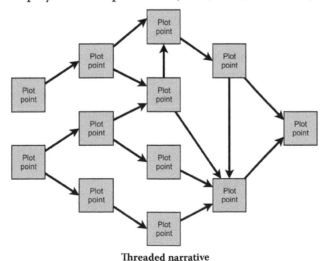

Threaded narrative

Limited Internavigability or Dynamic Narrative

Whatever you choose to call it, this method uses several mini-stories or story nests which the player can enter or leave at one or more points. These mini-stories are interconnected, and any given story nest can lead you to any of the other nests. This model eliminates a pre-defined ending in preference of a more open-ended experience, letting the player decide which plot threads to pursue and which to ignore or end. This approach can be challenging to execute successfully due to its complexity (Reeve, 2010e; Schreiber, 2009).

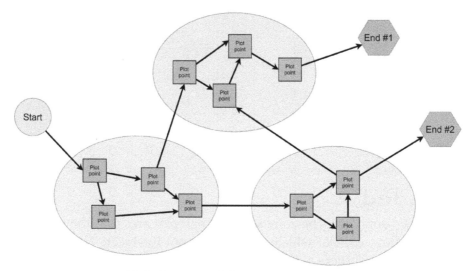

Limited Internavigability or Dynamic Narrative

You can probably sense at this point that some of these approaches are easier than others. Naturally, the more separate branches the plot possesses, the more work it will involve. Any of these approaches can work or even a combination thereof. I find it useful to begin the process of writing and then see which one of these approaches the game is naturally falling into before picking a specific strategy. Since each person's approach to writing games varies, you will have to decide for yourself whether to begin or finish with one of these approaches to creating a plot for your game.

Story versus Game

The tension between story and game is a topic beloved by video game theorists such as Jesper Juul in his paper "A Clash between Game and Narrative." One of the fundamental components of a game is choice. Players can choose what they want to do and how they are going to react to the choices in the game. If a game doesn't have any choices it isn't a game; it's a novel. However, if you put too many narrative paths into your game, it might lose any sense of story and narrative. Getting the right balance between story and player choice has vexed game designers for years with no clear consensus ever emerging. You can always use a good story to make the players want to keep playing the game (Lievano, 2010). In a TTRPG, like the one we are using for our adventure, the options available to the players are even broader than in any video game. Technically, nothing is stopping the players from skipping the setup you are writing and just going to the next town. The video game designer can structure their game in a way that carefully limits player choice. Since you cannot do that in a TTRPG, you have to focus on motivating your players to complete your adventure. The story is an excellent way to do that. One powerful method we can use to weave the story into a game is by providing meaningful choices to the player (Costikyan, 1994; Morrison, 2013; Schell, 2008, 210–211).

Meaningful choices occur when the player cares about the outcome of each decision (Costikyan, 1994). Making the player care about their choices in the game is the job of the story. A good story makes players feel involved in the outcome of the game and care about the characters in it. Establishing a connection between the players, the characters, and the NPCs in your adventure is the hardest part of designing a game. Making the player care about the choices in the game requires that each decision has the following components:

1. The player must know that they are making an important choice.
2. The choice must impact the course of the game.
3. The player must understand how the choice impacts the game.
4. The player must live with the consequences of their choice.

Morrison (2013)

Reinforce the plot of your game with a good story, interesting non-player characters, and meaningful choices, and you will have a recipe for a successful game! Each meaningful choice you create in your game forms a natural decision gate for your plot which you can use to map out your game flow.

Using Story in Your Game

The story provides context to the choices in your game. It sets the mood and drives the dramatic impact of events home to your players. Luckily for us, storytelling has been around, well, forever, and so there exists a wealth of practical advice for creating good stories.

Dramatic Structure

Formulas for the dramatic structure have deep roots in literature with examples going all the way back to Aristotle is a standard model for dramatic structure. Unsurprisingly, it contains three acts: the beginning, middle, and end.

The beginning is where you introduce the setting and backdrop to your story. It is also where the trigger for the chain of events that will become your story occurs. By the conclusion of this act, your heroes are committed to the adventure.

The middle is where the heroes of your adventure pursue their goals and face many obstacles, challenges, and puzzles. It may seem like the heroes will never be able to complete their quest or achieve their goals and things may look bleak indeed.

The end is where you resolve the questions of the adventure and reach some solution for the problems the players encountered. In a traditional story, this is where the character reveals what they have learned from their experience. In a TTRPG this is where the players learn the consequences of their actions. They also get to divvy up the treasure and progress to the next level of experience and power as their character progresses up in level.

While this traditional structure can work for games, it does need some tweaking to do so. It takes effort to include enough story cues and foreshadowing for the players to be aware of the importance of their choices. You can reinforce the sense of drama by appropriate setting and description. The more detail you put into the description of something the more you draw your players' awareness to it. If the sword they've just found is going to be an essential piece of the plot, then take pains to describe it in detail. The difference in impact is enormous between finding a magic +2 sword and finding a curved, single-edged long sword with a wrought hilt covered in gold filigree and set with precious rubies with the name of long-lost kings engraved upon the blade. The same thing holds true for your combats. If you want to emphasize the importance of a particular battle, then make it a big one! Throw in a big boss and some minions and challenge your players in such a way that they know this is an important fight. Players remember the tough combats so if you want an encounter to feel important make it as difficult as you can without killing them all or ruining the game! Try to provide spectacles and surprises for your players. Spectacles can be grand vistas, interesting NPCs, or anything visually stimulating. Use the elements of discovery and revelation to create a sense of surprise and wonder in your players. Provide something new to your players to keep them on their toes and interested in what is happening in the game. Use tough encounters, detailed descriptions, and surprise to emphasize the crucial elements of the story to your players. It will help maintain the narrative of the story.

Writing Tips

After all of that theory, it might help to have some practical advice as well. The following tidbits from Michael Moorcock and Lester Dent, two world-famous fantasy and action-adventure authors, should provide you with a few helpful hints. Together these two authors have written hundreds of novels and short-stories so be sure to heed their great advice.

Start things off with a bang! Throw the players immediately into the action. Try to make the nature of the initiating event unusual without being too clichéd. This event should provide something for the players to enjoy and whet their appetite for more. Your villains should have a goal that they are seeking. It could be money, power or something much more esoteric. Whatever the villain's goal is should provide a powerful motivation for the scoundrels to act the way they do throughout the story. The menace of the story should continuously threaten the characters. Throw wave after wave of problems at them once they become engaged with the story. Begin the adventure with an issue that the heroes must resolve, then double the danger, then double it again. Draw them into the story as deeply as possible. It is only when it looks like they will drown under the weight of their problems that you provide the release, solve the mystery, and conclude the adventure (Dent, 2013; Moorcock, 2010).

Make sure that you research everything that you will include in your adventure. Place the story in an unusual and unique locale that you have thoroughly researched and know the details about. It is an all too common failing for writers to skimp on their research and end up with vague and unconvincing stories because of it. Go out and collect a bunch of pictures or drawings for reference, list the descriptive words you want to use, and come up with a color palette or emotion that you'll keep referring to throughout your adventure. Provide the players with a clear goal. That way they are never searching for what to do next. If the players are solving a mystery, then keep adding more elements to add to the enigma as you go. Each clue reveals new riddles and puzzles to solve up until the big reveal and conclusion. Whatever you do, you must keep things logical. Even in a magical setting, the world obeys specific laws. Break these laws, and you lose the suspension of disbelief so vital to fantasy stories. Logic also applies to the plot as well. Establish all of the main characters, themes, and challenges in the introduction, roughly the first third, of your adventure. Doing so sets up a three-act structure where you can develop the plot further in the middle section and resolve things in the end. If you are worried about the players stalling, or not chasing the storyline fervently enough, then go ahead and add in a time element to quicken the pace. For example, there's the great line from the movie *Flash Gordon*, "Flash, I love you, but we only have fourteen hours to save the

Earth!" The ticking time bomb's clock never stops with 7 minutes left on the clock. The protagonist always disarms it with only a fraction of a second left. Including a time limit on the quest provides a steady drumbeat that can be used to drive the plot, and the players, forward (Dent, 2013; Moorcock, 2010).

Conclusion

Now that you have some idea for how plot, story, and narrative can be structured and intertwined with each other you can begin planning out how these elements will work in your adventure. Take your time when planning this stage out. It is critical that you get things right. You can always make changes, but the more developed your adventure becomes, the more rewriting it will take to implement any changes you decide to make.

Assignment

Create an outline of your plot and story. It doesn't have to be anything definitive, just a rough overview of how the story should go. You'll probably change things quite a bit as we go.

Example

A local branch of a sinister cult has set up shop near the town of Wolfshead. They have been charged with feeding and raising a cub of Fenris. To do this, they've been acquiring dead bodies and living victims to feed the cub a "proper" diet and prepare it to participate in the upcoming Ragnarok. The priests throw living victims into the pit for the cub to fight and devour or they hang dead victims up in the temple to be seasoned by cultic rituals for a while before being fed to the cub.

The characters are hired by the local magistrate to investigate a series of disappearances that have been happening in and around the nearby forest. The characters proceed along footpaths and trails into the woods for a day or two before encountering the site of a cult attack upon a merchant caravan. The characters follow various clues which lead them deep into the forest and a series of helpful or deadly encounters. Eventually, the players arrive at the secret wolf temple deep in the thick woods and must decide how to deal with it. If they win against the cult, certain letters, written upon flayed human skin, in the cult's possession will point players to the next installment of the adventure series.

The example above is a straightforward linear plot or perhaps a linear plot with detours. If I added in a full description of the town of Wulfshead, complete with a lot of NPC write-ups, then it might become more of a non-linear, threaded, or even dynamic narrative instead. The more I flesh out the environment, the more non-linear options open up for the GM and players in the adventure, and the more time and effort I would have to invest into the product.

Chapter 12
Adventure Outline

Overview

The hardest part is just to get started. Creating an outline is a great place to begin. Once you've built that skeleton, you can start to add more material and start putting flesh on the bones of your adventure. We can use the content we've written so far as a jumping off point. Once you reach a certain point, the momentum will build up, and you will begin to flesh things out.

Diving In

Now that we have enough material to start appropriately developing the adventure, we can dive in. There are a few locations we've thought up with the town of Wolfshead, the Wolf Forest, and the Wolf Temple that can serve as our starting points. I briefly considered changing the theme from wolves into squirrels for a more humorous slant on things, but I think it'd be more interesting to go with the original rather dark wolf theme. To begin, let's list the setting elements we've got so far and put them in the order the players will likely encounter them. Deciding where precisely the adventure will take place will put things into perspective as to how much work we will need going forward.

1. Wolfshead Town
2. Wolf Forest
3. Wolf Temple

OK, now let's go in and fill things in a bit by adding what the characters will do in each place. With the three-act structure in mind, we can break down events by the beginning, middle, and end.

[*Beginning*: the introduction to the setting, story, and initiating action.]
Wolfshead Town
- Adventurers arrive in town
- Observe and experience the (evil) town
- Get involved:
  a. The adventurers are asked by a local to save his kidnapped/lost child.
  b. The head of thieves' guild asks the player characters to investigate rumors about an evil temple subverting his bandits.
  c. The adventurers are tasked by a secret agent of the King to find the root of this evil and corruption.

[*Middle*: obstacles, challenges, and puzzles]
Wolf Forest
- Attacked by the bandits.
- Track the bandits back to their camp.
- Discover evidence of the temple.
- Go to the temple.

[*End*: resolution and solution]
Wolf Temple
- Attack the temple.
- Defeat the cult.
- Save the child, solve the rumors, or root out the evil.

[Epilogue]
Return to Wolfhead Town
- Receive rewards and acclaim.

I added the epilogue so that the story can be thoroughly wrapped up and any remaining questions answered for the players. Now just add a bit more detail and think a little more about how these places will line up with our dramatic structure. The plot structure looks like a parallel paths type. Let's throw in some options for a few side quests to pad things out at different stages and make the adventure a combination of the parallel paths and linear plot with detours types, a sort of parallel with detours type. With that in mind, what are a few short side quests or encounters I can throw at the players? After a brief consideration about what might be interesting I came up with a few options:

- Evil wolf pack
- A wolf priest hunting with a pack of wolves

- Evil pilgrims
- Insane dryad (a type of wood nymph)
- Ogre

Each of these encounters would be good for a digression or two while the players are exploring the Wolf Forest. It isn't necessary to create all of these, but if I can narrow down the list to three or so solid encounters it should work. These encounters should provide an opportunity to give a few clues to the players and maybe furnish an item or two to help them in the climactic battle they will have at the end of the adventure.

Now that we're thinking up some different bits of the adventure we really ought to consider how difficult we're going to make things for our players. Adventures for TTRPGs in the classic old-school *Dungeons & Dragons* vein like *Glory of Yore* tend to fall into one of the following categories.

- *Low-level*: TSR, the company that created *D&D* back in the day, made a large number of these introductory adventures for characters at levels 1–3. A brief list of these introductory modules includes *Keep on the Borderlands, Against the Cult of the Reptile God, The Village of Hommlet*, and *The Sinister Secret of Saltmarsh* to name a few.
- *Mid-level*: These are adventures usually targeted at player character levels 4–7. Again there were a lot of these that got published. Some of the better examples of this type of module include *Scourge of the Slave Lords, The Hidden Shrine of Tamoachan, The Ghost Tower of Inverness, Dwellers of the Forbidden City, Ravenloft*, and the *Desert of Desolation* adventures.
- *High-level*: Normally representing a range from 8 to 14th level these weren't as common as the previous types. The list of these includes some of the most famous and best written examples of adventures ever made such as *Against the Giants, Descent into the Depths of the Earth, Vault of the Drow, Queen of the Demonweb Pits, Tomb of Horrors* and *White Plume Mountain*.
- *Epic-level*: Written for characters higher than 14th level, these are pretty rare fare. Not many campaigns or characters made it this far, so there was a lot less demand for these products. Those that did get published include *Labyrinth of Madness, A Paladin in Hell*, and the *The Bloodstone Pass* series.

Since this is the first adventure that you are writing it is a good idea to keep things as simple as possible. Writing for low-level characters is more straightforward than creating a challenging adventure for more powerful characters. This is especially true if you are new to the game. So with simplicity and ease of writing in mind, let's target our adventure at introductory level characters of a 1st–3rd level.

Just What You Need

One critical consideration is how long of an adventure are we trying to write? Our adventure includes a town, a forest, and a temple. We could easily enough write one hundred pages just detailing the town! An equal number of pages could be devoted to the forest and maybe even the temple if we made it large enough. Since this is supposed to be a short demo adventure, not a boxed campaign setting, we can aim for something significantly briefer such as 10–15 pages. The single most common mistake in production is to be too ambitious with your goals. An outstanding practice is to go through and identify which elements of your game idea you absolutely must include, things you'd like to have, and stuff you can add if you have the time to do so. Let's break down our setting components and list the events we need to happen, want to happen, and optional stuff for each place.

[*Beginning*: the introduction to the setting, story, and initiating action.]
Wolfshead Town
- Optional > adventurers arrive in town
- Optional > observe and experience the (evil) town
- Needed > get involved:
  a. The adventurers are asked by a local to save his kidnapped/lost child.
  b. The head of thieves' guild requests the player characters investigate rumors about an evil temple subverting his bandits.
  c. The adventurers are tasked by a secret agent of the King to find the root of this evil and corruption.
  d. The characters are attacked by wolf cultists while traveling through a lonely forest.

[*Middle*: obstacles, challenges, and puzzles]
Wolf Forest
- Wanted > track bandits back to camp
- Wanted > discover evidence of temple
- Needed > go to the temple

[*End*: resolution and solution]
Wolf Temple
- Needed > attack temple
- Needed > defeat cult
- Needed > save the child, solve the rumors, or root out the evil.

[Epilogue]
- Optional > Return to Wolfhead Town
- Needed > receive rewards and acclaim

[Side quests]
- Optional > Evil wolf pack
- Optional > A wolf priest hunting with a pack of wolves
- Optional > Evil pilgrims
- Optional > Insane dryad
- Optional > Ogre

Time to make a few tough choices. First, I moved "getting attacked by bandits" to the beginning. Doing so creates a useful shortcut for involving the characters in the adventure. By simply throwing them into the story I can eliminate the entirety of Wolfshead Town from the adventure or merely mention it as an option that the GM can flesh out if they choose to do so. This one decision removes over a third of the module content that I would otherwise have had to develop. Starting the adventure off this way also serves to begin things with a bang and get the players immediately emotionally involved. Eliminating the town also makes the "return to Wolfshead Town" epilogue a moot point and lets me reduce the writing load even more. We can now rewrite our outline and condense all of the events into a more manageable narrative.

[*Beginning*: the introduction to the setting, story, and initiating action.]
Wolf Forest
- Get involved:
  - The characters are attacked by a wolf priest and cultists out hunting with a pack of wolves while traveling through an evil forest. They discover evidence of a secret evil temple located in these woods and hints of a fabulous treasure to be found there.

[*Middle*: obstacles, challenges, and puzzles]
Wolf Forest
- Track the cultists back to the temple. As the party goes through the vile forest, they have the opportunity to encounter a few interesting things.
  - Optional side quest > Evil wolf pack
  - Optional side quest > Evil pilgrims
  - Optional side quest > Ogre

[*End*: resolution and solution]
Wolf Temple
- Attack the wolf temple
- Defeat the wolf cult and root out the evil.
- Recieve rewards

So we've trimmed down the outline, condensed it, and moved our optional encounters into the section where they make the most sense. I've included a few more details to some of the headings. With the current outline in hand, we can now go into the next phase of our planning.

Genre

Ask yourself what type of adventure are you writing? What are the primary elements that form the core of the adventure? Once you have figured this out, you will have decided what genre your module is. The genre is merely the literary category your module falls in. The list of possible genres you could work in is quite broad, open-ended and flexible. It is entirely possible for your work to fall into several different classifications at once or be a straightforward example of just one. Due to the game we are using, and the type of work we are writing, some aspects of the genre are already determined. *Glory of Yore* is a fantasy game with elements of myth and historical fiction in it due to its Arthurian setting. You can choose to add additional flavors to your writing. For example, you could add a comedic, mystery, drama, horror, or even a romantic focus to the adventure. If the player characters have to solve a crime, then you have a mystery on your hands. If they are overwhelmed by nightmarish evil, then it is a horror game. If it is a love story at heart, then it's got elements of romance. You don't have to make the entire storyline about one topic. You could easily include a side adventure that involves a love story between one of your player characters and an NPC, add a comedic interlude, or present a minor mystery or two for the players to solve as part of the grander scheme of things. The choice is up to you. Being aware of what genre or genres you are working in and maintaining your focus are the important things. This way your comedy doesn't morph into a romance and then into a horror game as you write it.

In our example adventure, we have a dark and scary forest full of monsters and a murderous evil cult. There's a fair amount of journeying as well. It looks like we have a straight up sword-and-sorcery adventure in the style of Robert E. Howard's *Conan* short stories. There are elements of horror, action, and adventure involved, and it falls squarely in the fantasy genre. There should be a lot of fast-paced combat, terrifying encounters, and a dangerous journey. When we eliminated the town and bandits to save space we got rid of the mystery part of the adventure, so it wouldn't make sense to try to weave that back in. We could add in something like a romantic interest or two if space allows for it at the end of the adventure to give the module a little variety.

Wilderness Adventures

Since a large part of this adventure is going to be trekking through an evil forest, this officially makes the trip itself a significant portion of the story. Monte Cook, as always, has some sage advice to offer in his Dungeoncraft segment in Dragon magazine 317. While one approach would merely say, "it takes you three days to reach the evil temple," it might be more fun in this instance to detail things out. The goal in our example adventure is to find the source of trouble, go there, and solve the problem. That being the case, we can list out all of the potential difficulties that can beset our adventurers during their travels:

- Getting lost, you could run out of supplies and starve to death.
- Weather, nothing like a blizzard to make things fun!
- Impassable terrain such as flooded streams, cliffs, washed out trails, and so forth.
- Fellow travelers could be merchants, pilgrims, beggars, robbers, refugees, or potentially anyone.
- Marauders, orcs, bandits, or other monsters.
- Since this is an evil forest, there isn't much traffic, and you won't find much in the way of inns or taverns on the road, just campsites.

Cook (2004c)

Established paths won't take the characters into problem areas unless the danger has happened since the road was built. The characters will need food, water, and proper gear. If they didn't think to bring this stuff then you could be in serious trouble, especially if you get lost. If you are off the path and exploring you will end up walking right into impassable terrain, animals, monsters, or who knows what. It is best if you have a local guide you can trust who knows the area since navigating a thick forest is a challenging feat to accomplish. Since it is possible to meet anything or anyone on the road, it provides an opportunity to have some fascinating encounters for the party (Cook, 2004c). When it comes time to detail some of this material out, we can add in a weather table and maybe some rules for navigation and survival.

Resources and Themes

Now that we've settled on the genre and style, take some time and gather together any reference material you think you might need. Some pictures of unnatural evil wolves, the evil wolf god of Norse mythology, Fenris, Vikings, and gloomy forests are called for by our story. You can create a mood board out of these images and pick a few themes and colors to reference throughout your adventure to enhance the mood of each scene. For color, let's say a dark, ominous blue-green, bright blood red, and black. Our themes are wolf related such as teeth, claws, mangy fur, grim forests, blood, gristle, and bone. All of these themes are suitably dark and exciting! We can refer to these words, colors, and ideas throughout our adventure and give it the feel of a unified whole.

Conclusion

We now have a working outline of what the adventure will look like, and we have successfully established the tone and mood of our product. We have fixed the theme in place and determined our setting. Creating this sort of outline lets us identify critical elements like our genre, theme, and locations and gives us hints as to what our plot points and story arc can be.

Assignment: Outline/Flow Chart

Create an outline or flowchart for your adventure. Using an outline or flowchart can help you visualize your game's narrative structure and make the progression of events clear to you. These frameworks can be useful for identifying problems such as having too much or too little material. Frequently when beginning a game project, the initial concept is too ambitious and has to be toned down significantly. An outline can help you identify the core aspects of your game idea and let you focus on them. Depending upon the type of story you are trying to tell, and the nature of the narrative structure you are using the result of this exercise can be anything from a simple outline to a complicated flowchart. An excellent way to get started is to get a stack of index cards. On a single card write down either one major plot point, a single important decision the players must make, or a place or person they might encounter. It is vital that you put only one thing on the card—each card represents a single significant event, decision, or encounter in your adventure. Once you have your initial ideas put onto cards, place them on the floor and start arranging them. You can add new events by writing up a new card or throw out any that don't seem to fit in or make sense. You can use string, straws, or cards with arrows drawn on them to indicate connections. Add color and make notes in a notebook or on the reverse side of the card if you need to. Do whatever helps you to figure out how the players will progress through your game and how their choices will affect the outcome. Once you have finished, take a photograph or draw a picture. You can now use this to help you design your adventure!

Chapter 13

Rewards

Overview

Gary Gygax gave us the truism that fame and fortune await our bold adventurers in fantasy table-top role-playing games. Indeed the rewards that people can earn for playing form a key component for any game. The fact that characters typically gain experience points for the value of any treasure found indicates that treasure is central enough to the game to be woven into its core mechanics. The types of rewards used can vary enormously depending upon the nature of the game and the audience that the game is trying to appeal to (Gygax, 1979a). That said, there are certain qualities that all in-game rewards possess and which can be used to categorize these rewards into a format useful to the game designer. Each reward possesses various core qualities which in turn can be broken down further into different attributes or categories (Hallford and Hallford, 2001, 158–160; Gazzard, 2011). Once you have settled on the overall nature and frequency of your rewards, you will have to get down to the nitty-gritty process of defining each one in detail.

Rewards

Hallford and Hallford describe the four basic types of rewards as follows:

1. *Rewards of Glory*: This type of award has no real effect upon gameplay but provides some emotional impact for the player. Glory rewards can range from a high score in an arcade game, a bonus character skin

unlocked after a tough mission, medals for feats of arms, winning by completing the game, or even just an engaging narrative experience that the player can brag about (Hallford and Hallford, 2001, 158–160). Something as simple as positive encouragement by the local NPCs would qualify as this sort of reward (Phillips et al., 2013). An excellent example of this found in the *World of Tanks* video game are the medals rewarded to players for excellent gameplay. Medals such as the "Top Gun", "Tank Sniper", and "High Calibre" achievements serve to commemorate the players' prowess. These medals have no impact upon gameplay whatsoever, but they still serve to encourage further play.

2. *Rewards of Sustenance*: Sustenance rewards enable the player to keep playing the game. Anything that helps the character continue on the adventure qualifies. In a fantasy RPG like we're working on this can include healing potions, magic spell scrolls, armor, weapons, or even a good mule or horse the player can use to lug around more stuff (Hallford and Hallford, 2001, 158–160).

3. *Rewards of Facility*: These rewards grant the character new abilities or enhance their existing attributes providing the player with more gameplay options (Hallford and Hallford, 2001, 158–160). A magic ring that lets the player character turn invisible would represent such a reward.

4. *Rewards of Access*: Typically rewards of access allow players to reach new areas that they couldn't access beforehand. These items typically have no other use other than serving as a key and frequently only work once (Hallford and Hallford, 2001, 158–160). A potion of water breathing that lets the character access a new location such as the sunken city of Atlantis would be an example.

Duration

The type of reward can be qualified by the length of time each reward is active. Phillips breaks down duration into four variants.

1. Timed rewards are only active for a fixed duration. A magic scroll that grants a one-time immunity to dragon's breath weapons for the next ten turns would be an example of this.

2. Transient rewards exist only while a specific situation exists or until specific in-game events occur. The reward is only active for one particular circumstance, or while within a fixed location. A magical blessing the characters receive while defending the holy temple of Nomnom from an invading army of mutant kobolds would be an example of this.

3. Permanent rewards provide a continuing boost or enhancement to the character. The classic example of a permanent reward in a TTRPG is leveling up to the next level which grants a range of new abilities for the player character.

4. Consumable rewards let the player decide when the reward's effect will come into play. Typically these types of rewards are one-use items or have a limited number of times the player can activate the reward. A magical potion of healing is a perfect example of this type of award. Once the character drinks the potion and gets healed the potion has been consumed and is gone.

It is perfectly allowable to have rewards that fit under more than one category. A potion that doubles the character's movement speed is an example of a consumable, transient duration reward as well as an award of sustenance and facility too.

Schedule

Now that we've got a grip on the different types of rewards, we need to figure out how often these rewards should occur. Rewards tend to happen based upon one or more of the following four reward schedules.

1. Fixed ratio schedule: the player receives a reward after a fixed number of actions.
2. Variable ratio schedule: the player gets a reward after a random number of actions.
3. Fixed interval schedule: the player receives a reward after a fixed interval of time.
4. Variable interval schedule: the player gets a reward after a variable interval of time.

Lee (2016)

Each of these schedules is useful in different ways within the game. In his 2001 article for Gamasutra the head of User Research for Bungie, John Hopson, explains that fixed ratio schedules such as those found in the typical TTRPG leveling system are good at providing long-term goals and rewards to the player. The problem with this sort of schedule is that the gap between the rewards tends to increase along with the increasing value of each award. Eventually, the time between each reward becomes so long that it isn't enough to continue motivating the player. The fixed nature of the reward does mean that players aren't always having to focus on winning the reward. These rewards happen after a specified amount of actions occur. Variable ratio schedules are suitable for producing a constant level of engagement. The player, in this case, knows that their actions will generate rewards, but they do not know exactly which action will trigger the reward.

Interval-based rewards schedules provide a reward after a certain amount of time rather than a number of actions. Interval-based rewards are easier to implement in a video game than it is in a TTRPG, though you can approximate the effect by having a reward triggered after a certain amount of play time or by hitting different locations, either fixed or random, in the adventure. Interval-based rewards typically generate a more even pace of activity in players than the ratio schedules.

This methodology of type, duration, and schedule can be a useful approach when thinking about rewards in an abstract sense but can be a trifle difficult to translate into practice. A more practical way of looking at rewards is to denote their nature, usage, and frequency in the game as played. Rewards should appear irregularly in the game matched to the challenge level of the encounter (Barwood and Falstein, 2006). Rewards shouldn't always follow a cause and effect relationship since you don't want your players thinking that every time they kill a troll, they'll find a pot of gold or some such reward immediately afterward. Not all monsters should possess a treasure, while those that do should have a reasonable enough amount to stir the greed of players. It is vital that whatever treasure the players find suits the nature of the monster(s) that possessed it (Gygax, 1979a). Always make the players work to acquire wealth (Barwood and Falstein, 2006)! The amount of reward should be commensurate with the difficulty the players had in obtaining it and reasonable for their character level (Gygax, 1979a, 91–93). Give them meaningful rewards only after they complete significant challenges or overcome difficult obstacles (Barwood and Falstein, 2006). Remember that great rewards should come only with great gameplay. By the end of the adventure, the surviving characters should be more powerful, impressive, and wealthier than they were beforehand and they should feel like they've earned it. Whatever the reward, always make sure that the allure of the treasure equals or outweighs the risk involved in acquiring it (Barwood and Falstein, 2006). Whether or not the reward turns out to be quite what the players thought it would be is a different matter entirely.

Traditionally, rewards in a *D&D* style game can take many different forms each with their use. A brief list of these various forms of reward includes the following:

1. Advancement (Finch, 2008; Gygax, 1978a; MacDonald et al., 1981; Perrin and Turny, 1978).
2. NPCs and contacts (Granato, 1995).
3. Monetary treasure (Gygax and Arneson, 1981, 45).
4. Continuation (Greenwood, n.d.).
5. Magic items (Gygax and Arneson, 1981, 45–50).
6. Cosmetic ("5e: How…," 2016; Phillips et al., 2013).

7. Status (Dunnell, 2000; Granato, 1995).

8. Combinations, permutations, and miscellanea ("5e: How...," 2016).

Let's examine each of these different types of reward in turn.

Advancement

One of the hallmarks of the vast majority of tabletop role-playing games is their built-in system of character advancement (Finch, 2008; Gygax, 1978a; MacDonald et al., 1981; Perrin and Turny, 1978). Normally the character advancement phase occurs at the end of the adventure or designated stopping points (Gygax, 1979a, 86). All we have to do is use this built-in system appropriately. In our sample adventure, we can award the characters enough experience points to allow them to advance from the first to the second level after they have completed the forest section of the module but before they take on the temple itself. That way the characters get a little taste of the rewards to come at the conclusion of the adventure and are better able to handle the challenges of the temple itself. This bit of character advancement serves as a reward and will better match the power levels of the characters against the monsters in the temple. When awarding experience points, you have to keep in mind the amount of danger the player characters were actually in. A group of five goblins is a dangerous threat to a small group of first level adventurers, while to an experienced group of fifth level characters they're no threat at all. Defeating these goblins would be worth a notable experience reward for the first level party but would earn the higher level group nothing at all (Gygax, 1979a, 84). The level of the award should match the level of threat (Barwood and Falstein, 2006).

NPCs and Contacts

Rewards can be valuable new contacts, hirelings, friends, or henchmen ("5E: How...," 2016; Granato, 1995; Gygax, 1979a, 34). Slaying the dragon and saving the princess might earn a character entry into the royal family as the princess's new spouse. The little town might not be able to pay the characters in gold, but they might be able to offer free room and board to the heroes instead (at least until the heroes outstay their welcome). The local sheriff might appreciate the job the characters did cleaning out the nest of bandits so much that he recommends their services to the local baron who just so happens to need some adventurers for a difficult job. The wolf pups a character rescues from the temple might eventually become valuable traveling companions. It can pay off handsomely to think a little bit outside of the box when it comes to this type of reward. After all, the world works at least as much on a who you know basis as it does on a what you know basis. Add elements like this into your game to put some extra zest to it.

Monetary Treasure

Cold, hard cash—or in this case gold doubloons, silver drachmas, or copper pennies make the fantasy game keep going (Gygax and Arneson, 1981, 45). Monetary treasure in a fantasy game frequently takes the form of coins, gems, and jewelry, but this doesn't always have to be the case. Valuable paintings and other works of art such as sculptures, carvings, tapestries, furs, and rugs can all form part of a treasure. These types of valuables can form part of the adventure as the characters try to get fragile or bulky items somewhere they can sell them (Humphrey, 1992). Just make sure that the characters can succeed in this, a treasure they can never profit from is no treasure at all, and the goal isn't to punish them for being acquisitive (Humphrey, 1992). That's just a way to lose your player's interest. Treasure can even be composed of much cruder stuff such as valuable ores, minerals, and ingots of precious metals such as mithril, adamantium, and even copper or iron. A barrel of spices, a cask of fine wine, rare books, or even a barrel of maple syrup would all make a suitable treasure for some adventurers in desperate need of money. A low-level adventuring party will be thrilled by a few hundred gold pieces worth of treasure while a high-level party might barely notice it (Gygax, 1979a, 91–93). Treasure can be more than just pure cash. You can be creative with your coins and jewelry. Take a look at this table of medieval English currency for example.

£1 pound = 20s shillings = 240d pence

and

1 Guinea = 21s
1 Pound = 20s or 240p
1 Mark = 12s 4p
1 Noble = 6s 8p
1 Crown = 5s
1 Florin = 2s
1 Shilling (s) = 12p
1 Sixpence = 6p
1 Groat = 4p
1 Threepence = 3p
1 Penny (p) = 1p
1 Halfpenny = 0.5p
1 Farthing = 0.25p

The old English system includes additional coins such as the "tanner" and "groat" all utilizing a lovely non-decimal base system (Emsley et al., 2017; Sanders, 2014). It would be worth a little effort to create a few oddball currencies for the different kingdoms in your campaign setting to add a bit of reality to your treasure. Money can take all sorts of strange forms such as salt, seashells, beads, or weird stuff such as decorative iron axes, gigantic spearheads, or dog's tooth necklaces (Quiggin, 1949, 52–55, 63, 127). Then there's downright strange currency such as the giant wheel-like Rai stones of Yap island (Quiggin, 1949, 144–147).

STONE MONEY OF UAP, WESTERN CAROLINE ISLANDS.
(From the paper by Dr. W. H. Furness, 3rd, in Transactions, Department of Archæology, University of Pennsylvania, Vol. I., No. 1, p. 51, Fig. 3, 1904.)

Rai currency stone of Yap Island (Furness, 1903)

Some of these stone wheels are so large as to be immovable but this doesn't matter much since the locals know to whom each stone belongs no matter where the stone currently resides. The most notable example of this is a gigantic stone that sank to the bottom of the ocean, but that doesn't matter since everyone on the island acknowledged a particular family as still owning the rock. Something akin to this currency could form a puzzle in and of itself. Imagine the characters surprise when they learn that the item they stole isn't considered theirs! The locals still think it the original owner's property no matter who has possession of the actual thing itself (Quiggin, 1949, 146).

Continuation

Treasure can also come in more abstract forms such as something that enables play to continue ("5e: How…," 2016; Greenwood, n.d.). Maybe it is just a compelling story or tidbit of information from a local sage, an old treasure map found in the goblin king's lair, juicy rumors overheard in a tavern, or the queen's secret love letters. This kind of treasure can lead the players to new adventures or a possible side quest. A sealed letter or map can be used to guide the players to the next phase of the narrative. A deed to a castle, tavern, or other property can be a fun twist for players letting their characters become landowners or set up shop and develop their characters further (Granato, 1995).

Magic Items

Master of the genre, Gary Gygax, suggests offering magical items as rewards when they can serve as an effective power boost in the game. These items serve as a significant form of power boost in the game, and their distribution should be handled so as not to unbalance the game (Wizards RPG Team, 2003, 212). Rewards of magic items and other treasure should be proportional to the level of work and risk involved in getting them (Barwood and Falstein, 2006). Providing a low-level character with an all-powerful rune-sword for winning a bar fight isn't going to be very satisfying to the player. On the other hand, providing such a powerful magic weapon to the character after they defeat the main evil villain of the story after several dozen or more game sessions might be a balanced reward well earned. Luckily, most pen-and-paper RPGs come with lists of pre-made magic items that are balanced for the game and come with instructions on when they form reasonable rewards for characters of different levels (Gygax, 1978b, 120–169; Wizards RPG Team, 2003, 216–282). If you are designing magic item(s) yourself, it can get a bit trickier (Wizards RPG Team, 2003, 282–288). One excellent way to get some food for thought is to reference a real-world item and then create its magical equivalent. Ask yourself what the thing is designed to do? Is it a weapon like an AK-47—then make it into a type of magic wand or staff. What about a car? A flying carpet or chariot pulled by ghostly steeds. Maybe the magic item keeps the bearer well groomed and fragrant smelling? Whatever you decide to try, don't make the link between the modern item and its fantasy equivalent too obvious! Don't forget to include a detailed description of the object and its function in your adventure module.

Cosmetic Rewards

A particularly fun type of reward is just something that changes the appearance of the character. Anything that enhances or alters their appearance will work so long as it is compelling. A spectacular tattoo, an unusual piece of jewelry or equipment, or something even more distinctive can all become precious accoutrements to a player character. I once played a character who wore an out-sized beard made out of alpaca wool that had been used by ancient dwarves to practice their beard decorating skills on like a cloak. The character had no idea about the history of the thing. They just saw a beautifully decorated and bedazzled mantle made out of fine strips of delicate wool. Another character received a blessing from the moon-god and always glowed like pale moonlight ever afterward. Neither of these rewards had any mechanical effect on the game, but both certainly made a difference in the play of it!

Status

Status was even more valuable than wealth in medieval societies. There's no reason part of the reward for completing a remarkable adventure couldn't include rewards such as titles of nobility, knighthoods, estates, honors, feasts or even a parade. Promotion to the nobility, a knighthood, or the award of a title or property were tremendous rewards in medieval times. If you choose to provide this sort of reward, make sure that the players have earned it. Nobles obeyed a different set of laws, had different taxes and led a completely different sort of life from the peasantry or middle class. Maybe instead the local king grants the players a distinctive form of address such as "Dragonslayer," "Ogre-bane" or something similar. What happens if the king grants the players a trade monopoly on pepper, purple dye, or kumquats? Maybe the reward is in the form of service. Perhaps the village the player characters saved provides one of them with a local NPC to serve as a squire. Maybe the locals can provide valuable information, housing, or followers as a reward (Dunnell, 2000; Granato, 1995). Think about what would happen in the game if after saving the village the local elders offer each adventurer a spouse? As you can see, there's no need to limit your imagination when choosing rewards to give out to your players. Be creative, and they'll thank you for it!

Combinations, Permutations, and Miscellanea

You can, of course, combine these different effects and modify them as you see fit. Perhaps the characters find the long-lost crown of a prince who went missing a decade or so ago. If they try to sell it to someone who recognizes it, they could get into a great deal of trouble and have quite a bit of explaining to do. Depending on how they deal with the local authorities this might get them an introduction to the local nobility and an assignment to go find out what happened to the missing prince or a trip to the local jail. Maybe the characters find a musty old tome that contains a few rare spells and hints to the location of an enormous magical trove, but the act of opening the book breaks a magical seal that lets a demon lord have access to this plane of existence once again after four hundred years of banishment. The possibilities are wide open when designing such stuff! Just make sure that the level of the reward matches the effort it took to acquire it.

Theme the treasure you provide to your adventurers according to your campaign setting, adventure, and the type of monsters or foes they are fighting (Schroeder, 1978). For example, a witch might have a magic broom or crystal ball or an ogre's lair might be full of things collected from the dead heroes it has slain, or in an ice cavern full of frost giant Viking types you might find a giant slaying sword (Gygax, 1981; Schroeder, 1978). There might be serious repercussions for showing up in town with particularly valuable or noteworthy items—the former owners might want the item back, thieves, assassins, or even tax collectors might target the characters (Schroeder, 1978). Think what would happen if someone came into town carrying jewelry the local villagers recognized as coming from a missing person? Many famously, valuable gemstones have allegedly bloody histories as people fought for their possession (Lovejoy, 2016). Imagine what people will do to possess a powerful magic item? Maybe the treasure is broken and no longer functional (Williams, 1991). Of course, even a broken gold crown is still worth quite a bit of cash and maybe even more if it can be repaired. Then there are loads of treasures that aren't quite as obvious. Things such as the monster's pelt and body parts, fragile or bulky items, or other less obvious things can all be valuable if the characters bother to think about it (Humphrey, 1992). One of the greatest treasures any of my characters ever found was in Gygax's Tomb of Horrors. The doors to the dungeon were made out of the some of the rarest metals in the campaign setting and were worth more than everything else in the adventure combined!

As an example, your characters might find a potion of healing after a dangerous encounter with a boss monster. The potion is a reward of sustenance, consumable, and found after a fixed ratio of actions, e.g. in a specific location within the adventure). Maybe the characters find "Foe-cleaver," a magical bronze axe crafted by ancient dwarven battle lords, buried deep in the refuse of a troll lair. When the characters get back to civilization, they discover that all of the local dwarven clans have a burning desire to possess the axe since it is a sign of their god's favor. If the players concede to this, then they can gain the friendship of one dwarven clan and a few choice dwarf-made magic items plus the enmity of the families who didn't get it. Of course if the players keep the axe then assassins and thieves are in their future as the less noble clans will go to any lengths to acquire it. The weapon, therefore, counts as a reward of glory, sustenance, facility and even access depending upon how the players utilize it as well as being either a permanent, transient or consumable reward! Perhaps the players find a simple magical ring that provides a basic +1 bonus to saving throws. The ring might later turn out to be a key to a hidden dungeon level or signify the inheritor of a magical kingdom or even both. The ring is a reward of sustenance, facility, and access. The GM could easily put a time limit on any of the items mentioned earlier to add an extra quality to any of them.

One final note when rewarding characters is that the rewards need to be mechanically suitable to the characters at their current level. Giving out powerful magic weapons to a weak party can destroy the game balance and ruin the game. You can moderate the power of an item by limiting its duration or effectiveness. The uber-sword of ultimate slaying might only work on the big bad boss at the end of the module. Otherwise, the sword is merely a +1 or +2 sword with a fascinating backstory. Always consider the repercussions the item or reward might have in the game before doling it out.

Conclusion

The different types, durations, and schedules of rewards are not mutually exclusive. Combine them in unique ways to reward your players and achieve the pattern of play you seek. Be creative in what you provide your players. Include a backstory to the items, flavorful description, or make the rewards personal for the characters if you can. Whatever the combination of qualities the rewards you provide to the players possess, they all serve the same purpose: to keep your players engaged with the fiction that is your game and keep them playing it.

Assignment

Create ten different creative rewards for your players which you can integrate into your adventure. Break each one of these rewards down by type, duration, and schedule like we did for the potion of healing example. Try providing a backstory to each item.

Chapter 14

Quests and Goals

If you want to make your game fun you have to make it challenging, otherwise it will just be boring, and no one wants that. You have to provide quests and goals to make the players feel like they're accomplishing something and to offer a sense of progress within the scope of the game. The objective is never to block their progress completely. The puzzles should not be so severe that they have to "look up" the answer somewhere. The obstacles should never be so great that they become frustrated or the monsters unbeatable. Everything the players need to overcome the challenges within the adventure should be accessible. The players should have to work for them, but the solutions exist. As the designer, you will have to strive very hard to create challenges that are balanced for your players. This will undoubtedly involve playtesting and some tweaking. No one gets all of this right the first time out of the gate. Take your time and have fun!

Quests

One simple approach to providing an incentive is to dangle a carrot in front of the characters. This can be a long-term goal, "we've got to get the ring of power to the mountain of doom," or it can be something more short-term, "that thief just stole your wallet." Either way, keep the carrot dangling in front of the characters and the resolution always just out of reach. The thief keeps dodging into doors and throwing obstacles in the players' path. The journey to the Mountain of Doom has a seemingly never-ending supply of monsters and obstacles in the way. Whenever the characters need a little boost, provide some extra clues or aid in some form. A helpful eyewitness can describe the thief or knows where he can be found. A sympathetic elf queen might provide some rest or much needed magic items to help in the characters' quest. You always have to provide direction for the players. Never leave them guessing which way to go or what they should be doing next.

If the adventure is going to take a long time, then you will likely need to periodically provide the characters with places they can rest and recuperate. This can be any relatively safe spot where they can sleep and heal up or re-equip. These locations can range from simple campsites where their foes likely won't find them all the way up to an entire town where the characters can buy much needed supplies. These safe spaces can also serve as a location where the characters can find many helpful NPCs or quests. This sort of base is known as an adventure hub. How frequently you provide these will dramatically affect the tempo and feel of the game. Frequent safe resting spots mean that the characters hit each stage of the adventure fresh and at full power. An adventure that has no resting spots becomes a grueling and dangerous endurance slog as the characters' strengths are slowly whittled away. Either approach can be made to work, the designer just needs to be cognizant of how the choice will affect the gameplay.

When designing a quest of any scale, be it small or large, there are three main components to take into consideration:

- *Objective*: Every quest needs a goal. The characters might need to rescue a prisoner, acquire an item (or items), acquire wealth, defeat the big villain, get from point A to point B, or accomplish some combination of these tasks. Whatever the end goal is you have to be sure to provide sufficient motivation for the players to want to complete the job at hand. Otherwise, they'll never experience the adventure you have built for them.
- *Obstacle*: All of the things that stand in the way of accomplishing the objective. These obstacles can include things like the big villain and their minions, impassable terrain, or difficult tasks. Overcoming these obstacles might be as simple as defeating a monster, or it might involve multiple side-quests or a lengthy multi-part mission.
- *Solution*: The solution is how the players can overcome each obstacle. There might be one way or several ways to do this. You should always try to allow the players to use a bit of creativity to do so. It will make the experience feel more rewarding and ensures that the players don't feel railroaded down a particular path.

How each of these three elements is presented to your players is something that you will need to determine. They can be evident and up-front, for example, the town mayor asks your group to clear the forest of goblins. Events can also be thrust upon the characters. Perhaps a player character bumps into a mighty wizard who accuses the character of stealing an item. Whether your adventure has a clearly stated goal or has events that are thrust upon the characters is something best decided upon at the beginning of your developmental process.

According to Barwood and Falstein in their "The 400 Project Rule List" there are a few guidelines to keep in mind when designing your obstacles and challenges:

1. As the story advances towards the conclusion, the challenges should get progressively more difficult overall. This is a very straightforward way of providing a sense of flow to the game. However when using this approach make sure that the challenges have some variance to their difficulty level. You don't want the players to be able to reliably predict the difficulty of the next encounter. Modulate the difficulty of each encounter around an ever increasing median. This will keep the players guessing and more engaged.

2. Vary your threats. Don't just use smaller versions of your big bad as minor obstacles. An endless parade of the same monster only at increasing levels of difficulty gets boring fast.

3. Allow for multiple solutions. Let the players solve each obstacle from an array of possible solutions. Letting your players feel clever in how they deal with a challenge will encourage them to continue in the quest. Providing multiple possible solutions will also help avoid bottle-necks in your plot. Let the players choose from some combination of magic, combat, skills or dialogue to overcome their challenges. Don't let one solution dominate all of the others. For example, don't let combat be the only solution to every situation. Make some challenges combat oriented, others centered upon dialogue, and still others skill or magic based. Variety will keep things interesting for your players and give each of the different types of characters a chance to shine.

4. The solution should require some skill, not just luck. Never put the resolution down to purely chance. Random chance trivializes the player's role in the game.

5. Balance encounters to the median skill level. Begin by considering the average character(s) that will go through your adventure. Create your first batch of encounters as average difficulty level challenges for your ordinary player characters. Once you have sorted out the average encounter level for the party or player characters, you can begin to adjust each battle to make things more or less challenging as the story requires.

6. Never make your players feel stupid or punish them. Doing so will cost you players. Don't trivialize the player's roles in the game by

having a more powerful NPC come along and solve their problems for them.

7. Give a sense of depth to the quests and NPCs by providing a backstory for them. These elements don't have to be presented to the player directly. They can just be inferred from the NPC's actions and dialogue or show up as background elements. Regardless of how you choose to present things you must make sure that everything in the game makes sense and flows logically from one thing to another.

8. There is a joy to discovery. Give the players the opportunity to explore the setting and story that you have created. Exploration isn't just about new places on the map. It can include surprise encounters, plot twists, puzzles, and mysteries for the players to unravel. You don't need lengthy explanations or backstories for everything in your game. Often it is enough to hint at things and imply a greater depth than what is written. Your players have an imagination; let it do some of the work for you! You cannot write up every possible scenario—and you shouldn't try to.

Frequently the heroes might need a little help overcoming the obstacles in their quest. This can take the form of clues the characters can uncover, items or keys they can acquire, or just helpful advice from NPCs. Whatever the form of the help, make sure that you write it down in detail. Specify the nature of the aid, where it is found, how it can be acquired, and any specific results to be gained from using it.

While on the quest, make sure that you provide your players with a sense of progress in the accomplishment of their goals. Nothing is as frustrating as not knowing whether or not your character is actually proceeding towards their goal or drifting further away from it. These clues can take many forms. Show the players a bit of progress by having the challenges get more difficult, the rewards get better, and by changing the description of what is around them. If the dungeon is getting darker and more frightening as they go on it will give the adventure a sense of direction. It is evident that you're making progress when the landscape is changing around you. Provide the players with equipment and rewards that alter their character's appearance (Barwood and Falstein, 2006). If the NPCs start treating the characters with more deference and respect the players will feel like they've really accomplished something with their character's development.

It helps to provide additional interest to the story by introducing a few red herrings or diversions into the plot. These can range from side-quests that are genuinely unconnected to ones that can have a bearing on the final outcome. For example, a sickly old beggar might plead with the characters to help him find his lost daughter. If the players assist the old man, the side-quest might lead them to a boon such as the location of a magical healing spring in the woods which the old man reveals if the players help him. On the other hand, the old man might be an agent for the character's arch-nemesis trying to lure them into an ambush! When designing these sorts of things remember to provide a mix of potential outcomes. If every side quest ends in disaster, then the players will start ignoring them. Remember that your players want to be involved in your game! Make sure you give your players plenty of opportunities to engage themselves with the different storylines you have created for them (Barwood and Falstein, 2006).

At the end of the quest, there should be some sort of reward. This acts as an encouragement to your players and can take many forms. A story reward advances the story or points the characters toward a new location to explore or quest to undertake. The experience gained during the adventure feeds into the game's built-in leveling system to reward successful players with new abilities and powers. In fantasy adventures like the one we are writing, rewards are frequently in the form of magical and mundane treasure, that is, cool stuff and gold. A low-level endeavor like ours might result in each character acquiring anywhere from a few hundred to a thousand or two gold coins worth of monetary treasure plus one or two minor magical items, each depending upon the overall level of challenge involved. These treasures don't have to be simple. They can present their own problems or be the key to future adventures in their own right. A simple magical +1 sword might turn out to be a lost royal heirloom bearing the seal of the vanished crown prince. The monetary treasure might include a painting which contains hidden clues to the location of a lost city. The valuable treasure might be a priceless large marble statue, and the challenge is now getting it back to civilization!

There might be multiple possible outcomes to the adventure depending on how the players solved each challenge. You should detail out a few of these potential outcomes. If the players ultimately succeed in their quest, fail at it, or get some degree in between, there should be consequences for these actions. If the players defeat the dragon and the city is flattened as a result of the battle, the locals won't be thrilled with the results! At a minimum provide some guidelines for if the players succeed entirely, partially, or fail.

Conclusion

We've gone over a lot of the theories and practical advice for designing the challenges, obstacles, and rewards for your players. Remember that these are just guidelines. You can break these rules, but you have to know when doing so is appropriate. Learning when to follow this advice and when to ignore it is a large part of becoming a game designer. In the upcoming chapters, we will apply these rules to our adventure.

Assignment

Look over the elements of the adventure that you have already developed. See if there is any your material that you need to revise to fit the advice you have read in this unit. Note where in your adventure you are presenting the objective to the players, challenging the players with obstacles, and providing for solutions. Make sure that all of these elements flow logically into each other and that the players always have an understanding of their state of progress in achieving their goals. If you see any problem spots in your plot now is the time to fix them before you write up the rest of the adventure in detail.

Obstacles and Challenges

Creating Challenges

In addition to combat, you can confront the players with a wide range of hazards, obstacles, puzzles, traps and other types of challenges. These can be used to break the pacing of the game up a bit and are useful tools in your design kit. Hitting the players with the same sort of challenge over and over again becomes tiresome. Use the array of ideas presented in this chapter to develop some innovative obstacles that will keep your players interested.

When creating these challenges, it is a good idea to consider how each problem fits into the overall path to completion for the whole adventure. Each obstacle should maintain the theme of the entire experience and reinforce the plot in some way. Make sure that you are providing multiple paths to completion for each challenge and the adventure as a whole. The players should be able to use a variety of tactics and abilities to accomplish the goals of the module. This is true regardless of whether we are talking about a specific objective like getting across the chasm, defeating a particular group of foes, or achieving the end goal of the adventure as a whole. Letting your players solve problems through combat, negotiation, stealth, or however they choose avoids potential bottlenecks in your plot and helps alleviate boredom by preventing repetition. A useful approach when handling a sequence of obstacles and challenges is to have success over one obstacle to help the players solve the other difficulties. The player's achievements should have an incremental and cumulative effect on improving their chances at each additional problem (Barwood and Falstein, 2006). Building upon their previous successes like this provides the players a sense of progress and forward momentum within the adventure and will help to keep them engaged with the story. Always remember to give the player a fair chance. Provide some hint that there's danger ahead or a clue on how to solve the problem. If there's an exploding orange gem on the floor surrounded by charred remains, then an ingenious player will have a clue that something is up (Gygax, 1978b). You do not want your players to feel that the game is ever unfair to them (Saltzman and Bleszinski, 1999). When you are creating your challenges, it is imperative not to make things confusing or too complicated. Keep in mind that the players won't have easy access to the answers to any puzzles or mazes that you create. What might seem to you, the designer, a relatively simple thing could turn into an impassable barrier for your players. You can provide subtle clues to your traps, mazes, and puzzles in the descriptions you write up of each one. Perhaps the wall that moves to reveal the secret passage is slightly wetter than the other walls in the room or has a different fresco, rune, or moss growing on it. The maze the evil priests use to guard their entrance might have a slightly more worn path on the flagstones from centuries of priests trotting down the correct trail. Subtle clues like this will reward diligent players for paying close attention to your descriptions.

In-Game Challenges

Two broad categories of challenges exist, in-game challenges and out-of-game ones. In-game challenges are relatively simple to create. They utilize standard game mechanics to determine whether or not the character can solve the problem at hand. To create an in-game challenge, describe the nature of the problem in as much detail as possible then decide upon the game mechanic used to overcome that obstacle. Frequently this involves rolling one twenty-sided dice, adding in a modifier based upon one of the ability scores such strength, intelligence, wisdom, and such, plus any situational modifiers or a bonus based off of character level, then comparing that total with a fixed difficulty number. The character succeeds at the task if the roll plus all of the modifiers is higher than or equal to the difficulty number. If the designer is feeling a bit lazy, they can make the target number equal to the character's saving throw number. The quandary when designing in-game challenges lies in assigning a reasonable difficulty number to the task and describing it engagingly.

Out-of-Game Challenges

Out-of-game challenges are more difficult to design. These challenges require a considerable amount of effort to develop depending upon the nature of the problem you are trying to represent. Frequently this involves having the player(s) solve a puzzle, riddle, word game, or other tasks. These can be trickier to create since as a designer you can't assume much about the capabilities of your eventual players. You do not want to create an impassable block inside of your adventure or cause your players too much frustration. The reward for solving the puzzle must always be worth the challenge involved! The upside of this type of problem is that it allows you to be quite creative when designing them since it frees you from the standard game mechanics of the role-playing game system. Most often these types of problems test the players' knowledge and problem-solving ability since these are relatively straightforward to represent with puzzles, riddles, or word games. Tests of strength, dexterity or constitution are a bit trickier to design but can be simulated as well.

Designing Challenges

First, decide upon which attribute the problem is testing. Is it a test of strength, intelligence, wisdom, dexterity, constitution, or charm? Physical challenges are best based upon either strength, dexterity or constitution, whereas intellectual or abstruse dilemmas use intelligence, wisdom, or charm. If you aren't quite sure which attribute you should test then refer to the following:

- Physical attributes
  - Strength involves feats of vigor, energy, power, and physique.
  - Dexterity relates to finesse, skill, nimbleness, and precision.
  - Constitution requires endurance, toughness, and resilience.
- Abstract Attributes
  - Intelligence affects battles of wit, puzzles, riddles, rhymes, or questions.
  - Wisdom represents willpower, experience, sound judgment, or moral fiber.
  - Charisma or Charm uses persuasion, seduction, or even intimidation to get what you want.

Decide if you want it to be an in-game challenge for the player's characters or an out-of-game challenge for the players themselves. If it is an in-game challenge, then you must decide what system you want to use, a simple saving throw or the slightly more complicated ability check system. If you go with the saving throw system, then you can also decide whether to make the roll easier or more difficult by assigning a modifier. You can use the ability score modifier as well as a situational modifier of (usually) +5 (very easy) to −5 (very difficult) to the roll. The result looks something like this:

d20 roll + ability score modifier + situational modifier => target number

The designer can set the target number, or you can use the character's saving throw number. For example, in *Glory of Yore*, a first level character usually has a saving throw number of 14. Let's say the character has to swim a swiftly flowing river for a challenge. You can ask the character to roll a saving throw and add the character's strength modifier with a −2 modifier for the swiftness of the cascading water. The result ends up looking like this:

1d20 + Strength modifier − 2 => saving throw number

If the modified d20 roll is equal to or higher than the character's saving throw number, then that character successfully swims the river. Of course, there are quite a variety of different mechanical systems out there for rolling this sort of skill or ability check within these sorts of fantasy RPGs, and you can use whichever method you desire that works with your chosen RPG system. Make sure you are familiar with how the system works before using it. Using an in-game resolution to overcome a game challenge provides an easy way of letting the characters do things. The drawback is that it doesn't make for terribly exciting gameplay. It is just a roll of the dice. You can heighten the tension a bit by making the cost very dear; in our previous example, the character might drown if they fail the roll. This sort of high stakes single dice roll can be somewhat frustrating to your players though. Frequently it is better to provide a fallback or two. For example, if the character fails the initial roll then they get to try again at it with an extra −1 penalty next round. Each time they fail the roll the penalty gets more severe, by an extra −1 per fail, until after 3 tries the character either succeeds or finally drowns. You always have to balance the difficulty of the task with the potential payoff and degree of frustration with the game. Too many save or die situations becomes tiresome. On the other hand, if there aren't a few severe consequences to their failures then the gameplay becomes meaningless and without any real sense of victory over difficulty.

Things get a lot more interesting (and complicated) if you decide to simulate an obstacle with an out-of-game challenge. You still must determine which ability you are testing. Is it a physical trait like strength or a more abstract one like intelligence? Once you've decided upon what attribute you are checking you need to figure out how you intend to test it. For some challenges, such as one for intelligence, you can occasionally hand the actual task to the player. If the problem is to solve a riddle, then you can hand over the riddle to the players and let them have a crack at it. For more physical challenges this isn't appropriate, you can't very well ask your player to swim a river, for instance. In that case, you need to assign a reasonable substitute for the task. If it is a task of strength, then you can have the character arm wrestle the GM for instance, or play a round of rock, paper, scissors to determine the outcome. The point is that you can be creative when it comes to creating a resolution system for an in-game task. Just try to have the player's action match the theme of the character's activity to provide a degree of verisimilitude for everyone. You can use this approach to break up the nature of events in the game a bit and offer a diverse range of experiences when playing your game. It can be a nice feature if you provide both in-game and out-of-game systems, to resolve the challenges in your game. Doing so lets the game master running the game choose which approach to use based upon their knowledge of the players.

Hazards, Traps, and Puzzles

The flavor of each obstacle is arguably even more important than the mechanics you use to simulate each challenge. Obstructions can be natural hazards, traps, and puzzles. Each of these types of barriers has its uses and flavor. Let's look at each of these types in turn and explain them in more depth.

Hazards

The term hazards encapsulates natural phenomena such as inclement weather or troublesome terrain. The severity of the danger can vary enormously. Anything from an intense rainstorm, which can make travel more difficult or wash away footprints, to a raging forest fire or volcanic explosion, can put a big dent in an adventuring party's day. If you want to develop some ideas for natural hazards, think back to that camping trip you once took. What types of obstacles did you potentially face out in the wilderness? Getting lost, a lack of food or water, wild animals, bogs, swamps, fallen trees, severe weather, flooding, or impassable terrain, perhaps. You could include any of those in your adventure. Maybe the characters have to climb a mountain, negotiate a crumbling cliff face, or cross a raging river or deep gorge. You could throw in something more exotic such as lava pits, boiling mud flats, or a few native monsters, perhaps. The trick when developing these is to make sure that they fit the theme of your adventure and add flavor to the campaign without becoming too frustrating for the players to overcome. The results of the hazard can vary wildly in severity. Inclement weather such as a blizzard might call for a wisdom modified saving throw or check to avoid getting lost, a constitution check to prevent frostbite, or a dexterity check to maintain the character's footing when negotiating an icy trail. Here's a fully developed example:

> The players must navigate an underground river that has flooded the subterranean complex they are exploring. Parts of the area they must traverse are entirely underwater.

The challenge here is holding your breath long enough to get from point A to point B without knowing how far the distance is. An additional complicating factor is that unless the characters have a magical source of light (it's a fantasy game after all!) the entire trip underwater will also be in the dark. If you wanted to make it more difficult, you could throw in one or more underwater monsters for the group to fight or have a few side passages that terminate in dead ends. If you don't provide the rare safe place for them to catch their breath, then this hazard becomes very deadly indeed. If we keep it simple then we use the following rules:

> Each character can hold their breath for a number of rounds equal to their constitution score. Each character must roll a swimming check (saving throw adjusted by their strength modifier) to swim the distance against the river currents. A player who fails their swim check makes no progress that round. The characters must complete the underwater portion of their journey before their breath runs out or they drown.

Characters can resolve most natural hazards through a combination of climbing, swimming, jumping, riding, or some other non-combat physical skill. These challenges are usually more physical in nature, though you could simulate more intellectual natural hazards such as identifying which mushroom is safe to eat or building a raft. For instance, if we wanted to lower the difficulty of our water passage, then we could eliminate the completely underwater parts and have each character make a swim check to see if they make it. Maybe smart characters could use the debris lying about to fashion a makeshift raft (an intelligence check), or realize that there must be another route into the remote section by noticing the breeze wafting in from that direction (a wisdom check). Developing these hazards is limited solely by your imagination.

An example of a natural hazard (© 2018 Greg Johnson)

Traps

Traps are human-made hazards designed to delay, diminish, or destroy anyone who gets within range. Much like natural hazards, traps tend to be physical in nature though, again, this isn't a strict requirement. Traps have a wonderfully long history, and they are well documented in fiction and fact. There are even some handy U.S. Army manuals on the subject (McChristian, 1965, 145–167; Department of the Army, 1967, 27–53). There is quite a lengthy list of simple traps such as the spike trap box, spike pit trap, collapsing bridge, arrow trap, spiked bamboo whip, caltrops, punji stakes, deadfall, sliding walls, collapsing floor, flooding chamber, one way passage, needle traps, and dart traps just to rattle off a few (McChristian, 1965, 144–167; Department of the Air Force, 1985, 224–227). You can model a trap off of a carnivorous pitcher plant or Venus flytrap. Have a one-way passage that slowly narrows until the character notices there are forward facing blades preventing them from crawling back out. You can bait a trap with treasure and add poison or filth to make the trap deadlier or cause infection. If you want to mimic the design of exploding traps, then add magic. An exploding glyph, potion, or other magical object can adequately simulate the blast of a grenade or mine allowing you the full use of a variety of modern approaches even though the use of magic would substantially increase the cost of the trap to the original maker (Wizards RPG Team, 2003, 67–76).

You can always rely upon the simple pit trap which is just a hole in the ground covered by a trap door of some type. In *D&D* style games falling does about 1d6 points of damage for every ten feet fallen (Wizards RPG Team, 2003, 303).

So just a ten-foot deep hole covered with a trap door will do a small amount of damage if one of the player characters steps on it. You can add spikes to the bottom of the pit to add a bit of extra damage, say one or two extra dice of damage (Wizards RPG Team, 2003, 71). If you are feeling a bit vindictive, then coat the spikes with poison and force the unfortunate victim to make a saving throw or sustain additional damage (Wizards RPG Team, 2003, 74). Triggering the trap is automatic if the characters aren't taking any precautions. If the players are cautious, then allow a saving throw to notice the trap with a positive or negative modifier of say, up to ±5 for how cautious and carefully they are searching. If a thief is leading the party, have them roll a skill check to allow them to detect the traps. In *Glory of Yore* you use the "Thieving" skill, in *OSRIC* and some of the older *D&D* flavors the "Find Traps" skill is used to detect the trap before triggering it (Norvelle, 2016, 21; Marshall, 2008, 23–24). If the characters fail to recognize the trap, then the first character to traverse over the trap triggers it. That character takes 1d6 points of damage from falling 10 feet plus an additional 1d6 damage from the small spikes set in the bottom of the trap. At low levels, this is enough to kill a character. A medium level party 1d6 of damage would be a hindrance, while a high-level group wouldn't be affected much at all. You could have the trap set off an alarm which causes a group of foes to rush out from a hidden room to attack the party while one or more of the party members are stuck in the pit! Even nastier would be to have these foes dump a flask of burning oil down upon the trapped character for another, let's say 2d6 points of damage plus catching them on fire for 1d6 continuing damage for the next 1d4 rounds. That is how you can take a simple trap like a pit trap and start off doing a minimal amount of damage (1d6) appropriate for low-level adventures and scale the trap's damage upwards until it becomes a significant threat to even a high-level party.

Let's write up one full-blown example of a simple trap. We need something that our wolf cult can make out of primitive equipment that won't be too deadly against our party of first level adventurers. The real purpose of this trap is to make the adventurers a bit paranoid and more cautious. Making the group a bit skittish dovetails nicely with the adventure plot since we don't want the player characters just charging in and getting swamped by the number of foes present at the temple. That in mind, we can place these traps on the trails leading up to the temple complex just before the characters get there. Thoughtful players will slow down and start to look before they rush in. A simple enough trap for our purposes is the spiked ball trap.

Spiked ball trap: This is a large clay or mortar ball up to two feet in diameter and weighing forty pounds or so that has spikes sticking out at all angles from it. The clay can be fired to make it harder. Hang the spiked ball by a rope attached to the trees and triggered by a tripwire on the trail. When the tripwire is triggered, the ball sweeps down along the trail striking everyone in its path (Department of the Army, 1967, 53). Have the players roll a saving throw to notice the tripwire or, if the party has a thief, have the thief roll a "thieving" skill check to detect the trap. Otherwise, when sprung the spiked ball attacks every character in a ten-foot line at +1 to hit and doing damage 1d6+1 to anyone struck.

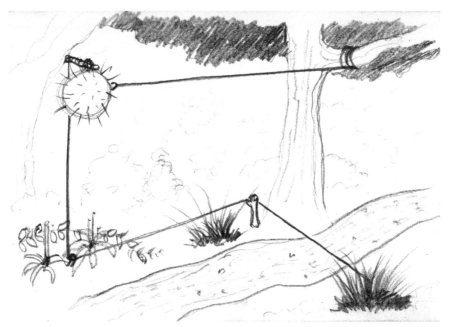

Spiked ball trap (© 2018 Greg Johnson)

Puzzles

The final type of non-combat obstacles we will discuss in this chapter are also the most difficult to adjudicate in many ways. Puzzles are a non-combat task or tasks that the players must complete to move forward with the plot. This problem can be as simple as finding the key to unlock the gateway to the next level or as complex as a functional mini-game. What exactly constitutes a puzzle is quite varied. The term covers word games, logic problems, riddles, lateral thinking puzzles, spatial reasoning, and more (Brathwaite and Schreiber, 2008, 43–48). In fact, there is so much material regarding puzzles that you could fill a library about them! You can create a puzzle based off of a medieval game such as chess, checkers, backgammon or something more obscure such as the Philosopher's Game. You can create something like a game of chess where the players become living chess pieces and engage in combat and compete for their lives (Hammack, 1980, 10). The variety of puzzles is limited only by your imagination. In word puzzles alone we have anagrams, acronyms, rebuses, completions, hidden words, reversals, homophones, homographs, and metatheses. While we don't have space to go over every possible type of puzzle, we can at least talk about a few of the more common or relevant ones.

Riddle Me This

The riddle is a time-honored classic in fantasy literature showing up most notably in Tolkien's *The Hobbit* and innumerable ancient Greek myths. Studying this particular type of puzzle is important since it holds such a noble place in the halls of fantasy. A riddle is simply a question or statement presented in such an obtuse way as to require a fair amount of cleverness to ascertain the answer. Mark Anthony in his article, "The Answer is … the Riddle!," in Dragon magazine 175 provides the following steps for creating a riddle:

1. Decide upon the theme for the riddle. What is the riddle about?
2. Describe the subject of your theme in as much detail as possible.
3. Take your descriptions and turn them into sentences.
4. Now find the most obtuse way possible of saying each sentence (Selinker, 2001). Swap each word out using a thesaurus and a rhyming dictionary. Try out different metaphors, obscure words, comparisons, puns, or personifications to further obscure what you are talking about.

Let's try one out, shall we? Step one, I need something familiar to most gamers. My first thought is to use "dice." There will probably be a handful or two of dice on the table under the players' noses which will only add to the fun. Step two, describe "dice." Small, a variety of geometric shapes, generates random numbers, throwable, used in gambling and games, can be loaded to cheat with, built for amusement, and they're polyhedral. So onward to step three, putting it into sentences.

> They're small and multi-hued
> Polyhedral
> They generate random numbers
> Used in games of chance and fun

It's pretty obvious I'm talking about game dice at the moment so let's proceed to step four and obfuscate these sentences.

> Many in hand a rainbow.
> A geometrician's dream of unconsidered range.
> Lady Luck throws haphazard.

Done! I combined the polyhedral reference, a "geometrician's dream" with the random numbers portion of "unconsidered range," unconsidered being a synonym of random and range a reference to the mathematical range of numbers the dice generate. Lady Luck references gambling. Throws being a throw of the dice, and haphazard being another synonym of random. Overall not a difficult riddle but I could leave out the Lady Luck line to start with and only add that in if the players need help solving it. If we wanted to increase the difficulty level, then we could add in a time limit (Brathwaite and Schreiber, 2008, 49). Now we can hand this riddle to the players for them to solve as part of an adventure maybe the next time they encounter a sphinx or a wizard with an odd sense of humor.

Cryptograms

A cryptogram is a message concealed by using a substitution rule. These can be quite difficult to decipher depending upon the complexity of the substitution rules, whether or not you alter the spelling, word order, or reduce the number of symbols used (Selinker, 2000). We'll use a step-by-step process for creating your cryptogram.

1. The first thing to do is to decide upon your message.
2. Now write out the alphabet and assign a new letter, symbol, or code to each letter.
3. Transcribe your sentence using the encryption alphabet you designed in step 2.

Let's see, what would be a suitable message for our wolf temple to encrypt like this? How about, "When the Blood Moon rises between the Jaws of the Wolf."

Now let's transpose it. I'm going to do the consonants separately from the vowels to make it a bit harder too. I used a different increment for the vowels and the consonants, but I kept the shift regular and didn't do a random letter assignment. That might have been too hard ever to decipher.

original: A E I O U Y, B C D F G H J K L M N P Q R S T V W X Z
transposed: O U Y A E I, J K L M N P Q R S T V W X Z B C D F G H

So this:

"When the Blood Moon rises between the Jaws of the Wolf."

Turns into this:

"Fpuv cpu Jsaal Taav zybub jucfuuv cpu Jofb am cpu Fasm."

Before using this as a puzzle in a game you really would want to test it out on some other people first to make sure that it isn't too obtuse. It could be just as much fun to translate the original phrase into a proper period script such as futhark runes and use that instead or even translate the encrypted phrase into Futhark and stump the players. Be careful about making a difficult puzzle like this essential to the plot. This sort of challenging problem always requires provision for an alternate solution, so the players don't get stuck (Barwood and Falstein, 2006).

Rebus

A rebus uses images as substitutes for words in a visual pun (SirotaSOFT, 2014). It was a popular enough trick in heraldry during medieval times that there is a specific term, canting arms, for it. Canting arms involves converting the name of the noble into images (Velde, 1997). For example, Sir Beesmith might have a shield with a bee or bees and an anvil or an arm grasping a smith's hammer on it. Lady Bowbridge would have a bow and, you guessed it, a bridge. If you take an entire sentence and convert it to images, then you go beyond canting arms and are playing with a proper rebus. For example our phrase, "When the Blood Moon rises between the Jaws of the Wolf" could be turned into a picture of a moon, followed by an upward pointing arrow, then a wolf's jaws. We might be able to simplify it into just a blood red moon rising out of a wolf's open mouth below it.

An example rebus (© 2018 Greg Johnson)

Conclusion

The spectrum of hazards, traps, and puzzles presented in this chapter serve as models for a variety of non-combat challenges you can include in your adventure. Anything that prevents the player characters from achieving their goal qualifies as an obstacle. In this unit, we're using the narrower sense of it excluding combat and opponents since we have dealt with those elsewhere. The critical thing to remember is that almost anything can form an obstacle to your character's progress if you set it up that way—inclement weather, puzzles, natural hazards, traps, even plain old misinformation.

Assignment

Write down a list of everything that could hinder your players in your adventure. Drop any obstacles from your list that are boring, don't stimulate your imagination, or that don't fit the theme of your module. Now decide whether each specific challenge is best as an in-game or out-of-game challenge. Write up a detailed description of each obstacle then define the game mechanics that will implement your hazard best. Try to write up at least five or six fully fleshed out obstacles in this way.

16

Non-Player Characters, Foes, and Monsters

Who are These People?

Adventures are full of characters. Some are usually just in background like the barkeep, blacksmith, or a crowd of local farmers. Others form the centerpiece of your story such as the main antagonist, friendly wizard, or hapless noble that needs rescuing. Making these characters interesting, believable, and appropriately detailed is one of the biggest challenges of writing an adventure or game. Get it right and your game will be a joy to play, absorbing, and fully immersive. Get it wrong and your adventure will fall as flat as month-old soda.

Inspired Character Creation

It helps to have some inspiration when you begin developing NPCs. Try practicing your first-hand observation skills. Watch your family members, friends, or even strangers. If you described one of these people how would you do it? What sets them apart from each other? Describe that person in 2–3 concise sentences. Sources for inspiration can be very diverse. You can use television or movie characters, famous or historic people, or even your pets as a starting point for an NPC.

For example, I have three cats, each one has a unique personality. I'll start off by describing each one as succinctly as I can.

Kermit: A big strong and fluffy guy. He is very friendly and fond of people. He dominates whatever space he is in with his presence and tends to sprawl out as large as possible.

Franklin: A lithe athletic cat who is a skilled jumper. Rail thin, he is always elegant and well poised. He is rather aloof with people he doesn't know well and trust.

Princess: This old girl is quite the scruffy lap cat. Lazy and not very bright, she is still the friendliest cat around. If you have a lap, she is there.

So this is my starting point. Next, I will alter each description to fit a fantasy character. Let's turn Kermit into a fantasy dwarf.

Kermit: A big strong dwarven warrior with an enormous, woolly beard kept immaculately clean. He dominates whatever space he is in with his friendly presence and enjoys sprawling out whenever he relaxes.

Franklin: This lithe, athletic thief is quite acrobatic and skilled at breaking into upper story rooms. Rail thin and well poised he is always elegantly dressed in the latest fashions. He is good looking but nevertheless aloof with people he doesn't know well and trust.

Princess: This charming old dowager princess no longer cares much about appearances. She avoids the court preferring to spend her time in the palace conservatory or library where she will merrily chat with anyone for hours about the trivialities of her life.

A fair amount of adjustment had to take place to smooth out the shift from talking about a pet versus a person, but the overall gist is still there. One excellent trick is to replace the original adjectives you used in the initial description with synonyms. Hopefully, the new descriptors will also suggest further refinements and let you add some more detail to the character write-ups.

Finally, I give them a new name. There are plenty of name generators and name search tools available on the Internet, or you can create your own.

Names

One of the things that give developers grief is how difficult it is thinking up new names for characters and places. There are a wide variety of approaches to naming things. The names you come up with need to have the right feel for whatever you are naming. They don't have to be wholly original but try to avoid names that are overused or closely associated with famous people or characters (Miller, 2009). Whatever you do, don't name the halfling Bilbo or Frodo!

For something more original start with one to three adjectives that describe the outstanding qualities, characteristics, or history of the person or thing being named. For example, Kermit is big, fluffy, and sprawling. Go look up a bunch of synonyms for the descriptors you used. Aim for the most inspiring or obscure words available. Looking up synonyms for big gives me gargantuan, gigantic, great, Herculean, mountainous, and prodigious. Fluffy provides downy, fleecy, flocculent, velutinous, and velvety. While sprawling supplies me with accumbent, couchant, patulous, procumbent, and supine. If one of these new words works for a name, then you're done but, as in this case, if nothing feels right, you can move on to the next step.

Take one or more of these words, break them down into syllables, then rearrange and combine them.

Choosing the following synonyms for my original terms "gigantic," "flocculent," and "patulous," I break these words down into the syllables "gi·gan·tic," "floc·cu·lent," and "pat·u·lous." Then I can rearrange and combine the syllables into the following new names:

Ganfloc
Ganlent
Ganlous
Gantic
Gilent
Ticcu
Ugan
Lentu

You can misspell, modify, and mispronounce the name. Try saying the word very fast, slurring it, or emphasizing different syllables to arrive at variations on these names. Trying these techniques out I get;

Glentic
Teekoo
Lentoo

The process is really about getting a name that feels appropriate to the person more than anything else. "Lentoo" and "Teekoo" sound like they'd fit a sci-fi character more than a fantasy one, so that leaves us with "Glentic." Try to give NPCs from the same regions similar sounding names (Miller, 2009). A classic example is the naming convention for Vulcans found in the Star Trek franchise where Vulcan males frequently had names starting with "S" and ending in "K" while Vulcan females often had names starting with "T'P" (Memory Alpha, 2018).

You can also take a few place names, features, or descriptive terms and combine them. Names like Greenesthorpe, Silverleaf, and Cragrock can be made in this way. A similar method takes a word and combines it with either a prefix, suffix, or both (Achberger et al., 2017).

Prefixes	Suffixes
a-	-ant
be-	-ed
en-	-est
mid-	-ing
pre-	-ion
re-	-t
up-	

Using a starting word like "bear," the technique provides new names such as Abear, Bearant, or Upbeart. There are dozens of different prefixes, suffixes, and similar morphologic affixes you can combine with various root words to get a wide array of new names. For added variety, you can use root words and modifiers from other languages.

If you have the time to develop it, the use of a random syllable table can be a fantastic way to generate new names. Below is a straightforward syllabic table. Roll 1d6 (that is to say one six-sided dice) once on each column; A, B, and C and combine them.

A B C

1. Ka ba la
2. Ke be le
3. Ko bo lu
4. Je ma k
5. Jo me zo
6. Ju mu zum

Doing this gives us names like Jumulu, Komak, and Jobola. The system works better with more complex and well-prepared tables, but even a simple table like this one serves to illustrate the technique.

A different approach is to take a regular name and tweak it to fit the character and setting. Names like Jontic, Paulgan, Theolous can be quickly drummed up in this manner. Always take the precaution to Google the name you choose to see if any unwanted meaning, connotation, or association pops up in connection with that particular name (Miller, 2009).

Another classic method involves using a medieval or historical name. These ancient names can be run through the array of tools presented above to change them into something more unique or just used as is. Names like Tyrkir, Unnulf, and Ethelstan can easily be dug up from archival records and name lists online ("Authentic Names", 2004).

Alternatively, you can use an onomatopoeia; a word based upon the sound the object makes. Kablahp, for the note a mace makes when hitting a goblin, or Phing for the sound of an arrow flying true. It takes a bit of imagination, but this can be a handy way to create some original names.

Try taking the root words through a language translator and turning the words into a new language. You can go so far as to combine words from two or more different languages for a fresh approach (Rourensu, 2017). Try combining elements of Hungarian with Chinese, Esperanto and Khmer, or Maori and Russian. Anything goes when trying this approach.

If you are up for it, try creating a constructed language, or conlang, in the same way that J.R.R. Tolkien built Elvish from bits and pieces of Anglo-Saxon and old English (Achberger et al., 2017; Tolkien, 1937). The Omniglot website (www.omniglot.com/links/conlangs.htm) has information on building conlangs.

If all else fails, try randomly pounding the keyboard with your hands then tweaking the results into something legible (Rourensu, 2017). Doing this gave me, "ggpijger pojy'herwn", which I turned into the names Pidger, Podgy, and Herwyn.

After all of this development work I ended up with;

Kentic Kragrock: A big strong dwarven warrior with an enormous, woolly beard kept immaculately clean. He dominates whatever space he is in with his friendly presence and enjoys sprawling out whenever he relaxes.

Theolous Komak: This lithe, athletic thief is quite acrobatic and skilled at breaking into upper story rooms. Rail thin and well poised he is always elegantly dressed in the latest fashions. He is good looking but aloof with people he doesn't know well and trust.

Princess Herwyn: This charming old dowager princess no longer cares much about appearances. She avoids the court preferring to spend her time in the palace conservatory or library where she will merrily chat with anyone for hours about the trivialities of her life.

All of these descriptions and names derived from my cats and a bit of research and ingenuity.

A good name and a brief character description will work just fine for the majority of secondary characters. The only time you need to go deeper is when you are working on significant villains or other primary characters for your game. Keep in mind that the amount of detail you need to provide should be based upon how much time the players will interact with that character. There's no point whatsoever in writing up Joe the Wooden Bowl merchant if the characters aren't going to speak with him for more than a minute or two. On the other hand, if Joe is secretly the famous assassin Jaebolino of the Black Hand who is on a secret mission to slay the king which forms a central part of the story, then he probably needs a much more thorough treatment.

Factions

Let's start developing some additional details now. Factions are just groups of people who share a common goal, interest, outlook, or background. These factions can be based upon almost any reason: class, race, religion, creed, even something as trivial as which sports team someone supports. Practically anything will serve as an excuse for a group of people to organize themselves into a faction. Factions help connect the various non-player characters to the place that they live. Start by asking questions. Who lives here? Why do they live here and not somewhere else? Who runs the place? What type of government does the place have? For example, is it a local king whose family has governed for generations or is it a new conqueror who only recently seized the throne? Is there a power behind the throne that actually runs the city? Take a look at England in 1067 after William the Conqueror had taken control of England. The land was divided into the Anglo-Saxon peasants and their Franco-Norman rulers. Tensions created by this sort of situation can serve as the basis for a good storyline. In the time of King Arthur it was the invading Saxons who were wresting control away from the Romanized British people, but the idea of conflict between the rulers and the ruled is a timeless one. Doing this sort of us versus them development process is part and parcel to developing the different factions in our setting. A handful of interesting factions can provide you with sources of conflict that the players in your adventure can be tasked to solve. Factions tend to have different views on things and these views in turn generate the conflict that an adventure needs. Which faction the players decide to support can set the course for a whole campaign of adventures.

Factions operate on many different levels with each member possessing a different level of commitment to the various factions they are members of. Each faction member self-identifies with their group and this forms a deep-rooted part of their sense of self. This identity is very difficult to break or adjust and it usually takes a life threatening event to change someone's sense of identity. Make sure that you note not just what factions a given character belongs to but their strength of allegiance to that faction.

To try this developmental approach out, test it on yourself. As an exercise, write down the factions you belong to then prioritize the list from most to least important groups. For example, I am a member of the following groups currently:

1. Academia
2. Middle-class
3. American
4. Anti-authoritarian
5. Cat owner

Membership in various factions can lead to conflict since the goals of each faction may not align with each other. These memberships be a source of conflict between different characters or even the source of an internal struggle within the character as they are forced to decide which group they care about the most.

Factions comprise the different groups the players will encounter in your game. A place can have multiple factions operating in it. Nationality, religion, ethnicity, politics, and socioeconomic factors can all serve to define the various factions present. These factions are not exclusive to each other and their overlap can create interesting details. Any given non-player character might be a member of one or more factions just like in the real world. The players in our adventure might encounter a local young woman named Wulfhida who is a desperate Anglo-Saxon outlaw. Each of these major factions, poor, Anglo-Saxon and outlaw, can be subdivided into smaller factions to provide more detail. Perhaps she is a member of a secretive pagan cult that reveres Feondulf, a Saxon version of the evil Nordic Fenris-wolf. She is an outlaw because no sane villager would want a priestess of this bloodthirsty god anywhere near them. She is poor because she isn't welcome in any town and has to eke out a subsistence level existence from the forest and what few offerings she can coerce out of the local villagers. By creating a few factions and providing some detail, we are well on our way to developing a good villain in this case.

In the local city of Wolfshead, we might have the following factions:

- Thieves' Guild
- Corrupt city leaders and constabulary
- Fences and other unscrupulous merchants
- Forest brigands
- The secret cult of Feondulf
- Local peasants
- Church of Yagnaris the Healer

Now let's go in and add a bit of detail to each of these factions.

The Thieves' Guild is the power in this area. They run everything in town either directly or indirectly. To cross this group is to ask to get your throat slit as many of the more outspoken townsfolk have discovered.

Corrupt city leaders and constabulary gleefully take bribes to look the other way. The Guild would get rid of them, but they're afraid the King or other powerful nobles might notice so bold a move.

Fences and other corrupt merchants, someone has to buy and sell all of that stolen merchandise. Profits are good enough that this unscrupulous lot don't ask many questions about the origins of the goods.

Forest brigands are the ones who do the dirty work of highway robbery and theft. A rough crowd that spends much time in the Wolf Forest. Quite a number of them have joined the cult of Feondulf.

The secretive cult of Feondulf is slowly inducting the more vicious and bloodthirsty criminals into its ranks. Eventually, it will come out and try to seize power openly once it feels it controls enough of the Guild.

The poor peasants, farmers, and foresters suffered greatly at first and were the victims of grievous violence. Practically all of the upstanding and virtuous members of this group have either been killed or driven away. The ones who are left have accepted things the way they are.

Church of Yagnaria the Healer is the religion of the local mother deity whose pews are empty of late. The former high priest was an outspoken critic of lawlessness and the first person the Thieves Guild murdered to set an example. Now only a cowed deacon remains to give services and try and hold things together.

Now that we've established some of the local factions you can see how the setting is starting to develop some exciting details and real flavor.

Character Outline

Once you start generating the non-player characters who will populate your world, you must ask yourself how much detail each character needs? Exactly how much back-story and development does each of these NPCs require? The answer depends on how important they are to the story. A minor NPC that the characters might briefly interact with might only merit a single line or two of descriptive text. Just their name, faction(s) they belong to, and any outstanding trait about them. A critical villain or recurring character merits a more in-depth treatment. For essential NPCs, you can use the following guidelines to write up a summary of that character. Write a couple of sentences for each one of the headings listed below, and you will have done a reasonably in-depth portrayal of that NPC. We'll use an old character I played as an example here and run him through the process described in C. M. Cline's "The 7-Sentence NPC" article from Dragon magazine 184.

Bosco the Obnoxious

Physical description

Start off by describing the character in as much detail as one or two sentences will allow.

Example: Bosco is a balding middle-aged male dwarf with watery brown eyes, a fringe of white hair and a scraggly beard. He is covered in warts, has exceedingly foul breath, and a malodorous smell which is only outdone by his obnoxious personality.

Occupation, attributes, and skills

Write down the NPC's job plus any outstanding or distinguished features and abilities here. Whether the NPC is an honest blacksmith or an ignoble knight should be listed and fleshed out with any notable skills or attributes not inferred by their job. Try to be descriptive in your language.

Example: Bosco is a notorious bandit who thinks of himself as a noble adventurer. He is skilled at working a forge but is infamous for his abrasiveness. The fact that he is impossible to catch due to his collection of magical goodies has been the only factor keeping him out of prison.

History

Write a summary of the character's backstory.

Example: Bosco has lived a charmed life of misadventure always managing to survive through his skills, wits, magic, and luck while his companions in arms died or got themselves arrested.

Values and motivations

What drives this character to act the way they do? Include information on any factions the NPC belongs to here as well.

Example: Bosco sees himself as a dashing and noble hero out of the epics. He is trying to live up to the standards of the great dwarven heroes of old, but his offensive personality keeps getting in the way.

How does the character interact with others?

Describe briefly in detail how the rest of the world interacts with the NPC.

Example: The rest of the world views Bosco as a repulsive offense against the senses and a wanted bandit to boot.

Useful knowledge this character possesses

Describe how the NPC serves in any way, shape or form to advance the plot or story here.

Example: Bosco can be used as a humorous interlude anywhere a good bar fight can occur. He is also able and willing to help out a down on their luck group of adventurers for as long as they can stand him and pay for his services.

Distinguishing feature(s)

Write down anything the truly stands out or is remarkable about this character.

Example: Bosco is an unwittingly offensive and repulsive character with a heart of gold. This dwarf cannot keep his mouth shut and spews out offensive commentary at the most inopportune time.

Fascinating Flaws

A flawed character is an interesting character. Whether we are talking about player characters, NPCs, or villains doesn't matter. A flawed character is more interesting, relatable, and memorable than a cardboard cutout. Our example NPC, Bosco, had the woeful misfortune to roll a "3" on his charisma. Bosco was hideously ugly, uncouth, rude, aggressive, offensive, and since he never bathed—smelled to high heaven. He was also blissfully unaware of the effect he had on others and thought himself a Don Juan character. There was not an NPC the group could encounter that Bosco would not, and did not, offend. The group considered leaving him behind, but he was just too good a fighter and a thief for them to do without him. He was one of the most fun and memorable characters I have ever played. People whom I don't even know have asked me about him—they talked to someone who had played in that campaign and heard about Bosco. Ten years down the road and while most of the details of that campaign are forgotten, everyone still remembers Bosco the Obnoxious. It was his flaws that gave him depth and brought him to life in everyone's eyes. The usual, unflawed characters in the game just weren't as fun or memorable. Bosco was also a very nice guy who would fight tooth and nail to defend the underdog. Between his offensive behavior and heart of gold, there was always ample opportunity to create adventure. Always try to encourage the development of unique character traits and background depth to your characters, villains, and NPCs. Doing so will provide endless options for stories and plots and keep your players engaged.

Bosco

The Unexpected

Since important NPCs should play a role in the plot, you should add in how they affect the game. You can provide each NPC with a secret, a fantastic ability, relationship or reward to offer the players (Winninger, 1999c). There's the classic example of "Luke, I am your father," or it can turn out that your love interest from the first movie is your sister, like in the original *Star Wars* movies (Lucas, 1980). Perhaps the NPC is a source of useful or misleading rumors, some handy advice or they can even provide aid in the form of an items, spells, or just extra muscle if the party is too weak to face down its foes (Winninger, 1999b). In our example of Bosco it just so happens that he has impressive abilities. Bosco possesses magic items that let him run as fast as a horse and walk through walls. Whenever things got sketchy, Bosco would take off in a straight line running at speed through any buildings in his way. The only reason he isn't in prison for his obnoxiousness was this fantastic ability.

Adding More

You don't have to stop with the outline suggested above. You can keep adding more details and bring the character to life if you choose to. Just make sure that the NPC merits this treatment. Reserve it for your main antagonist or other characters critical to the plot. Monte Cook's inestimable advice in his "Dungeoncraft: Characterization" articles in Dragon magazines 320 and 321 provide a few more suggestions. Describe the character's goals, motivations, fears, likes and dislikes. Speak to the NPC's mannerisms and emotional attitude. Maybe the NPC yawns incessantly, pick their ears, or fiddles with everything. Provide them with big and small goals, fears, likes and dislikes. Throw in a memorable catchphrase or quote to round out the NPC, and you'll end up with someone the players will honestly remember and enjoy dealing with. Use your friends and family as source material if stumped for ideas. Think about a famous movie character or well-known public figure and use them as a source for your NPC's personality, appearance or attributes. Remember that not all of your NPCs or monsters will be equally intelligent or personable. Make some as dumb as a rock and others smart as a whip (Cook, 2004a,b). The point is to give each NPC as much flavor and personality as possible. NPCs are defined by what they do, not their backstory (Barwood and Falstein, 2006). Make sure your NPCs act, not just talk or explain things. Having your NPCs take action will make them come to life instead of just being set dressing for your plot!

The Character Profile Worksheet

When creating an NPC or character that is critical to the game you can use the following detailed character profile worksheet to assist you. Start with the basics and fill out the sheet as best you can. It will force you to answer all of the essential elements regarding that character (Hedlund, 2010; Scholar, 1998). Use this approach when you need a fully three-dimensional character. For lesser characters, you can stick to the basics. Don't waste your time using the whole form on trivial or unimportant characters.

Basics

- Name:
- Nickname? Who uses their nickname?
- Nationality:
- Current social status:
- Overall intelligence level:
- Education:
- Hobbies:
- Skills, abilities, and talents:
- Current residence:
- Occupation:
- Family members (list):
- Describe their home and home life.
- Do they have a significant other(s)?
- Who is their best friend? How do they get along?
- Worst enemy? How do they interact?
- Who is the most important person to this character?

Description

- Height/weight:
- Body type:
- Species or race:
- Age:
- Hair color and style:
- Eye color:
- Skin color:
- Scent:
- Facial features:
- Describe the character's voice and speaking style.
- Describe their manner of dress, favorite clothing, and jewelry.
- Describe any distinguishing features (scars, tattoos, glasses, false teeth, injuries, stance, or other unique things).
- Item(s) special to character:

Behavior

- Describe their temperament.
- Describe the character's personality (happy, sad, polite, stingy, and so forth).
- Is the character introverted or extroverted?
- Mental problems, illness, or addictions?

- Favorite form of entertainment?
- What does this person fear, hate or love?
- How does the character see themselves?
- How do others see the character?
- How does the character cope with loss?
- With anger?
- Fear?
- What makes this person happy?
- Sad?
- Describe their sense of humor.
- Do they have any quirks or eccentricities unique to them?
- Describe the character's mannerisms and habits.
- How does the character act around others?
- Does the character have a catchphrase or a common saying?
- Does the character belong to any factions? List and prioritize them.
- Describe their religious or spiritual beliefs.
- Describe their political beliefs.
- Describe their prejudices.
- How do their beliefs affect them?
- What are their favorite foods?
- What are their favorite books?
- What is their favorite color?
- What is their favorite place?

History
- Describe this character's history.
- Have they ever killed someone? Why?
- Hometown:
- Provide a brief family history.
- What was their home life like growing up?
- Describe at least one formative or traumatic event in this character's past.
- How does society view this character?
- How do their family and friends see them?
- What do their enemies think of them?

Game
- What is the character's role in the game or story?
- What is this character's relationships with the other game characters?
- Does this character have any allies? Enemies?
- What does this person believe their goal to be?

- What is the actual problem this person needs to work through (is it different than their stated goal)?
- What is keeping them from their goal?
- Why do they desire this goal?
- How does this character evolve during the game?

Hedlund (2010), Scholar (1998)

Developing Villains

All it takes for your NPC to turn into a villain is to have them start hindering the players. As soon as the NPC sets himself up in opposition to the players' goals, voila, they're now a villain. Villains should actively oppose the characters (Barwood and Falstein, 2006). To make a villain genuinely evil, have them do something personal to the character. Setting up the villain's evil nature using backstory doesn't have the same impact as having the villain hurt the character or their loved ones directly in the game does (Barwood and Falstein, 2006). Overplay this card though, and you end up with characters who never grow attached to anyone. Remember to let your intelligent villains act intelligently. They'll retreat when it looks like they could lose, plot careful escape routes and fall back positions, call in reinforcements when needed, and persist long enough to get under the characters' skins. Remember that most intelligent foes won't fight to the death unless they have no other option.

Developing Monsters

All of the techniques we've talked about so far can be used to create monsters as well. Unintelligent monsters are just hungry, but more intelligent monsters can be generated just like other NPCs. If you are designing new monsters, then go out and do some visual research to identify which animals (or objects) you'd like to base your monsters on. Fortunately, research has revealed a few handy fear triggers that you can use for game monsters:

1. Staring eyes.
2. Predator mouth, full of sharp teeth.
3. A big, red tongue.
4. Menacing and sudden movements.
5. Blood.
6. Bones.
7. Darkness and the night.

Trout (2011)

You can leverage these primordial fear triggers to design an appropriately scary monster. You will have to make sure that your monster fits the setting and makes sense in the environment where you encounter it. Don't include a killer robot in your fantasy setting or giant squids in the forest (or at least explain why they are there)!

When designing challenges for an adventuring party, you can use the following basic formula. Add up the total number of levels in the adventuring party of characters to calculate the group's overall challenge rating (CR). For a typical party, this is usually about 4–5 characters, so a 1st level party has a challenge rating (CR) of roughly 5. A single monster is worth its die value of hit points in CR. So a 7d8 monster has a CR of 7.

If the Monster's CR is less than the Party's CR the difficulty is easy.

If the Monster's CR is equal to the Party's CR the difficulty is average.

If the Monster's CR is one or two die higher than the Party's CR the difficulty is hard.

If the Monster's CR is three or four dice higher than the Party's CR the difficulty is deadly.

If the Monster's CR is more than five dice higher than the party's, then the characters should run!

When encountering multiple monsters, you need to add up their total CR rating to compare it to the adventuring party's. The CR total will provide you with the final measure of the difficulty of the encounter that you need to balance things out.

Typically in an adventure, you can have as many easy or average encounters as you like. Use a few hard battles to get the player's attention or weaken them before you hit them with one deadly encounter which should be the climax of the adventure. Do not throw them up against an overwhelming encounter without plenty of powerful indicators that the outmatched players should be running.

Example

I need a monster to serve as part of the culmination of the adventure. Since we're talking about priests of Fenris, a giant evil wolf seems appropriate. The characters will probably be 2nd or even 3rd level by the time they reach the finale, so the monster needs to be tough. Each monster should have a fair amount of hit points, damage dice, and everything else. Since it will be part of an encounter that includes other NPCs and monsters, each monster shouldn't be too overpowering, or we might unbalance the encounter. We're probably looking at a total player's CR of about eight (8) by the finale of the adventure. Once we add the main monster, Skohl, (CR6) to the high priestess (CR 4) along with a couple of low-level minions (CR 1) we end up with a total encounter CR of 12 for the finale. That should be a very tough encounter that the players will remember!

Skohl
Hit points: 6d8 (27 hit points)
Armor class: 14
To hit bonus: +7
Damage: 2d8
Movement: 180 feet
Saving throw: 6
Special: immunity to cold damage
Size: large
Number: 1 (unique monster)
Treasure: special
Experience: 700
An enormous white wolf covered in frost. Skohl stands about 5 feet tall at the shoulder and is roughly 8 feet long and 700 pounds in weight. Skohl is intelligent and able to speak with wolves and the priests of Fenris. Skohl is immune to cold damage, but fire inflicts a +1 damage bonus per die rolled. Skohl's glistening pelt is worth 1d6×1000 gold pieces.

The 6d8 hit dice averages out to around 27 hit points when rolled up. A large number like this means that a group of adventurers can wail on this critter for roughly 3–6 rounds before it dies. Its armor class is relatively low since I want the players to be able to hit it. If we combined a high number of hit points with a high armor class, this thing would decimate any low-level party it came across. As is, I will probably need to give the party some sort of advantage when fighting this thing or it will surely kill half of them at least. It does a wicked amount of damage per bite, but smart players can use missile weapons to their advantage to help mollify that somewhat. Its movement is roughly standard for a wolf. I added the immunity to cold damage more for flavor since low-level parties aren't going to have any cold spells or magic items, so it doesn't add to the monster's difficulty rating. That cold invulnerability gives me an excuse for its fire vulnerability which is something the players could exploit. I give it a low saving throw number, so the party doesn't just charm it or otherwise one-shot it with a spell. That'd be anti-climactic if it happened. Roughly 100 experience points per hit dice seem appropriate, so it ends up being worth 600 experience points. Making the pelt the monster's treasure adds in a little more flavor to things and feels right.

Now we can write up the wolf's backstory using the character outline and character profile worksheet as guides. We'll do so in paragraph format because that is more useful for the adventure than making a bullet point list.

Skohl is a young pup of the evil Norse god Fenris the Wolf. One of a litter of a half-dozen pups he was given to the high priestess of this local branch of the Cult of Fenris to raise. Bringing up the puppy has caused the current crisis in the forest. This semi-divine offspring requires a great deal of feeding, so the cult took to abducting or killing anyone who traveled through the woods to serve as food and sport for the young pup. Dead victims directly served as food. Living victims were tossed into the pup's lair alive to teach the puppy how to kill its prey. Some captives were even armed with a knife to provide a better experience for the puppy and train it valuable lessons. Skohl is cruel and direct in his methods. He has become quite the selfish, spoiled brat due to the fawning overindulgence of the priests who regard him as a holy blessing from their god. Skohl is arrogant, petty, cruel, and feels entitled to whatever he wants when he wants it—which he frequently gets. Skohl's temperament exacerbated the priests' depredations on the forest since Skohl demanded "fun food" quite frequently and if a captive wasn't available a junior acolyte would do. This bad habit led the priests to scour the forest for victims and directly to the current state of affairs which got the characters involved in finding a fix for these same depredations. When Skohl chooses to speak, it is in a rather high pitched growled voice. He still is nowhere near to being full grown and might even mistake the characters for a priestly training session with more "fun food." All Skohl has ever known is the groveling service the priests provide. Only the high priestess herself has ever disciplined him, and Skohl will mind her though he does so grudgingly like a rebellious young child does when obeying their parents. When thwarted in any way, Skohl will howl loudly and may pitch a full-on temper tantrum though if he is seriously hurt he will quickly realize the danger and respond with deadly intent.

Since Skohl is not someone the characters will likely interact with too much, so we don't need a full treatment for him. Just enough to give the monster a sense of personality and purpose within the adventure.

Skohl (© 2018 Greg Johnson)

Conclusion

In this chapter you've learned how to flesh out everything from simple secondary characters to robust significant NPCs, villains and monsters. Developing characters is all about providing engrossing details and memorable quirks. Think about your friends and family. What makes each of them unique in your mind? What makes them stand out from everyone else in the world? Now apply that level of detail to your NPCs, villains, and monsters.

Assignment

Write up four NPCs. One should be a minor character, one a major NPC, another one your main villain, and the last one a new type of monster the players will encounter. Be sure to include all of the relevant statistics, catchphrases, and anything else needed to bring that NPC to life.

Chapter 17

Fleshing Things Out

To add the detail that our adventure will need there are a few things we will have to decide first. The critical elements we must develop are:

Victory conditions and goals
Encounters
Locations
Dialogue
Rewards
Story branches

Defining Victory Conditions and Goals

We'll start with the most critical one, what are the goals or victory conditions for our adventure? One of the universal goals of any TTRPG is for the characters to survive. Other standard goals include to acquire treasure, magical items, and become more powerful characters. Surviving, growing more powerful, and acquisition of wealth and magic are the default goals for almost every TTRPG adventure. Is there anything specific to our story beyond these universal goals? What hooks can we offer to our players to emotionally involve them in the adventure? The exact answer to this will depend upon the larger goals of your game. Are you shooting for a dark and gritty drama, a light-hearted humorous romp, or a beautiful spectacle? Only after you decide upon the tone and goal of your adventure can you begin crafting the story, non-player characters, and setting to match your goals.

Taking aim at a grim and emotionally intense battle filled drama, we might go with an epic good versus evil story such as seeking to defeat an evil cult. So what are the objectives of the cultists? After researching a bit of Norse mythology, I learned about the Norse myth of the Fimbulwinter, an apocalyptic winter that occurs after Fenris, their wolf god, eats the sun. Let's have the evil wolf cult try to bring about the Fimbulwinter. The Wolf Cultists have collected a mass of people they intend to sacrifice during a solar eclipse as part of a magic ritual to bring about the Fimbulwinter and destroy the world. We could have just used the fundamental TTRPG goals of surviving, becoming more powerful and getting more stuff, but it helps to have more ambitious goals to grab the player's imagination and emotions. If we hadn't eliminated the town for brevity, we could have used the relationships the characters built up in that area to provide a personal link to events. Maybe one or more of the character's family members has been abducted by the cultists, and the players are sent to rescue them? That would be easy enough to arrange as part of the introduction and backstory to the adventure. Along the way to save their family members, the characters can discover what the actual goals of the cult are and work to defeat them.

Let's write up the introduction to our adventure.

> Terror stalks the fringes of the Wolf Forest. Numerous people have disappeared in the night from the villages and hamlets surrounding the forest. Eerie howls and cries echo within its dark and twisted woods. Strange figures, neither man nor wolf, have been seen skulking through the shadows. Why has the forest become so dangerous? Who is behind the mysterious disappearances? What can be done about it?

> Doom is looming ever closer to people living near the Wolf Forest. Can your band of brave adventurers solve the mystery of the Wolf Forest?

That sets the tone for our adventure and introduces some of the primary motivations for the player characters to engage with the narrative.

Encounters

Let's start with our outline. We can go through what we've already developed and begin adding more details and specifics to each section. Luckily for us, the adventure is split into two parts: the forest and the temple. This allows us to focus on each section separately if needed.

It can be quite a painful process to commit to firm decisions while doing this. Consider your options carefully so that you don't have to go back in and rewrite extensively. Try to write for an hour or so each day to make steady progress. Eventually, the whole thing will start to take shape!

Balancing Encounters

When designing the encounter portion, you must consider the difficulty of each event. Each encounter should be adjusted to the overall level of the character party. Battles that are too difficult are frustrating while ones that are too easy are boring.

The 3.5 edition Dungeon Master's Guide by the Wizards RPG Team has excellent guidelines for balancing encounters. An average party for the adventure we are designing consists of four to five first level characters. We add up the total number of levels involved to find the overall average encounter level for the group, in this case, five. To figure out the power level of monsters or enemies to put into the encounter, use either the monster's hit dice amount or enemy character level. A standard battle involves five hit dice or levels worth of foes. A weak encounter involves four or less hit dice or levels. A difficult one has a higher amount of levels or hit dice than the character party but not more than double that of the party. For our module, this means six to nine hit dice worth of foes. An overwhelming encounter has more than double the hit dice or levels of the party (Wizards RPG Team, 2003, 48–50).

The idea is to pace the number and type of encounters in the adventure out. Begin by offering a few weak confrontations and maybe an average one or two to serve as an introduction to the story. In the middle offer up some more average encounters. The climax is served by a few fierce and maybe one genuinely challenging battle that is almost, but not totally, overwhelming for the big boss battle. Be careful not to crush the party with too many difficult confrontations. The player characters need time to recharge, rest, and heal between fights. A rapid succession of average encounters can be just as challenging as one or two big boss battles because you aren't giving the characters time to recuperate. Conversely, an adventure that allows the players to proceed at their own pace, fully recharged for every battle, can throw more difficult engagements at the party and still maintain balance.

Situational modifiers can change the difficulty of each encounter drastically. Providing the players with an advantage of some sort can help balance out otherwise overwhelming situations while putting them at a disadvantage can amp up weaker ones. Shooting goblins as they climb up a cliff face towards the party is pathetically easy, whereas having to climb a cliff face while goblins shoot at you is incredibly rough. One standard approach is to try and reward smart gameplay by providing opportunities for different situational modifiers. For example, if the players find the temple and just charge in, they wind up with a giant melee involving the entire cult—which will probably kill the players. On the other hand, if they sneak up to the temple and begin ambushing lone or small groups of cultists, they can whittle the cult down bit by bit until the final boss battles are quite manageable.

Part I: Wolf Forest

1. While traveling through an evil forest, the characters are attacked by a wolf priest and cultists out hunting with a pack of wolves. They discover evidence of a secret temple located in these woods and hints of a fabulous treasure to be found there.
2. The party tracks the cultists back to their temple. While traveling through the vile woods, the party has the opportunity to have a few exciting encounters.
   A. Optional side quest > Evil wolf pack
   B. Optional side quest > Evil pilgrims
   C. Optional side quest > Evil ogre

Part II: Wolf Temple

1. The party locates the Wolf Temple. They can scout it out by infiltrating it, observe it, capture and question a cultist or two, or directly attack it head-on.
2. The characters attack the wolf temple. Hopefully, they defeat the wolf cult and root out the evil. Afterward, they receive any rewards.

Note how I am reworking the material in the outline as I go. Iterating the contents and slowly refining it each time I do so. This framework provides a list of the places we will need on our map. Go ahead and sketch out a rough version of your key locations. Use a pen or pencil and paper to do it. Just get a rough idea of where things will be located. We will start with the Wolf Forest. While traveling through the forest, the characters get attacked by a wolf priest out hunting with a pack of wolves. On the dead priest, the players will discover evidence of a secret temple located in these woods and hints of a fabulous treasure to be found there. The goal in this section of the adventure is to introduce the players to the story, provide enough interest and encouragement that they want to engage with the plot, and throw in enough danger and excitement to keep things interesting.

Descriptions

We will need to write up descriptions and details for each encounter. Something evocative is preferred, but the account should match the importance of the site. A broom closet doesn't require much detail but the battleground where the players meet the final boss surely does. Let's start by describing the Wolf Forest.

Locale description: The Wolf Forest is a grim place full of gigantic and gnarled ancient trees where the shadows are deep and dark. A tumble of large moss covered stones, and fallen leaves carpet the forest floor. A few old logging paths lead through the forest, but these have fallen into disuse and are now heavily overgrown and choked with weeds. The path through the forest narrows and passes down a slight gorge with large boulders to either side of the track.

This description sets the default tone for the section of the adventure set in the forest. It will form a block of highlighted text that helps introduce our narrative to the players. Now we can move on to working on the first encounter. This initial encounter will establish the tenor of the whole adventure and thrust the players directly into the core of the action. We can start by describing the setting then provide all of the game mechanics and stats for our NPCs and monsters.

> *Trap*: As the characters pass down into the gorge have them each roll a saving throw. If they succeed, they are not surprised and can roll for the initiative like normal. If they fail the saving throw, then they are surprised for the first round of combat and can only act after their enemies have had one full round of actions. The Wolf Priest of Fenris, Manichi will leap down from his hiding place atop one of the boulders while he calls the wolves to the attack with a whistle and cry of "Blood for Fenris!"

One of the best ways to get players involved is to start things off with a bang. Throwing the players into immediate action and danger is a great way to get them hooked on the adventure. Even better, this encounter can happen almost anywhere along any random dark forest road. This allows the GM to drop the event into any campaign rather effortlessly. The battle also illustrates the way to describe a simple trap, in this case, an ambush.

Encounter: Manichi Wolf Priest of Fenris

Cleric 2, HD:2d8 HPS:12 AC:15 ATK:+1 DMG:1d6 MV:60ft

Spells: cure light wounds, command

Manichi wears mangy collection of tattered wolf pelts over his set of chainmail armor. The iron fangs mounted on his helmet are used to "bite" his opponents. He also possesses a pick shaped like a wolf's jaws which he can use as a backup weapon. Manichi is a true fanatic and believes his god will not let him lose, so he fights to the death.

3 Wolves

HD:2d8 HPS:8 AC:13 ATK:+1 DMG:1d6 MV:100ft

These black wolves have an evil demeanor and visage to them. The wolves will flee if the cleric is slain.

Since the evil priest doesn't have a whole lot to say, I've gone ahead and thrown in his little catchphrase of "Blood for Fenris!" This also provides the first clue to the players of what and who they are up against. Since Manichi fights to the death, it is unlikely that they will capture him and get any information from him so I don't need to go into detail about his personality or background. His role is that of cannon fodder, not a recurring villain.

When writing these encounters up, it is perfectly fine to be brief. A lengthy exposition about the setting, villain's motivations, and backstory don't necessarily help you tell the story. It's a good thing to leave some material to the player's imagination. You write down just the content that you need to tell the story. Nothing more. This philosophy translates directly into video game production. No professional company would waste time making stuff they didn't need to tell the story and play the game. The world is there to help you reveal the story, not the other way around.

The fact that the villain in this scene is ambushing the characters brings us to our next point. Make your enemies intelligent. Any good villain will use their head and fight to their own advantage. They'll set up ambushes, create traps, fortifications, and secret passages or tunnels to exploit. Only very stupid or animalistic opponents will charge in on sight every time.

Rewards and Clues

Since this is the start of the adventure, we have to include some hints that will lead the players to the next phase of the story. These leads should provide the characters with enough information to allow them to investigate things further and motivate the group to do so. In this case, the clue takes the form of a letter.

Reward and information: Once the players have defeated Manichi they find on his body 12 gold pieces, 60 silver pieces and a carved carnelian ring worth 40 gold. Remnants of a trade caravan he attacked and slaughtered recently. Carefully folded up around the money is a letter written on a piece of flayed human skin from the high priestess of his cult:

Manichi,

Capture or slay any travelers you find. Bring them back to the temple. Do not delay. The sacrifices must be fresh.

~Wulfhida

On the back of the letter, Manichi has sketched a crude map.

Manichi's letter and map

Hopefully, players will be intrigued enough by the money they find on Manichi and the nature of his orders to want to follow the map back to the temple. If not, you can use the following encounter with the destroyed caravan to provide a bit more motivation. Otherwise, you can just use the battle as a moral reinforcement of their quest.

Destroyed Caravan

Have a backup plan in case the players don't follow along. Try to avoid having the players feel forced into any course of action. Heavy-handedly shoving your players around becomes quickly tiresome for players and is a source of frustration in a LOT of games. The plot should flow naturally from motivating your characters to engage in the story with intriguing challenges, engaging NPCs, and rich rewards.

> *Description*: You hear the arguing crows before you see the horrific sight itself. Straddled across the trail lies the burnt out remnants of a wagon. Blood and gore cover the scene, but no bodies are in view. The crows flee at your approach, and you can see the ransacked remains of the farmer's goods scattered around the husk of a wagon.

> *Info*: If the players investigate, they find no items of any value remaining. Everything of any worth has been looted. Aside from the blood, there is no indication of any bodies. Large wolf paw prints and footprints are all over the place plus drag marks where the bodies were dragged off into the forest, but this is only apparent if the players investigate the scene carefully and look for tracks.

> If the party thinks to try, they might be able to track the pack of wolves and priests who did this slaughter back to the temple. Have each character trying to pursue the offenders roll a saving throw. If they succeed, then they can find the trail and follow it deeper into the woods. The players will have to roll a

tracking saving throw each hour they attempt to follow the trail. If they fail their rolls, they lose the path and end up lost deep in the woods. They need to make five (5) successful tracking rolls to locate the Wolf Temple since it lies roughly five hours away from the scene of this crime.

This encounter is just a description and a few clues. It serves to reinforce the need for the characters to continue on the adventure and solve the problem that the wolf temple represents. It also provides an opportunity to lead the players to the next section of the module.

The Sad Dryad

We'll do another example encounter to show a few non-violent options for encounter creation, the grief-stricken dryad. This encounter serves as the last chance for the group to get involved or as additional encouragement and motivation. It also helps reinforce the idea that the players don't have to fight everyone they meet.

> *Description*: The soft sound of sobbing quietly echoes through this section of the forest. Even the trees seem glum. Through their branches, you can see a beautiful woman with mottled brown skin and mossy green hair sitting underneath a tree crying her heart out over the body of a white deer. A large pool of blood spreads out from under the deer.

> *Info*: The deer has been attacked and slain by one of the roving bands of wolf priests. This magical white deer was one of the guardian spirits of the forest and a friend to the dryad. She is almost inconsolable in her grief and has not noticed the party approach. When she does finally see them, she shrieks in terror and rage but quickly calms down once she realizes they aren't affiliated with the wolf temple or priest. If they are sympathetic to her and do not attack or offend her, the sad dryad can prove to be a real boon to the party.

Provided the players don't attack the sobbing dryad she is willing to talk to them. This allows us to demonstrate a bit of sample dialogue.

> *Dialogue*: "Oh." As she wipes away a few tears and tries to make herself more presentable, she asks, "You are not part of the temple of Fenris?" Assuming the players confirm this, she continues, "those evil wolves have slain my friend. They pollute my forest and create such terror amongst my friends. I truly hate them now." If the players converse with her further or offer any sympathy or aid, she will help guide them to the wolf temple. "I know where to find the wolves lair. I can guide you there if wish."

This little bit of potential conversation is a straightforward example of a dialogue tree. In video games, these branching structures are critical since they include everything an NPC knows or can say. A TTRPG like the one we are making allows for much greater flexibility. Here we just have to define the personality of the NPC and maybe provide a few catchphrases or just the most important things they need to say to continue the plot. Everything else the NPC says can be made up on the spot by the GM running the adventure. While this does make our job much easier in this instance, it is essential to be aware that this is a principal point of difference between computer games and TTRPGs.

Even though this is supposed to be a peaceful, sad dialogue, there is always a chance the player characters will handle it poorly or aggressively and end up in combat. We'll include her statistics just in case that happens.

Encounter: Buttercup the sad Dryad, HD:3d8 HPS:15 AC:15 ATK:+1 DMG:1d4 MV:60ft

Spells: 3/3/2: cure light wounds, entangle, sanctuary, cure moderate wounds, hold person, zone of truth, cure serious wounds, speak with dead (already cast upon the deer)

Dryads are tree spirits bound to the largest oak tree in their forest. They resemble an elven woman with skin made of wood and hair of leaves or moss. These creatures are quite shy and only reveal themselves to people of good nature who love their forest. Dryads are powerful spellcasters operating like a 6th level cleric regarding spells.

Solving the situation sensitively and without bloodshed provides the same experience award that defeating her in combat would have.

Reward: If treated well, Buttercup will lead the players directly to the Wolf Temple. Otherwise, she will quickly run away from any rude or aggressive parties. She will defend herself if she is attacked, of course. If she is attacked and escapes she will spread the word to all of the forest inhabitants that the party is allied with the Wolf Temple and every creature of the forest will turn against the players from that point onwards.

Aggressive player characters will have a tough fight on their hands. Depending upon the type of party involved you can get wildly varying outcomes in TTRPGs. It is easily conceivable that an evil group might seek out the Wolf Temple to join it instead of fight it! While we can assume for the most part that they will be heroically inclined, it doesn't hurt to throw in a small tidbit or two for those who might tend otherwise.

Pacing, Mood and Random Encounters

An important aspect of storytelling is controlling the mood and emotional tension of your audience. You must keep your audience engaged in your story. This doesn't mean that you have to keep things at a fever pitch of excitement at all times, that quickly becomes tiresome, but you can't allow things to become dull, or you risk losing your audience. You have to provide a varied pace of excitement and recuperation throughout your story. Build up the tension, have a climax, a brief rest then repeat the process incrementally building up the story a little bit each time until you get to the crux of things and have your grand finale.

Professionals writers and artists will often use a variant of a mood board to plot out the emotional state they wish their audience to feel for each shot in an animated movie. The writers then carefully craft the color, action, and dialogue of each scene to fit the level of excitement and feeling they want. While we don't need this sort of emotional mood board for our game, it does illustrate a process that can be used by writers to visualize the flow of a complicated story.

Random Encounters

A straightforward ploy in the game designer's arsenal is to throw a battle at your players if they start to get bored or frustrated with their progress. These so-called "wandering monsters" can be injected any time the players begin to get bored, whenever you need to ratchet up the tension or just to keep the players on their toes. You don't want a continuous stream of monsters assaulting the characters though. The players will need places to rest and to recuperate otherwise the non-stop combat will quickly wear them down and increase the difficulty level of the adventure dramatically. Providing the occasional safe space that the players can use to rest and heal up allows their characters to be at maximum capability when dealing with their foes. Encounter design is a balancing act. You want to keep the tension high, but not so high that it becomes exhausting.

In classic *D&D* adventures such as "The Palace of the Silver Princess" or "The Keep on the Borderlands," random encounters are used to keep the players' level of apprehension up during the lulls in the adventure. These encounters take the form of a table of monsters that the GM checks occasionally to see if any of them show up. We can write up one of these wandering monster tables for our own adventure and then offer a few suggestions on how the GM can use them.

After a bit of thought about what sort of people and creatures the adventuring party could conceivably run into in the Wolf Forest, I came up with the following list.

Acolyte(s) of Fenris
Hunting party
Forest animal
Pilgrims
Wolves
Worg (tougher wolves)

These are all encounters that would logically make sense to be there for one reason or another. Either they just live here in the woods and haven't been eaten yet, or they are drawn in one fashion or another to the violence the temple to Fenris represents. Now we just need to detail out each encounter a little bit. Since these aren't significant parts of the story, we can keep these characters relatively flat and provide only a few details about each one. This will need to include their game stats and any other notes the GM will need to run the encounter appropriately.

Acolyte(s) of Fenris: Roll 1d4 to determine the total number of acolytes encountered. These followers of Fenris are out seeking things to hunt and kill. Unless the party makes some pretense of being fellow worshippers of Fenris, the acolytes will mark them as prey and attempt to slaughter them.

Acolyte, first level cleric, HD:1d8 HPS:8 AC:13 ATK:+1 DMG:1d6 MV:60ft

Spells: each cleric knows either command or protection for their once a day spell.

These acolytes are equipped with wolf hide armor and axes. Each acolyte has 1d20 silver pieces in their belt pouch.

So just a simple encounter with minimal details is provided. Again, these aren't essential scenes in our story just an event to keep the tension up.

Hunting party: A single acolyte of Fenris and his pack of wolves are out hunting for victims and sacrifices. He may try to capture the party and bring them back to the temple for a proper sacrifice.

Acolyte, first level cleric, HD:1d8 HPS:8 AC:13 ATK:+1 DMG:1d6 MV:60ft

Spells: entangle. Equipped with wolf hide armor and an axe.

Wolves, roll 1d6 for the number.

HD:2d8 HPS:8 AC:13 ATK:+1 DMG:1d6 MV:100ft

These black wolves have an evil demeanor and visage to them. The wolves will flee if the acolyte is slain.

Similar to the encounter with Manichi, just not as life-threatening to the party. This encounter should drive home how infested the forest is with these evil priests. It also provides another way to get the characters to the temple though if the priest captures them, then the GM will have to engineer their escape somehow.

Forest animal: Your party stumbles upon a frightened and terrified forest animal.

Deer - HD:1d6, HPS:5, AC:12, ATK:+0, DMG:1d3, MV:100ft

Rabbit - HD:1d3, HPS:2, AC:12, ATK:+0, DMG:1d2, MV:90ft

Squirrel - HD:1d2, HPS:1, AC:11, ATK:+0, DMG: 1 point, MV:60ft

Nothing spectacular here, it is just that animals live in a forest too. Resourceful adventurers can use them as food if they can catch them.

Pilgrims: This group of converts is traveling to the new shrine of Fenris they have heard about to worship. They're a grim, violent and humorless bunch with an intense distrust of strangers. They will not willingly reveal their intended association with the temple unless forced to. They possess a crude map to the temple's location.

Roll 1d6 to determine the number of pilgrims in the group.

Pilgrim: HD:1d8, HPS:7, AC:12, ATK:+0, DMG: 1d6, MV:60ft

They are equipped with a motley assortment of weapons such as clubs and axes and wear thick, padded furs and clothing as a crude form of armor. Each pilgrim has 1d12 copper and 1d6 silver pieces in their belt pouches. One has a golden wolf-shaped pendant worth 10 gold pieces on a leather cord around his neck.

This encounter also serves to guide the players back to the adventure if they are lost or otherwise distracted.

Wolves: Simply a pack of evil wolves without any priests or acolytes out on the hunt.

Wolves, roll 1d6 for the number.

HD:2d8 HPS:8 AC:13 ATK:+1 DMG:1d6 MV:100ft

These black wolves have an evil demeanor and visage to them. The wolves will flee if the biggest wolf is slain.

Worg: A gigantic unnatural wolf the size of a grizzly bear distantly related to Fenris himself. As evil and despicable a perversion of nature as can be found anywhere. This monstrosity will attack anything that crosses its path fearlessly.

HD:4d8 HPS:23 AC:14 ATK:+4 DMG:1d10 MV:100ft

This encounter serves merely to reinforce the evil wolf theme of the adventure as a whole. The giant wolf emphasizes the corrupt and evil nature of the temple as a bonus.

Now that we've written up our wandering monsters we can formalize how they can be used by the GM by creating a table and description for their use.

Wandering Monster Table

GMs can roll for chance encounters with the creatures on this table. Roll 1d8 at dawn, dusk, and midnight each day the players are in the Wolf Forest. On a 1–2 on the dice roll, they encounter something. Roll 1d6 to determine the type of encounter the adventurers have. The GM can use this table to provide some excitement anytime their players are getting restless or bored.

Dice roll	Wandering monster encountered
1.	Acolyte(s) of Fenris
2.	Hunting party
3.	Forest animal
4.	Pilgrims
5.	Wolves
6.	Worg

The encounters on our table are known as "Mooks" in common game parlance. These low-level antagonists are individually weak and frequently uniform in nature. They only provide a real threat when thrown at the players in considerable numbers. They're an excellent tool to provide weak to mid-level encounters which are not too threatening nor too easy. Because each individual mook is quite puny, scaling these encounter a bit harder or easier becomes as simple as adding more or less mooks to the battle. Mooks are great when designing simple encounters and combats. They scale with their numbers and don't present too much of a challenge to the players. Use them to provide a few clues and a taste of the treasures and rewards to be gained by finishing the adventure.

Conclusion

We've got our encounters written up and fleshed out, developed the story a bit, and provided a number of clues and story crumbs to guide the players to the next section of the adventure. While I could keep going and write out the rest of the encounters, what we've got so far serves as an excellent example of the development process. We'll keep working on things in the next chapter by creating some of the maps we will need. Hopefully, this guided process will illustrate a proper development path. Keep in mind that each developer has their process and what works for one might not for another. That said, organization, preparation, and a structured working process tend to be a successful recipe.

Assignment

Write down a list of encounters that you need for your adventure. If you're writing something substantial, then split things up into sections and just work on one part like I've done here in these examples. Everything should relate back to the overall theme of your adventure and reinforce the central motifs that you've decided upon. If an encounter doesn't fit in well or could take the characters down a wrong path then just eliminate it. You don't want to confuse your players as to what they're supposed to be doing. You can always use that idea in a different adventure. Make sure that you provide clues and pathways for the players to follow your storyline and keep up with the plot. You will need to understand the rules of the game you've chosen to use, so make sure that you play the game system you've chosen. Once you've detailed out your encounters, you can move on to the next chapter.

Chapter **18**

Big Finale

We've come to the crux of the adventure now, the big finale. The characters have found the location of the Temple of Fenris and have to destroy it. Before they can do that, we have to describe it and write up all of the encounters and other details the adventure needs. Since this is a low-level adventure and we're not talking about a grand temple complex, just a local branch of a much bigger cult, we can make this section relatively brief. Let's start by outlining all of the elements we need.

A setting with encounters, like our wolf temple, is a living ecosystem (Cook, 2003c). The bad guys don't build their lairs for the convenience of the player characters (Guss, 1996). These places are where the bad guys live and work. There should be security measures, storage space(s), living quarters, plus anything else the bad guys need. Whatever you choose to include should make sense, be functional, and enhance the believability of your location. It would be silly to have a gigantic temple complex or cathedral be the home for our secretive wolf cult for example. How would the cult hide its activities and presence if it possessed such a grand edifice? Your adventure has to be believable and make sense! Every place and building in your module should have a purpose, both for its inhabitants and for the narrative you are telling. You need to figure out what that purpose is and how it fits into your adventure. Ask yourself who built it, why they made it, and what function it serves now? This doesn't mean that you need to provide details for every hut in the village, but you do need to describe everything that is relevant to the plot (Guss, 1996; Cook, 2003c).

NPCs should have a life of their own outside of their interactions with the player characters. The world should keep turning and events unfolding even when the player characters aren't around. Doing so reinforces the critical concept of always implying that there is more to the world (Barwood and Falstein, 2006). It is why J.R.R Tolkien's books have such power; it feels like there's a real place due to the incredibly detailed world he created. The characters should exist within the setting. The world shouldn't be there merely for the sake of the characters.

When designing the rest of the temple complex, it is okay to leave some parts of it vague or relatively undeveloped. You can just mention some areas briefly and let the GM develop those places later. Perhaps there is a far scouting post located elsewhere in the woods or other pre-arranged ambush spots the villains talk about. Including a few tidbits about other places and events can impart a sense of their being a greater world out there than what you actually write down.

One element to include in your layout is to offer the players a few safe spaces to rest and recuperate. Otherwise, the adventure can turn into a very challenging grind for the characters. Including a spot for the characters to safely sleep, maybe in the dryad's home if they befriend her, would offer a distinct advantage for the players. This also illustrates an additional principle: the players' actions should have a lasting effect upon the world. The players' choices have an impact on the game world and their decisions matter. This establishes a connection between the setting and your players that will get them emotionally involved in the adventure.

Standing Stones and/or Runestone

There are a lot of standing stone circles located throughout the United Kingdom and indeed all over the world. A moderately sized one comprised of jagged stones that look like giant wolf's teeth ought to fit the bill for a creepy setting. We can cover them with Norse runes which can add a puzzle for the players to decipher. Use this to reveal a clue about how Ragnarok, the apocalypse of the gods, is coming soon and the cult's role in making the event come to pass. This can be used with some other clues we can throw in as a stepping stone to further adventures. There'd also be a sacrificial altar amongst the stone circle.

Pit Lair for Skohl

Since Skohl is such a spoiled and needy pup, the high priestess has just taken to living in the pit with him to prevent him from howling and whining for attention incessantly all day and night. Since she lives in the den with him now, she'd have the cultists carve steps to make getting in and out of the lair easier for her. She'd move her essential living gear down there too. I imagine she would keep any precious stuff in her old living quarters to keep Skohl from tearing up anything valuable, but she probably doesn't get to slip away from Skohl too much.

You can see how the character write-up of Skohl that we did is now driving the development of our setting. When doing this sort of developmental work you usually either start with your characters and then let their background and motivations drive the evolution of the environment, like we're doing now, or you can develop the setting in detail first and allow that determine what sort of characters you place in it. The Wolf Forest section of the adventure was an example of a more setting driven development, while the temple is being driven by our write up of the wolf pup we did.

Captives

There should also be some captives kept around. Keeping some live prisoners handy to feed the spoiled wolf pup seems like something the priests would do based upon what we've learned about Skohl in his character development process. We can use these captives as a reward. One of them might fall in love with their rescuer. Another might be willing to become an employee while yet another might have a family who will reward any rescuers for the safe return of their family member. It could be fun to throw in a young orphaned waif who will follow the character(s) around. Add in a few local peasants to round things out, and we can proceed to write the captives up in more detail later. Since the cult never keeps captives around for long, they probably just keep them in cages or maybe another pit. The prisoners are indeed in a really pitiable state.

Living Quarters

The priests, acolytes, and cultists all need a place to stay as well. Probably not too near the sacred standing stones or Skohl's pit. I'm quite sure the other members of the cult got a bit tired of his whines, growls, and howls a long time ago. The other wolves the cult uses probably just roam freely around and come and go as they please.

There are a few other vital elements the site ought to have that we can list out.

Kitchen
Larder
Latrine
Wolf kennels

There might be a limited amount of industry for things the cult needs and doesn't feel like traveling out for.

Smithy
Tannery

These last two are optional though and might be excluded just to save space as neither really adds anything to the primary focus of the adventure.

Breathing Life into It

Make your adventure a living, breathing place (Guss, 1996). Plan not only what the players could do, but also what they actually do (Cook, 2003c). Have the bad guys react appropriately to whatever the characters do. The bad guys probably aren't fools. Make sure they act like it. The enemies might have contingency plans in place for a lot of different situations. If so, write out what the triggers are for each of the contingency plans and what each scheme entails. If the bad guys have any organization at all, they'll have some sort of alarm system developed. In *Glory of Yore* you can have the baddies make a saving throw to detect the presence of the player characters. Have the GM use modifiers from +5 to −5 on these notice checks to reflect how difficult it is to detect what the players are doing. Difficult circumstances would use a penalty whereas advantageous situations provide a bonus to their rolls. Of course, if the players go around making a lot of noise and killing everything in sight, then you don't even have to roll for the bad guys to take notice! If the players are detected, then you need to write down what the bad guys will do about it. Will they run away, fight, negotiate, get ready for battle, or go get their friends? The bad guys will be sure not only to plan ahead but also react appropriately to what the players do. Always keep your story in mind. If something doesn't advance the story along it can either be eliminated or given only a brief description (Guss, 1996; Cook, 2003c). You do not need to create a complicated backstory for each NPC or a detailed history of the entire world, just enough to convey your story and provide sufficient flavor to keep your players interested. Just remember that you are trying to create a short adventure not a novel or complete campaign setting!

With all of this in mind, we can look at our temple again and fill in a few gaps. What about the guards? Since the temple has many wolves running around all of the time they can just use them as their early warning system. Have any wolf pack that finds invaders start howling. That will alert everyone for miles around that something is happening. The priests won't set out guards specifically beyond the roving packs of wolves and acolytes they have out capturing sacrifices or hunting down prey. After all, a wolf's senses are sharper than a human in general, and the priests feel pretty secure that they would be able to see something coming before it ever gets to their temple. The lack of proper guards also serves to make this introductory adventure a little bit easier for the players. This can actually be used to scale the difficulty level of the quest. If the party is having a hard time, then allow the priests to let their guard down a bit. If the adventure is too easy, then make the priests on the alert for intruders and have an organized defense planned in case anyone finds their temple. All that is required is to have the chances of encountering a patrol increase as the players approach the temple. Let's write it up.

As the party approaches the temple, the chance of encountering a roving pack of wolves or an acolyte lead hunting pack goes up significantly. The base chance of meeting one of these groups is 1 in 6 for the primary forest. Within 10 miles of the temple the probability goes up to 1–2 in 6, within 5 miles to 1–3 in 6, and within 2 miles up to 1–4 in 6. Any wolves encountered will howl loudly to alert the rest of the temple and even summon aid. Random encounters this close to the temple or either a wolf pack (50% chance) or a hunting party of acolytes and wolves (50%).

Wolfpack: A pack of 2d6 wolves led by a worg.

- Wolves: HD:1d8+1 HPS:5 AC:13 ATK:+1 DMG:1d6 MV:100 ft SV:14. These black wolves have an evil demeanor and visage to them. The wolves will flee if the alpha worg is slain.
- Worg: HD:3d8 HPS:16 AC:14 ATK:+4 DMG:1d10 MV:100 ft SV:11. A gigantic unnatural wolf the size of a grizzly bear distantly related to Fenris himself. As evil and despicable a perversion of nature as can be found anywhere. This monstrosity will attack anything that crosses its path fearlessly.

Hunting party: A single acolyte of Fenris and his pack of wolves are out hunting for victims and sacrifices. He may try to capture the party and bring them back to the temple for a proper sacrifice.

- Acolyte, first level cleric, HD:1d8 HPS:8 AC:13 ATK:+1 DMG:1d6 MV:60 ft SPELL: entangle. Equipped with wolf hide armor and an axe.
- Wolf, HD:1d8+1 HPS:5 AC:13 ATK:+1 DMG:1d6 MV:100 ft. Roll 2d6 for the number of wolves. These black wolves have an evil demeanor and visage to them. The wolves will flee if the acolyte is slain. Roll 2d6 for the number of wolves.

Designing the Encounters

After we have the list of locations, we have to start detailing things out. The combat encounters are first. What will we find in the temple that the characters will have to fight? Listed in order of increasing difficulty the enemies the players will have to deal with are:

Cultists
  Wolves
  Acolytes
  Priests
  Worgs
  High Priestess
  Skohl

It would be convenient to write up the base statistics for each possible encounter we could find in the temple just to have this on hand for use.

Cultist or Pilgrim: HD:1d6 HPS:4 AC:12 ATK:+0 DMG: 1d6 MV:60 ft SV:14

Wolf, HD:1d8+1 HPS:5 AC:13 ATK:+1 DMG:1d6 MV:100 ft SV:14

Acolyte, cleric 1, HD:1d8 HPS:6 AC:13 ATK:+1 DMG:1d6 MV:60 ft SPELL: command

Priest, cleric 2, HD:2d8 HPS:12 AC:13 ATK:+2 DMG:1d6+1 MV:60 ft SPELLS: command, cure light wounds

Worg: HD:3d8 HPS:16 AC:14 ATK:+4 DMG:1d10 MV:100 ft SV:11

High Priestess, cleric 4, HD:4 HPS:24 AC:17 ATK:+5 DMG:1d8+2 MV:60 ft SPELLS: command, protection, cure moderate wounds, cure moderate wounds

Skohl, HD: 6d8 HPS:27 AC:14 ATK:+7 DMG:2d8 MV:120 ft SV:6 immune to cold

What do the priests do if they hear the alarm? Mostly this should be up to the GM so she can scale the adventure to fit her party but a few notes about what the temple will do couldn't hurt.

If the temple hears the alarm, they will send out a hunting party as reinforcements. If the signal is close by, the reinforcements will be a hunting party that includes a priest and additional acolyte: 2d6 wolves, 1 worg, 2 acolytes, and 1 priest.

If multiple alerts come from the same area or the alarm is really close by, the high priestess herself will investigate with a large war party of reinforcements consisting of 3d6 wolves, 1d3 worgs, 2 acolytes, 2 priests along with the high priestess herself.

Now we get to the temple itself. We can use our outline of places that we described earlier as a starting place and begin filling in the encounters that can typically be found in each location. The ceremonies of an evil wolf temple seem like they ought to take place at night, preferably under a full moon. I imagine that during the day things are devoted to doing chores, labor, and other upkeep.

It is probably a good idea for balancing the adventure to come up with a total number of villains that the players might have to fight. We can then disperse these throughout the temple.

Total numbers:
    20 wolves
    3 worgs
    20 pilgrims
    4 acolytes
    2 priests
    1 High priestess
    1 Skohl

At any given time we can assume around half (or even more) of the wolves, acolytes, and priests are out patrolling or hunting. These aren't included here but can show up unexpectedly if the players are having too easy of a time of things. During the day, half or more of the inhabitants of the temple will be asleep. This includes the High priestess, Skohl, the priests, and half of the acolytes. Around midnight everyone is up and about for the daily ceremonies to their dark god. Afterward, the day shift gets to rest until morning.

Standing Runestones

There's always a few wolf packs roaming the compound plus pilgrims, a few acolytes, and at least one priest officiating minor ceremonies here. At night things pick up with a big turnout of the majority of the congregation and clergy.

Day:
    10 or so wolves
    1 worg
    2 acolytes
    8 pilgrims

At night:
    20 wolves
    3 worgs
    2 priests
    4 acolytes
    20 pilgrims
    Plus the High priestess who leads the nightly ceremony.

Hopefully, the players will scout out the temple before charging in. Otherwise, they might be in for a rough time if they attack during a ceremony!

Pit Lair for Skohl & the High priestess

This pit is Skohl's lair. His incessant whining and howling led to the High priestess moving into the den with him. The racket was otherwise keeping the whole temple up all night and making everyone miserable. Skohl is always here. The High priestess is here unless she happens to be officiating a ceremony. There are usually two or so unfortunate pilgrims here as well doing chores.

Cages for the Captives

This area consists of just two pilgrims acting as caretakers and guards. The prisoners are held in sturdy wooden cages and have been thoroughly demoralized by their harsh treatment.

The prisoners deserve some additional details. The following elements can be found amongst the captives:

- Love interest
- Annoying waif
- Henchman or replacement character
- Wealthy rescuee
- Peasants

Now we just add some flesh to this bare-bones list of NPCs. Including encounters such as this one which allows the players a chance to really role-play their characters and interact with the NPCs in a meaningful fashion will enable us to appeal to more than the fans of hack-and-slash amongst our players. It also provides a series of opportunities for the GM to integrate elements of the adventure into their broader campaign.

Love interest: One of the prisoners is exceptionally attractive and very taken with her/his rescuers. Use whichever name fits your campaign and player characters better.

"Olga or Olaf," attractive peasant, HD 1d8, HPS 5, AC 10, MV 60 ATK +0, DMG 1.

Olga/Olaf was part of a caravan that was hit by the cult last week. Her/his parents have already been sacrificed to Skohl, and Olga/Olaf is on tonight's menu for the wolf cub.

Annoying waif: Elsa is a young (6 years old) orphan. The kid sister to Olga/Olaf Elsa has been woefully traumatized by the events of the last week and will fixate on the most formidable player character in the adventuring party and proceed to slavishly follow that character around regardless of personal danger to herself.

"Elsa," waif, HD 1d6, HP 6, AC 13, ATK nil, DMG nil. Elsa does not speak. She just stares at you with large soulful eyes, clutches your leg and doesn't let go. The characters will have to tie her to a tree or the equivalent thereof to get her to stop following them.

Henchman or replacement character: If any player's character has died in the adventure so far use this opportunity to introduce a new character to the group. If all of the characters are still alive, then the group gets to meet a potential retainer.

"Gabby," Fighter 1, HD 1d10, HP 10, AC 11, ATK+3, DMG weapon+2; S 17, I 10, W 9, D 12, C 12, CH 7.

Gabby is friendly enough but is very difficult to understand due to his thick accent and gibberish sounding speech pattern. Gabby will gladly fight if given a weapon of some sort. He is willing to be hired on as a retainer to any honorable character for 100 gold pieces and half the standard share of party experience and treasure. Gabby was a caravan guard for the wealthy merchant.

Wealthy prisoner: This wealthy merchant is willing to offer a 500 gold piece reward to the characters for getting him safely back to his merchant's guild and civilization.

"Thurston," merchant, HD 1d4, HP 3, AC 10, ATK nil, DMG nil.

Thurston is a soft, old, greying man in his 50 s. He loves to brag about his business acumen and expects those in his pay to cater to his whims. Thurston was transporting a load of expensive glassware when his caravan was taken. If he sees any of his wares, he will steadfastly insist on the return of his property and a proper escort to his destination.

Peasants: A handful (1d6) of pathetic and worried local peasants. They will flee the scene as quickly as their feet can carry them. If they are escorted back to their village, they will be incredibly grateful and will happily reward the characters with as much porridge and vegetables as the players can stomach.

Peasant, HD 1d4, HP 3, AC 10, ATK nil, DMG nil.

High priestess's Old Quarters

Since the High priestess doesn't really stay here anymore, she's moved in with Skohl to keep his whining to a minimum, her old hut doesn't see much use aside from a place to store some of her stuff. A careful search of the premises does reveal some valuable items, which we will detail in the next section on rewards!

Living Quarters

Each group has its own encampment and huts or cabins. These are rather crude yet serviceable huts made out of rough-hewn logs, animal skins, and tree branches.

> *Priest and acolyte cabins*: There are always a few priests or acolytes bunking down due to their nighttime activities and odd schedules. These huts are a bit nicer and afford each occupant a bit more privacy than the communal living arrangements for the pilgrims.
>
> *Acolytes*: two acolytes are presently sleeping or studying their holy texts (50% chance for either).
>
> *Pilgrim huts*: This is a large communal timber hall. The accommodations are very primitive, really just a sleeping space on the dirt floor and a place to leave a few belongings while visiting the temple. Six pilgrims are sleeping, cleaning or otherwise busying themselves about the area.
>
> *Wolf kennels*: The wolf kennels are really just an open area for the wolves to gather and frolic or rest. There are two pilgrims here feeding and otherwise attending to the 5–20 wolves (5d4) present.
>
> *Kitchen* & *Larder*: A crude affair of large campfires and primitive cooking equipment. Nevertheless, the four pilgrims working in the kitchens and larder areas manage to keep the whole congregation adequately fed. It's best not to ask about what type of meat can be found in the larder.
>
> *Latrine*: The smell gives this place away. The latrine consists of an outdoor area amongst a wide splotch of dense bushes on the other side of a small hillock.

Conclusion

Of course, this first draft of encounter locations and monsters still needs further work. Thorough descriptions of each area and the rewards and treasure to be found therein are coming up in the next chapter. Placing the encounters in the appropriate locations gives us another framework to base the rest of our work off of. When you are developing any sort of complicated scenario, it is frequently a good idea to work in stages by starting with an outline and progressively adding more and more details in successive layers of writing.

Assignment

Go through your project and list out all of the possible locations that could be part of your adventure. Once you have an extensive list of the places that could theoretically be in the adventure whittle the list down to include just the critical locations and add the other nonessential sites in your adventure only if you have the time and room to do so. Go through and develop the encounters that will take place in each critical location. This allows you to balance the difficulty level of your adventure as a whole before you invest a lot of time adding extra detail (and doing more work on things). Be sure to include a variety of different types of encounters that will appeal to the diverse interests of your players.

Chapter 19

Creating the Scene List

Now that we've got an outline of the places and encounters in place it is time to go in and describe everything. We need a scene-by-scene description of each locale which is called a scene list. We must paint a vivid picture in the imagination of the players with the sights, sounds, smells, and other details of each location. This is the place to include any new game mechanics needed to round out the adventure. Components such as weather tables, survival rules, new spells or even new character classes can be written up and included.

We can start by taking our existing outline and writing up a detailed description of the lighting, look, and mood for each location then add in any information on rest areas and tactical notes such as firing arcs, hiding places, and so forth as well. This will be our scene list for the adventure. You can use the following format to write up each scene in detail:

Scene List Breakdown

Title:
Number/Identifier:
Location:
Description:
Encounter/Challenge:
Events:

Notes:

Rewards:

Title: This is the name for the specific scene. Try to use something descriptive and meaningful when naming things. Using meaningful names makes it a lot easier if you need to go back in and make edits or significant changes. Trying to figure out whether you need to fix "Tower A" or "Tower C" is more difficult than knowing that it's the "Wyvern's Roost" or the "Crow's Abode." Descriptive names also help the GM who is hurriedly flipping through your adventure trying to find the correct place.

Number/Identifier: A necessary numeric identifier you can later use as a reference point on the map you will eventually draw up and include in your adventure.

Location: This is just the name of the locale that you previously wrote up when creating your scene outline in the previous chapter. Now's the chance to place the location relative to the other places on the map.

Description: Now we have to do some work. Each of the locations you've previously outlined now has to be described in full. You've got to establish the mood for your adventure. To start off, write down a list of descriptors for your narrative as a whole. These are words you can use to provide a unified feel to your whole module and set a consistent tone throughout the work. For right now it is enough just to sketch out our terminology and develop a good feel for the place.

foggy	unpleasant
disturbing	snarling
eerie	biting
menacing	furious
ominous	berserk
weird	howling
dire	clawing
dread	bloody
gruesome	toothed
nightmarish	fang
threatening	

Sometimes it can help go even further and create a proper mood board for your game. A mood board is a collage of different images, words, colors, or even objects you can use to define the mood, style, and "feel" of a project. To create a mood board, think about what emotions are present in each location in the adventure. Now assemble some photos or illustrations that reflect what you are trying to go for. Be sure to include notes on lighting and color scheme as well. You can even create a bunch of different color swatches and try matching them to each scene. Put all of this material together. Now you can use this mood board to help you develop your written descriptions for each locale (Timmons, 2016; Wyatt, 2014).

Once you've got the mood set for the whole adventure you can begin to flavor each individual encounter. Some might have a lighter or more helpful mood while others will be extra intense or scary. Always keep your overall story and plot in mind when writing up your descriptions. The feeling of each scene in your adventure should serve to reinforce the overarching vibe of the story as a whole. Do not underestimate the emotional impact that dramatic lighting and sound can have on people. The whole forest in this adventure should be echoing with the eerie howls of various wolf packs, the slobbering growls of the worgs, the animal-like yapping of the priests, and the booming voice of Skohl reverberating through the dark forest.

It can be quite tricky to get started writing on a massive project such as this, especially if you are brand new to such an endeavor and are worried about what you will sound like. Get started by reading a lot of excellent authors in the genre you're working on beforehand and take note of any elements of style that you enjoy. Try to cobble together these tidbits of style in your early drafts. The amalgamation of the different forms can help you create your own unique style. Make sure that you do not submerge your own sensibilities, however, into any one other author's. The goal is to use the styles of other great authors to help formulate your own, not merely to copy theirs (*How to Write for the Press*, 1899, 7). Write and rewrite to make sure that the order of events is always in proper sequence. Strive to be as understandable as possible in your writing, then you will be headed in the correct direction. Your own style of writing will eventually evolve out of your own efforts, temperament, and personality (*How to Write for the Press*, 1899, 6–15).

Encounter/Challenge: Just fill in this section with the encounter details you wrote up in the previous chapter. This is one of the hardest parts of writing up an adventure and you've already done it! You can take the opportunity here to flesh out any of your encounters even further by adding in tactics and notes about how the combatants will react or behave. Remember that you can also use other challenges aside from just combat. Puzzles, riddles, and other obstacles can be used equally well. Maybe the problem is to figure out how to cross a deep ravine, how to safely open the magic puzzle box without setting off a deadly trap, or finding a route through a maze or any sort of obstacle that is preventing the players from making progress towards their goal.

Events: Put notes regarding any events that should occur in this scene. Do the prison guards try to grab a prisoner and threaten their life if they aren't allowed to escape? Do the wolves in the surrounding forest hear the howls back at camp and come running in as reinforcements? Does the High priestess try to negotiate and stall the characters long enough for more help to arrive? Maybe there's an earthquake that starts to collapse the ceiling? Anything that you feel ought to be scripted in as a hint for the GM on how to run that scene should be included here.

Notes: Add any additional elements that might be needed by the GM here. Things such as suggestions on how to run the encounters, information regarding the personalities of the people the players meet, historical context, possible outcomes of the meeting, or any other relevant information that might impact the characters or game.

Rewards: To properly motivate your players, it helps to have more than just a good story. Bribe your players with rewards! Rewards can take many forms from character advancement and growth to magic items or coin of the realm as discussed earlier in Chapter 13. Just remember that rewards work best when they are proportional to the level of effort involved in winning them (Gygax, 1979a; Barwood and Falstein, 2006). Too much can break the game and lead to disinterested and jaded players, while too little leads to grumpy players wondering why they even bother.

Now that we've covered the topics in our scene list, let's write up an example location derived from the outline we created in the previous chapter.

Title: Temple of the Wolf God

Number: #1

Location: This, the final objective is in the middle of the second map detailing the temple compound.

Description: The dark, overgrown forest parts to reveal a large circle of jagged standing stones reaching skywards like the black teeth of some gigantic wolf. Each stone is crusted with runes that catch the light and glitter like fresh frost in the morning. In the clearing amidst these relics squats a large crudely hewn stone statue of a wolf. In front of this cruel visage is a dark altar of rough stone covered by many centuries worth of blood stains. Littering the floor of the clearing are the bones of previous sacrifices piled up so thick that no grass can grow through it. Human priests dressed in wolf skins lope around the altar on all fours like beasts as groups of supplicants to the foul wolf god howl forth their prayers. Members of a menacing wolf pack prowl around the gathered ensemble pausing every so often to gaze at the dark, bloodstained stone altar at the heart of the circle.

If the players continue to watch, a horrific scene plays out. A struggling captive is brought forth, tied down upon the altar, then ceremoniously torn to shreds by the assembled pack of worshippers as the priests officiate the ceremony.

The wolf cultists are fanatics defending their sacred shrine so they will fight to the death or until their pack leader, the high priestess, is killed. If the high priestess starts losing the fight, she will begin howling for Skohl. The giant wolf cub has a 33% chance per round to jump clear of his pit and rush to her aid.

If the party members lose this battle, any survivors will be bound and sacrificed to their evil deity forthwith.

Encounter/Challenge: Precisely what is encountered varies depending upon what time the characters intrude upon this space. Hopefully, the players will scout out the temple before charging in. Otherwise, they might be in for a rough time if they attack during a ceremony! As the heart of the temple complex, it is always busy, but activities pick up at night since that is when proper services to Fenris occur. A few wolf packs are roaming the compound constantly plus a handful of pilgrims or acolytes, with at least one priest officiating minor ceremonies here. At night things pick up with a more massive turnout of the majority of the congregation and clergy.

1. Day:
    a. 10 or so wolves
    b. 1 worg
    c. 2 acolytes
    d. 8 pilgrims

1. *At night:*
    a. 20 wolves
    b. 3 worgs
    c. 2 priests
    d. 4 acolytes
    e. 20 pilgrims
    f. plus the High priestess who leads the nightly ceremony.

Events: The wandering wolves serve as a very efficient early warning system. Unless the party is cautious and approaches from downwind the wolves are almost guaranteed to notice them and start howling. This brings the whole camp to alert and draws attention to that area. If a fight breaks out reinforcements from the rest of the compound will begin to arrive within 5 rounds. Each round after that choose one encounter area and have the inhabitants join the fight. As the GM you will need to keep careful track of all of the inhabitants of the temple complex since there isn't a never-ending supply of opponents. After 8 rounds the High priestess will show up and confront the characters.

Smart players will avoid a direct fight and work to lure individuals or small groups out into the forest where they can be disposed of more easily. Perhaps by letting a wolf catch scent of one character and then fleeing into the woods to act as a lure for small hunting parties of cultists. This way the players can manage to some extent the size of the forces they are fighting.

Notes: Once the party slays the High priestess, any remaining cultists and wolves will flee abandoning the temple complex altogether. After a few months, these survivors will regroup and form a new temple at a different location and begin their predations once more.

Rewards: If the characters win, there is a fair amount of loot to be had.

Concealed in a small secret chamber set in the base of the altar (roll a notice check with a target number of 15 or a saving throw to find it if the party searches the statue) is the treasure of the temple. 5,000 copper pieces and three handmade gold wolf statuettes of an evil demeanor. These small statues are worth 300 gold pieces due to their gold content, but to a collector of unusual artwork, the statuettes might be worth up to 1,500gp.

Each of the temple's inhabitants possesses a certain amount of treasure, and there is even more concealed about the temple.

Each acolyte possesses 1d10 silver pieces (sp) and 1d4 gold coins (gp).

The priests have 1d20 sp and 2d6 gp on each of them.

The High priestess uses a magical silver battle-axe whose head is shaped like a wolf's skull. The weapon takes "bites" out of her opponents when it strikes doing an additional +2 to damage with each hit. The axe also possesses a +1 bonus to hit. This weapon is a sacred relic of the clergy of Fenris for many generations. The priesthood of Fenris will stop at nothing to retrieve this weapon. Its new owner will be a marked man in the eyes of the clergy of Fenris! The High priestess also bears a silver rune inscribed ring that provides the wearer with a +1 bonus to their saving throws.

A careful search of the altar will reveal a trapped secret compartment. Inside this compartment is a leather bag containing 100 gold pieces and 4 small moonstone gems each worth 50 gold pieces each. There is also a letter from the church hierarchy of Fenris to this temple's High priestess written upon human skin parchment with the symbols of Fenris upon it. The letter states:

Wulfhida,

We entrust into your care the pup Skohl. He is one of a litter born of our beloved Fenris. The time of Ragnarok approaches soon. May he be a terror to those who oppose us.

Bronthide

The contents of this small compartment are covered in a deadly poison. Anyone handling the bag of coins or letter without gloves must make a successful saving throw or suffer 4d6 points of damage.

Conclusion

The key to any large project such as this is to break down the larger goal into smaller more manageable chunks. The scene list provides a critical intermediary step between your initial outline and location list with your final document. Take your time and prepare your scene list with as much detail as you can manage. The more you can describe in your scene list the fewer gaps you will have to fill when preparing your final draft.

Assignment

Create a scene list to help finalize your adventure. Take the list of all of the different locations in your story that you prepared during the last chapter and using the Scene List Breakdown as a guide add in the relevant details for each site. Once you complete this process for each location, you should have no trouble at all compiling your final document.

Chapter **20**

Mapping Out Your Adventure

The Map

Quests happen in a physical space. Creating the locations where the encounters, quests, puzzles and other challenges in your game occurs is called level design. A simplified top-down view on grid paper works for most TTRPG maps. Occasionally hex paper or an orthographic map is used, but we can focus on the standard two-dimensional top-down view for our purposes. On our diagram, we will put all of the essential game-related information needed to help the GM visualize the playing space for the adventure. Descriptive elements such as lighting, coloration, and texture should be placed separately in a written description as part of the main body of the adventure document and not on the map. The goal is to have a legible map that only contains the information relevant to the gameplay of our adventure. Understanding how maps work in a table-top RPG is perhaps best learned by looking at examples. Classic examples of TTRPG maps such as that found within the adventure modules *G1-2-3 Against the Giants*, *B2 Keep on the Borderlands*, or any other of the dozens of adventure modules for any of the various flavors of D&D or OSR retro-clones will suffice as examples. Practically every adventure module ever made for a TTRPG includes a map of this type and would work as an example!

When you are laying out your map, it is imperative not to make things confusing or too complicated. Keep in mind that the players won't have easy access to the answers to any puzzles or mazes that you create. What might seem to you, the designer, to be a relatively simple thing could turn into an impassable barrier to your players. You can provide subtle clues to your map, mazes, and puzzles in the descriptions you write up of each environ. Perhaps the wall that moves to reveal the secret passage is slightly wetter than the other walls in the room or has a different fresco, rune, or moss growing on it. The maze the evil priests use to guard their entrance might have a slightly more worn trail on the flagstones from centuries of priests trotting down the correct path. Subtle clues like this will reward diligent players for paying close attention to your descriptions.

To make our map we can start with a list of encounter locations derived from our earlier material. First, sketch out your initial vision for the environment. Next, go into your sketch and identify each of the encounter locations on the map. These are all of the places you have written up as part of your scene list. If you've missed a position on the map, then draw it in now and make revisions. Be sure to include a scale reference on your map. Usually, each grid square on the graph paper represents 5 or 10 feet for an indoor plan. Outdoor charts generally have a much larger scale with one square indicating 60 feet (the distance a player character can move in one round) or even more, but it all depends upon how big the adventure area you need to represent is. Remember that you are just mapping out the elements you need for compelling gameplay, the fine details get put into the written descriptions.

Start with where the adventure begins. This area should be the place most familiar to the player characters and a place where they can outfit for the adventure ahead of them. Gameplay is usually a mix between resting and recuperating and actively adventuring so be sure to include a few safe resting spots for your players on your map (Winninger, 1999d). Your safe space can be a friendly village or just a hidden cave on an outdoor map or a long unused set of rooms in a dungeon setting. Providing sheltered locations such as this becomes less of an issue when designing high level (8+) adventures since such characters often have magical means of transport or safely securing a location against intruders. Conversely, the question of safe resting spots is critical for low-level adventures, that is, levels 1-3. A group of low-level characters can easily be devastated if they get attacked while they are not at full strength or are at a significant disadvantage such as when most of the party is sleeping! Since we are designing a low-level adventure, you will need to make sure you provide a few safe spaces for the player characters. Providing occasional respite doesn't mean that you have to forgive stupidity on the player's part. If the players lead the monsters directly to their campsite or do silly things like building a big fire out in the wilderness, then everyone for miles around will know where they are. The trick is to reward smart play, provide opportunities for such, and let the chips fall where they may otherwise.

Your map should make sense. Villages won't exist in a place where peasants can't earn an existence. If there's a town in the middle of the desert, then there needs to be a reason for it to be there. Maybe the settlement is located at an oasis and lies along a major trade route for salt and other goods like Timbuktu in Mali. Perhaps the desert town is atop a valuable deposit of gemstones like Coober Pedy in Australia. Cities, towns, and villages grow at spots that are useful or valuable for some reason. A deep harbor, defensible bluff, the junction of two rivers or trade routes all are suitable locations for an outpost of civilization. Sacred spots, access to a valuable resource or convenience are a few other good reasons to place settlements at a given locale. Remember that the locals have to eat, in a medieval society, this means that they have to either grow their food, forage for it or steal it. While you don't have to flesh out a complete societal background for every location in your game you do want to put in at least a passing consideration to these issues to preserve an air of believability in the fiction you are crafting. The NPCs and monsters should feel like they have lives outside of just interacting with the player characters. Not making the players the center of the world will make the world feel alive and more believable to the players and add a richness and depth of play to your game.

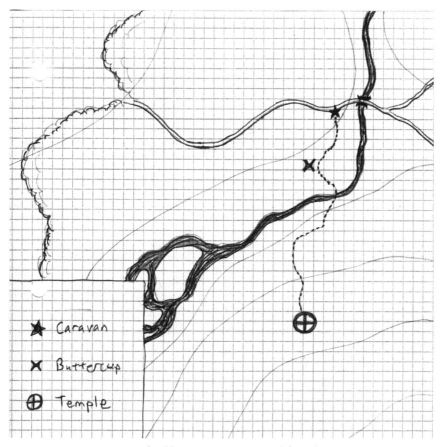

Rough wilderness map (© 2018 Greg Johnson)

Map Locations and Key

Labeling each area on the map is an excellent way to organize your adventure. You can use the labels as reference points when you start writing up all of the descriptions for each location on the map. It also makes it easier for anyone using your adventure to find the correct material for each area. You can use a map key as a sort of visual shorthand. This way you don't have to write every bit of description on the map but can instead "link" each location to a section of your text. Each map location will need a thorough explanation of that locale plus details about any quest or puzzle elements there, an encounter description and game stats, as well as any dialogue, rewards, or other information relevant to completing the adventure. Try to be as detailed and complete as possible in each of the steps. An unclear lead or connection could steer the players into pursuing the wrong quest, take them into uncharted territory, or otherwise make the adventure impossible to complete. When matching up your scene list to the map you are designing expect to have to go back in and make adjustments to fit the layout to the scene list and vice-versa. Editing and adjusting things before publishing is just part and parcel of the design process. Make sure you proofread your material thoroughly! Nothing says unprofessional like forgetting to run a simple spell check on something before turning it in for publication. Everyone who reads through what you've created is going to take note of your attention to detail or lack thereof.

Monte Cook's article on Dungeoncraft in "Dragon Magazine 310" offers plenty of sage advice that neophyte level designers can leverage. For instance, how and why did the builders create this place? A thing will only get built for a reason. Figuring out the why is a critical first step in the design process for your map. For instance, castles are filled with narrow corridors, steep staircases, ceilings with murder-holes, and other such contrivances to make the place easily defensible. A house, on the other hand, is designed for living and comfort, a temple for worship, an amphitheater for sporting events and so forth. Once you decide the reason the place got built, you can make intelligent choices to its design. That said the current inhabitants might not be the original ones. The castle may have been conquered and have fallen into ruins which are now inhabited by scavengers. The temple may have been abandoned long ago and now be used as a local tavern, though woe to those who inadvertently offend the ancient god! Buildings can have complicated histories. Think about some of the local structures in your town. What happens to these properties once the original owners are finished with them? You can use this sort of history to give your maps and game locations a rich history and level of believability (Cook, 2003b).

As Cook astutely observes, people usually do the minimum to get the job done. What was the space designed to do? Rooms and passages are typically just big enough to get the job done and no more. Exceptions include work done to impress and awe such as palaces, temples, or any other place designed to overwhelm visitors. Such sites tend to be built to a grander scale and level of ornamentation than would ever be practical to impress visitors with the power and grandeur of its inhabitants. Be sure to provide a variety of different rooms to keep your players interested. The list of places to include should include a variety of necessary living spaces such as family room, sleeping quarters, a meeting room, maternity room for infants, water well or other water access, kitchen, toilet, and a washing room (Cook, 2003b; Thompson, 2002). The entrance to the lair might be camouflaged or even trapped (Thompson, 2002). A lot depends upon the strength of the inhabitants. Operating on the principle of least effort, i.e., people only do what they have to, intelligent foes who aren't afraid of being attacked won't have much in the way of concealment or defenses. On the other hand, opponents who regularly face attack will have built up a lot more defenses and concealment. Think about how often the inhabitants of your adventure are challenged by their opponents. If they have frequent fights then there will be various traps, guard posts, ambush spots, and defensible areas set up (Cook, 2003b; Thompson, 2002). Pit traps, deadfalls, and other nasty surprises will abound in such a case. Overconfident foes unused to challenges might let their guard down and not even set up a watch! Some rooms or areas might have traps or natural hazards. Perhaps a chasm from a recent earthquake stretches across the floor of your ruined ancient temple, or maybe a room with a collapsing floor protects the inner sanctum of a dwarven fortress? If the locale is inhabited, you can be sure that the locals have either found a way around the trap or hazard or avoid it altogether. Include some areas that are secret or hidden. Maybe the old goblin king a century ago didn't trust his retainers and hid a magical necklace in a secret hiding spot so good no one has discovered it until now? Of course, this doesn't mean that the players will find it either—especially if they aren't taking the time to look! Some rooms will be empty, forgotten, or used as storerooms. Paranoid inhabitants will create a secret escape route that exits some distance away from the main encampment. Ostentatious rulers will have a throne room and private quarters for themselves and their significant others. You may set aside certain rooms as a key to access the other levels of the maps, i.e. you have to flip this switch or bring item X to location Y. Some places on the maps might serve specific story purposes to advance your plot. The trick here is to sit down and really think of the where, what, and why behind everything you are including in your adventure. It all needs to make some sort of logical sense and hold together as a story. The better you think things through, the more believable the fantasy you are trying to convey will be (Cook, 2003b; Thompson, 2002).

When designing your map, include a few hard to reach areas that are nevertheless visible to players early on. These areas should be utterly unreachable until the adventuring party completes a significant part of the adventure. Called "weenies," the purpose of these areas is to motivate the players to continue to explore the environment. Tantalize the players with hints of the treasure and rewards to be found within these areas and give them something worthwhile if they manage to get there (Rogers, 2010, 221; Winninger, 1999e). Your goal throughout the adventure is to provide a continuing set of reasons for the players to keep playing. New challenges, glory, and lots and lots of treasure should always be over that next horizon!

Get out your pencil and some graph paper and begin laying things out. Typically maps get laid out in either an alley or an island pattern. Alleys provide the characters with a goal, a fixed path, and a set number of obstacles and encounters in the way of reaching that goal. Islands offer the players an open space to explore in any way they want. Alleys are easy to design but can feel like they're forcing the players down a particular path (because they are) whereas islands are more challenging to develop but offer the players a great deal of freedom and room to explore (Rogers, 2010, 219–223).

Rough your map out first in pencil and do a play test with some friends. After trying the map and adventure out you can go in later and polish your work. Once you have everything the way you like it you can use your rough pencil map as a basis for creating a professional version on the computer using vector or raster software such as the Adobe Creative Suite, GIMP, or Inkscape.

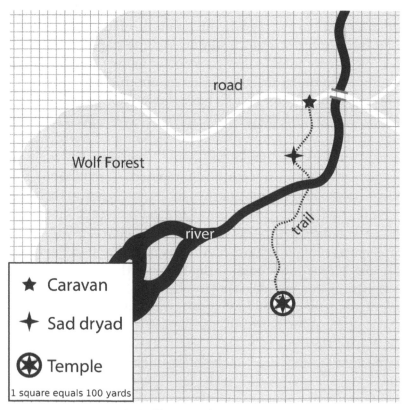

Refined wilderness map (© 2018 Greg Johnson)

Each map should include a key, a list of features and their visual emblem that you will use on the map to indicate that thing. A key is just a shorthand way of showing different items on the map. Fortunately, these keys have become pretty standardized over the last forty years of use, so there's a lot of reference material on the subject. Below is a sample of some of the most common elements that you can use when designing your maps.

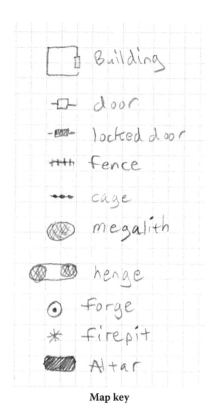

Map key

Each area noted on the map will need to have a description plus details on any encounters, challenges, and rewards to be had at that location. If there's some vital plot point or piece of dialogue that needs to occur or an NPC the players need to meet, then you must make a note of it. It isn't enough to have only thought it out in your head. You need to write everything down on paper and be as organized and detailed in how you present the material as possible. Your goal is to display your concept in as clear and intelligible a manner as possible. Avoid including areas where there isn't much to do. If it isn't relevant to your adventure in some way why include it at all?

Part of the essence of each place is the people you meet there. A good approach is to list out all of the NPCs that the players can encounter in a given area. Be sure to include the reason the NPC is around. They might be there to provide a clue, plot point, sell or buy something, or perhaps just to add a bit of flavor to the encounter. Include the type of interaction the NPC will provide or any dialogue required. An alternate approach is to list out and describe the important NPCs and their goals in detail and let the GM interpret the interactions with the characters as she sees fit. This approach can be useful if you aren't particularly adept or comfortable writing dialogue. If you do write up the dialogue make sure you say it out loud before including it to make sure it sounds OK and fits the character saying it. Just because it looks good on paper doesn't mean that it will make sense when said aloud. Don't forget all that you've learned about describing NPCs, their motivations, and personalities when writing your material. You will also have to include all of the challenges, encounter statistics, rewards and plot points for each encounter. While not every room needs to be brimming with content, an endless succession of broom closets and empty rooms will get boring fast.

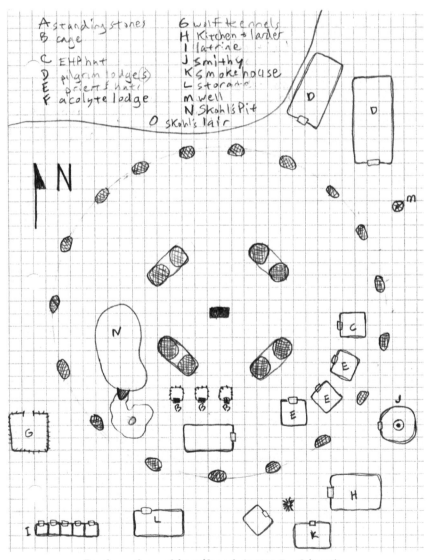

Rough pencil map of the wolf temple (© 2018 Greg Johnson)

You must enable the players' sense of disbelief. It is entirely up to you to write up descriptions, plots, and NPCs that are vivid enough to spark your players' imaginations. You will have to include hard enough challenges so that the players stay engaged but not so severe that they become overwhelmed (Ryan, 1999a). A range of difficulty levels that work towards a climactic encounter which coincides with the resolution of your plot and story tends to work best. There should be enough clues and hints for the players to progress through the adventure instinctively without resorting to forcing them down a specific path. The players must always feel like they have control over their characters and their own choices (Taylor, 2013). Forcing the players down a particular path will break the immersion of the game, and doesn't lend itself to very delightful play. The real trick is getting the players to want to do the things you have planned for them. The players should always have a sense of what they should be doing, where they are supposed to go, and how they can get there (Stout, 2012). According to Dan Taylor in his article "Ten Principles of Good Level Design (Part 1)," this knowledge can be imparted to the player using three crucial narrative aspects you can utilize when designing your level.

1. Explicit, merely telling the player what they need to do.
2. Implicit, using clues, hints, and descriptions or visuals to suggest to the player what they should do next.
3. Emergent, this is the story that emerges from the actual gameplay of what you have designed.

Use explicit goals to set the players down their path towards a stated goal. This goal can be assigned by the local magistrate telling the players what they need to do, the hapless victim screaming for help, or a powerful opponent issuing a challenge to all comers. Whatever shape it takes, the goal of the adventure must be stated clearly to the players. Emergent narratives are more difficult to manage and have to be approached indirectly. You cannot force an emergent experience; you have to set the stage, nurture it and hope it develops in gameplay. Implicit narratives are difficult to construct. One approach is to offer multiple possible objectives and let the players approach these goals in whatever order they like (Taylor, 2013). Another method is to have the challenge of each encounter ramp up in difficulty to help build up tension and progress the plot (Stout, 2012). This approach allows the player to come to grips with their enemies and master how to effectively deal with them which can provide a satisfying sense of mastery to your players (Stout, 2012). With either approach, successfully concluding each section offers a bit of help in finishing the next objective until the final goal is accomplished. Vary the pacing of the game to provide times of high-intensity excitement and cool down or rest periods to let the players catch their breath and maybe relax their guard before hitting them with the next surprise or twist (Taylor, 2013). Uncertainty is a central ingredient to fun. Surprises, plot twists, NPCs, and actions are what makes a scene or encounter memorable and engaging. As soon as something is predictable, it becomes boring. The trick is keeping the player in the enjoyable zone between things being too hard and frustrating or too easy and tedious (Mandryka, 2012). To make sure things don't become predictable you will have to vary the challenges, rewards, risks, and costs for each encounter and story path. Present different problems requiring alternate approaches or catering to different player abilities or play styles to maintain player interest. Each group of players should be allowed and encouraged to solve the challenges you present to them in their own way (Ryan, 1999b). Providing plenty of leeway for creative problem solving is a significant part of developing material for TTRPGs.

Your setting should reinforce the mood and story of your adventure. The lighting, color scheme, and environment can serve to create the basis for how the players feel and should provide a strong hint about how they should be reacting. This approach has been used reliably in filmmaking for a century. You know things are about to get violent when the lighting or color scheme in the show goes red. If things turn blue then something sad is happening, green for something spooky, and yellow for a happy event. You can do the same thing with architecture. Dark enclosed spaces will make you feel nervous while a wide open sunlit field of flowers offers a clue towards a happy scene being underway. While occasionally you will find these things inverted for effect or parody, the lighting, color, and setting are universal clues for the mood of whatever scene is occurring at the moment. Film noir with its dark shadows and high contrast lighting isn't famous for its happy vibe. Bright illumination and cheerful colors don't provide the backdrop for a horror movie! The main difference between leveraging color, lighting, and setting in film and your adventure is that here you have to write it all out evocatively enough to convey the mood you desire. Go through your module and carefully note how the player should be feeling at each critical juncture of the story then make sure the scene matches that vibe.

Conclusion

Use the sample included here for reference on how a map can be drawn up for your adventure. The map should support and reinforce the mood, vibe, and story that you are trying to tell in your narrative while at the same time encouraging engaging play and player immersion. The map should always provide help to the players reminding them of what they are doing at the moment and providing clues as to what they should be doing next. The setting should convey a sense of history and give depth to the game world and fit naturally into its environ. While the manner one should progress through the level might not be entirely obvious, it should never be a complete mystery to the players. Keep your design engaging, challenging, and fun.

Assignment

Now that we've talked at length about how to design a map, let's put it to use and create a map for our example adventure. Using the key included in the text and the sample map as a reference point go through and draw up a map that matches your scene list as closely as possible. You can revise your written material to match your chart if you need to do so.

Chapter 21

Revisiting the Narrative

We're now at the stage where we ought to revisit the narrative and make sure that it is shaping up properly. Thus far, we have the following outline and a significant part of the story as well.

[Beginning: the introduction to the setting, story, and initiating action.]
Wolf Forest
- Get involved:
  - The characters are attacked by a wolf priest and cultists out hunting with a pack of wolves while traveling through an evil forest. They discover evidence of a secret evil temple located in these woods and hints of a fabulous treasure to be found there.

[Middle: obstacles, challenges, and puzzles]
Wolf Forest
- Track the cultists back to the temple. As the party goes through the vile forest, they have the opportunity to encounter a few interesting things.
  - Optional side quest > Evil wolf pack
  - Optional side quest > Evil pilgrims
  - Optional side quest > Evil ogre

[End: resolution and solution]
Wolf Temple

- Attack the wolf temple
- Defeat the wolf cult and root out the evil
- Recieve rewards

Not too shabby, but it is a relatively straightforward plot. There aren't any twists or turns that would surprise the players in it. To have a solid story, we need to have a hero, a strong villain, and a reason for the conflict between them (Haas, 1975). The player characters will play the part of the hero. It might be tempting to include a batch of pre-rolled characters inside the module and use their backstory to provide a rationale for the characters wanting to go on the adventure. Doing so is a rather weak approach. Forcing the players to use specific characters might be considered bad form in a table-top role-playing game. The more detailed the pre-generated character you provide the player is, the harder it becomes for the player to project themselves into it (Smith, 1999, 2). In addition to those reasons, the whole setup feels like a cop-out. It would be far better to actively engage the players and make them want to participate in the adventure. Of course, you would run the risk of the players choosing to do something else, but that is part of the magic of table-top RPGs. Letting players generate their own characters makes the game a lot more fun and provides an inherent connection between the player and the character. The player has already invested time creating the character and thinking up their backstory for them after all. The villain is the evil high priestess and Skohl. After doing the write up for Skohl, I think we've got a pretty firm grip on our villainous duo. The conflict begins when the players discover the annihilated wagon. Any adventuring party worth their salt should be immediately concerned about who did that ghastly deed. That said, players can be a finicky lot and sometimes need to be coaxed a bit more into doing what you want them to do. For example, what if none of the characters are particularly heroic? Maybe they're just greedy murderous hobos or outright villains themselves. Regardless, it might behoove us to add in a bit more motivation for our players to engage with the story.

The Distraught Child

To add a bit of sure-fire motivation let's use a helpless waif as a plot device. We can add the child in at the end of the destroyed caravan scene.

Destroyed Caravan

Description: You hear the arguing crows before you see the horrific sight itself. Straddled across the trail lies the burnt out remnants of a wagon. Blood and gore cover the scene, but no bodies are in view. The crows flee at your approach, and you can see the ransacked remains of the farmer's goods scattered around the husk of a wagon.

You hear a soft moan and whimper coming from the woods nearby. Upon investigation, you find a small, blood-covered girl-child, barely conscious, yet still clinging to life. She seems grievously wounded by both bite and dagger wounds which cover her body though no one wound is particularly severe. If woken, she will scream hysterically until comforted.

Info: Shelby is the sole survivor of the ambush upon the caravan. She will recover if tended to though she is quite distraught at the memory of her entire family being killed before her very eyes. If questioned Shelby will relate that she slipped into the woods and hid in a bush while the attackers were distracted by something else. She is unable to provide anything more than a fairly generic description of the wolves and cultists who attacked her family. Thoroughly traumatized Shelby will attach herself to the kindest member of the adventuring party. The first day afterward she will act entirely devastated, but later she will quickly heal up and recover. Perceptive characters will notice her becoming progressively more upbeat, energetic, and aggressive as time wears on. After 2–8 (2d4) days of this, she will transform into a young wolf during the night and scamper off to join one of the cult's wolf packs.

Witnessing a young child turn into a wolf ought to terrify the players, alert them that something far outside of the ordinary is going on, and tug at their heartstrings. This event lets the players know that something profoundly evil and magical is happening in the forest. A smart and capable party might even be able to track her to the temple itself. The party might be tempted to try to save her somehow. We could add a spell scroll or potion at the end of the adventure to do just that, or perhaps it only requires a good old "Remove Curse" spell to fix. Since this is a first level adventure, the characters aren't going to have access to this spell, but this might serve as a springboard to another adventure to get the cure from a friendly high-level priest. Having the girl turn into a wolf will also put the question in the players' minds about the nature of all the wolves they must kill in the later parts of the adventure. Are all of those wolves former villagers or other innocents as well? By adding in this additional hook, we can create a bit of a moral dilemma in an otherwise clear-cut tale.

Let's amplify the emotional drama a bit. By tweaking her description when we introduce her, we can make her a bit more identifiable.

> You hear a soft moan and whimper coming from the woods nearby. Upon investigation, you find a small, girl-child, barely conscious, yet still clinging to life. Her tousled copper-colored hair is matted with blood, and she seems painfully wounded by both bite and dagger wounds which cover her body though no one wound is particularly severe. If woken, she will scream hysterically until comforted her green eyes filled with tears.

Now that we've planted that seed we can leverage it later on. Once the players find the temple, have them observe a copper furred and green-eyed wolf running with the pack. The players now have a moral quandary on their hands whether or not to try and save the girl. Maybe the player who was kindest to the girl can befriend this particular wolf and use it in a ploy to take down the temple? We can use this additional hook we've created to draw the players deeper into the story and add a bit of emotional depth and psychological complexity to the narrative. She can take the place of the Elsa the annoying waif the party would otherwise encounter at the temple later on.

None of this might work. Just because you give your players a particular option or opportunity doesn't necessarily mean that they will take it and run with it (Murray, 2017, 44). The players are involved in creating the story and things can and will go sideways as they think of solutions the writer and GM could never imagine or react to events in wildly unpredictable ways.

In his handwritten notes on how to make a good western novel, Ben Haas promotes the idea of a so-called "Double Snapper" where right after the heroes think they've resolved the story, another significant problem or villain reveals itself and forces one last ultimate showdown upon the players (Haas, 1975). The so-called double snapper is nothing more than one final plot twist, but it is still good advice. What can we include to have just such a last encounter? Let's brainstorm a few extra ideas.

- A hunting party and wolf pack returns and joins the fray.
- An envoy from another temple shows up to check on Skohl's progress.
- A gateway opens up to the mystical lair of Fenrir himself, and a mighty servant of his appears.
- We could have Skohl reappear somehow.

Let's analyze the flaws and merits of each of these ideas.

Letting a hunting party show up as reinforcements makes a great deal of sense, but it doesn't have very much emotional punch to it. Adding a hunting party might be worth including to ramp up the danger level if needed.

An envoy might work, but it would be challenging to explain why they showed up just when they did. Having some powerful antagonist pop out of the woods feels a bit forced too.

Having a mighty servant of Fenrir appear and smack the characters around is tempting, but we're writing heroic fantasy here not just strictly horror. Overwhelming evil is a hallmark of the horror genre, but in heroic fantasy, the protagonists should be allowed to win.

Skohl reappearing could provide a good fit. Maybe the dark god Fenrir reanimates his dead body. Perhaps he animates the high priestess too.

I rather like the idea of the power of the dark god bringing his favorite cub back to a semblance of life to test the player characters in an ultimate battle. It feels like the climax of a story.

As the battle at the temple proceeds, a dark thunderstorm builds over the unholy site. The brilliant flash of lightning striking the stone megaliths adds a thunderous boom to the last sounds of battle. A final dazzling bolt of lightning bursts from the sky enveloping the bodies of the high priestess and Skohl in a flare of energy. Infused with unholy power the corpses rise to begin the battle anew.

Undead Skohl
Hit points: 6d8 (27 hit points)
Armor class: 14
To hit bonus: +7
Damage: 2d8
Movement: 180 feet
Saving throw: 9
Special: undead immunities
Size: large
Number: 1 (unique monster)
Experience: 700

Glowing with a grisly green radiance Skohl's torn and bloody body is now infused with unholy energy.

Skohl is still immune to cold damage, but fire now inflicts double damage to him. What intelligence he once had has left him, and he is now an engine of divine vengeance. Undead are immune to charm, cold, death, disease, hold, paralysis, poison, sleep, and mind-affecting spells and effects.

We could add in the evil high priestess as well. Just use the stats for a ghoul straight out of the monster section of the *Glory of Yore* rulebook for the encounter.

The ghastly wreck of the high priestess shambles into unlife in a twisted parody of her former beauty.

Undead Evil High Priestess
Hit points: 3d8 (14 hit points)
Armor class: 14
To hit bonus: +3
Damage: 2d6 claws and bite
Movement: 60 feet
Saving throw: 13
Special: undead immunities
Size: medium
Number: 1
Experience: 300

Her touch is infused with dread power and can paralyze the victim for 2–8 (2d4) rounds if the target fails a saving throw. Undead are immune to charm, cold, death, disease, hold, paralysis, poison, sleep, and mind-affecting spells and effects.

By including these monsters, we give the GM an additional arrow in their quiver of tricks. The GM doesn't have to use them at all if they don't want to. It just provides a robust way to add one last dramatic flourish to the final encounter. Fighting a couple of unholy monsters while lightning crashes around you and a storm rages provides a grand culmination to the events in our story. After the fight ends maybe the players can recover the wolf-girl-child and either keep it as a pet or try to get her cured. I'm sure any good priest that hears the party's harrowing tale would be sympathetic to their cause enough to cast a "Remove Curse" if they can.

This battle also fits into our three-part narrative, creates extra tension, and provides a nice twist for the end of our tale. The whole story also fits nicely into what is known as the hero's journey or heroic cycle.

The hero's journey is a framework for building stories based upon the work of Joseph Campbell as outlined in his book, *The Hero with a Thousand Faces*.

The hero's journey

Though the exact structure varies with each story, the heroic cycle is a pattern that shows up persistently and repeatedly in almost every myth ever told. The heroic cycle forms a useful framework for understanding and creating heroic narratives even if not every story contains all of the stages of the journey. Campbell details out seventeen stages in his original exposition of the subject, but simplified versions have been presented by other authors who have followed in his footsteps (Campbell, 1949; Cousineau, 1990; Vogel, 2007).

The outline below is a somewhat simplified version of the stages and elements commonly present in the heroic cycle.

Departure
1. Call to adventure—the refusal of the call
2. Mentor and aid
3. Crossing the threshold—guardians of the threshold

Initiation
4. Friends and enemies
5. Trials, tribulations, and temptations
6. Death and the abyss

Return
7. Rebirth and transformation
8. Atonement
9. Return and the gift

Again there's quite a lot of variation in each stage and even in the order that things occur, but the following definitions for each element generally hold true. The departure correlates with the beginning of the story. The hero is introduced, and the dilemma that confronts him is outlined. The departure nominally consists of a so-called call to adventure, a mentor who offers the hero aid and ends with the hero crossing the threshold.

Departure
1. *Call to adventure*: Some event or message reaches the hero, which starts him or her on their epic quest. It could be an omen, a prophecy, or something more mundane. Whatever the nature of the message, the hero frequently refuses to answer the call of destiny immediately and often rejects or hesitates before events force an inevitable acceptance of the quest.
2. *Mentor and aid*: The hero finds a mentor who assists him. Frequently this aid is supernatural in nature, but it can also include a gift or helpful advice. This aid provides the hero with some comfort and protection in their upcoming dangerous quest.
3. *Crossing the threshold*: The hero leaves behind the safe, familiar world and enters into the unknown. The threshold often has a guardian who offers the hero their first challenge and a taste of the hazards that await. Once the hero has crossed into the unfamiliar territory beyond, they begin the process of testing and transformation.

The initiation serves up challenges and opportunities for the hero as it tests his metal and begins to change him into what destiny demands. This portion of the tale forms the main body of the story.

Initiation

4. *Friends and enemies*: The main character meets various friends and helpers who will assist him in his quest. The number and level of assistance these friends provide vary considerably from story to story. This portion is the place where you introduce and love interests the story might contain.

5. *Trials, tribulations, and temptations*: Problems, problems, and more problems beset the hero. The exact nature of the challenges the hero faces depends upon the story being told, but sexual temptation, physical combat, and emotional struggles are all appropriate inclusions. The character may fight against nature, other people, or even his inner demons during these trials.

6. *Death and the abyss*: The death here is a symbolic one. Typically the hero doesn't actually die. Instead, the course of events takes the hero to his lowest emotional point. Doubt and defeat loom heavily over the hero at this stage. This segment forms the pivot point of the story.

Return

The return marks the conclusion of the story. The plot lines are completed, and the conflict is resolved.

7. *Rebirth and transformation*: All appears lost until the hero finds some inspiration to power through this experience. At this stage, the balance begins to shift to the hero's favor as he completes the transformation into a real hero. Before this, the character is still in the process of becoming a hero. Afterward, he has become one, though he still needs to act upon his new found knowledge and capability.

8. *Atonement*: The hero defeats the big bad villain, resolves the crisis, saves the world, and so forth. Whatever goal the hero set out to gain is achieved.

9. *Return and the gift*: The mighty hero now returns from the adventure back into the ordinary world. The hero may have to be forced to leave whatever paradise he has found, or the return may involve a narrow escape. The friends and allies of the hero often assist the protagonist in this final journey. Frequently the hero will have a prize they bring back or, conversely, will receive a reward for having completed their mission.

The Hero's Journey shows up frequently in movies, books, and games. *Star Wars, The Hobbit*, Sergio Leone's spaghetti western *A Fistful of Dollars*, and the *Epic of Gilgamesh* all contain variations of the heroic cycle (Lucas, 1980; Tolkien, 1937; Leone; Sandras, 1972). We will use these four stories to illustrate how the heroic cycle has been previously implemented.

1. *Call to adventure*

   In the movie *Star Wars*, the original 1977 film to be specific, the call to adventure is when Luke finds the message hidden inside of R2D2.

   In the book *The Hobbit* the call to adventure arrives in the form of a group of dwarves who barge into Bilbo's home.

   In *A Fistful of Dollars* the call to adventure is the story the innkeeper tells the "Man with No Name" which sets him on a path of confrontation with the two rival gangs in town.

   In the *Epic of Gilgamesh*, it is Gilgamesh's own bad behavior that spark the gods to challenge him.

2. *Mentor and aid*

   The mentor in *Star Wars* is the old Jedi Obi-Wan Kenobi. Old Ben teaches Luke the ways of the Force and gives Luke's father's lightsaber to him.

   The mentor character in *The Hobbit* is the wise wizard Gandalf.

   The friendly barkeep serves as the mentor in *A Fistful of Dollars* providing food and drink to the hero.

   The *Epic of Gilgamesh* has the wildman Enkidu befriend and assist Gilgamesh in his travails.

3. *Crossing the threshold*

   In *Star Wars* the threshold is crossed when Luke returns home to find his aunt and uncle murdered by stormtroopers and goes with Ben to Mos Eisley spaceport. The violent drunk who picks a fight with Luke serves as the guardian of the threshold in this scene.

   In *The Hobbit* it is the point when Bilbo leaves the Shire with the group. The guardians of the threshold are the trolls they encounter on the road.

   In *A Fistful of Dollars* the "Man with No Name" begins his quest for money by shooting a gaggle of desperados for laughing at his mule.

   In *The Epic of Gilgamesh* the journey begins when Gilgamesh and Enkidu travel to the distant Cedar Forest. The guardian of the threshold is Humbaba, lord of the Cedar Forest.

4. *Friends*

   Luke gains several notable friends during the movie; Leia, Han Solo, Chewbacca, C-3PO, and R2-D2.

   Bilbo befriends the dwarves.

   The "Man with No Name" befriends the undertaker.

   In Gilgamesh's story the gods send Enkidu who first challenges and then later befriends Gilgamesh.

5. *Trials, tribulations, and temptations*

   Luke's enemies consist of the stormtroopers and other servants of the Dark Side.

   Bilbo fights goblins and struggles against the wood elves.

The "Man with No Name" struggles against the members of the Baxter and Rojo families.

The goddess Ishtar and her servants serve as powerful enemies to Gilgamesh.

6. *Death and the abyss*

Luke watches the Darth Vader kill his mentor Obi-Wan during a lightsaber duel.

Bilbo gets separated from his companions and then gets lost in the goblin caves.

The "Man with No Name" gets beaten to near death by the Rojos after they discover his perfidy.

Gilgamesh watches his friend Enkidu die from a wasting curse brought on by their slaying of Humbaba.

7. *Rebirth and transformation*

Luke hears the voice of Obi-Wan speaking to him from beyond the grave telling him not to lose hope.

Bilbo finds the One Ring in Gollum's cave and defeats Gollum in a battle of riddles.

The "Man with No Name" hides in a cave and rebuilds his strength.

Gilgamesh adventures forth and finds the immortal man Utnapishtim who offers him a quest for the secret of youth.

8. *Atonement*

Luke destroys the Death Star and saves the rebel base.

Bilbo uses the One Ring to outwit the dragon Smaug.

The "Man with No Name" has a shootout with Ramon.

Gilgamesh acquires the plant of youth from the bottom of the sea.

9. *Return and the gift*

Luke returns to the rebel base and receives a medal from Leia.

Bilbo returns to the shire with a small chest of treasure and a chainmail shirt made of mithril.

The "Man with No Name" rides his mule out of town having brought peace to the little village.

In the epic, the plant is stolen from Gilgamesh, and he returns home without it finally accepting his mortal fate.

From the first story ever recorded to modern classics, versions of the hero's journey show up as the backbone of each story. As you can see from the examples, the details of each implementation vary enormously, but the broad strokes of the cycle remain. You can use the heroic cycle yourself to help you develop the storyline from your module. Let's see if we can adapt the framework of the heroes journey to the adventure we've produced to help round it out a bit and fix any remaining holes in the narrative.

1. *Call to adventure*

   The adventure could begin with the destroyed caravan and the party discovering the distraught survivor. This encounter should be enough to pique the interest of the players and get them to investigate further.

2. *Mentor and aid*

   The sad dryad Buttercup serves the role of advisor and helper to the group. She can provide some more material support as well as leading them to the cult's temple. I could easily append something along the lines of the following to her description.

   Buttercup can also supply the group with the following items if they are helpful to her or exceedingly charming.

   a. One potion of growth

   b. A scroll with two cure light wound spells written on it.

3. *Crossing the threshold*

   The group moves deeper into the forest and encounters Manichi and the first group of cultists.

4. *Friends*

   There aren't many of these available in the adventure until the party reaches the temple. The prisoners there have the potential to turn into friends of the party. I don't think this will be much of a big deal since the adventuring group is itself formed out of a group of friends who can fill this role adequately.

5. *Trials, tribulations, and temptations*

   All of the hazards and encounters along the way to the temple comprise this element of the cycle.

6. *Death and the abyss*

   Getting the party to come up with a good plan and take on the temple. If the party can come up with a reasonable idea, the GM should be instructed to let it work. The point is for the players to conquer their fear and face up to the challenge of being heroes. Groups that accept the trial should be rewarded.

7. *Rebirth and transformation*

   Facing down the evil high priestess and Skohl will transform the characters into real heroes. If the party gets into trouble, it might be a good idea to have an ally or someone help them out. We could have the prisoners take up arms and join in the fight as one option. A better one might be to have Buttercup show up with a herd of angry forest animals to distract the cultists while the party deals with the priestess and Skohl.

8. *Atonement*

   The atonement is where the group defeats the cultists, the priestess, and Skohl then is forced to deal with the undead versions of the latter two.

9. *Return and the gift*

If the party is victorious, they should get to keep all of the treasure the cult has accumulated during its robberies. It might be appropriate for Buttercup and the creatures of the forest to give them some parting gift as well. Perhaps a blessing of some sort; the ability to speak with the animals of the forest, a green thumb or maybe a crown of laurel leaves so that any elves, fairies, and forest creatures react positively to the rightful wearers.

Conclusion

A heroic cycle is a powerful tool when correctly used. The trick is to remember that you don't have to use all of it literally. The hero's journey provides a robust framework of principles for you to build your story around or, much like we did here, to offer a bit of advice on how you can round out your plot.

Assignment

Use the nine elements of the heroic cycle listed here to see how your adventure fits into the framework. See if the hero's journey provides you with any suitable options for any remaining plot holes in your story then modify your module accordingly to fill in those gaps.

Chapter **22**

Building the Final Document

Now that you've created the components for you adventure you will need to put them all together and build your finished product. Start by listing all of the elements you need for the final publication. This list will serve as a framework into which we can fit the material we've developed so far. An outline like this is useful to make sure that we don't forget anything significant and will help smooth out the final development process. We can later use the outline as a starting point for our table of contents for the adventure as well. The initial list for what we've created so far in this book looks like this.

Initial Outline:
Cover
Maps: forest, temple
Introduction
- Notes for the GM
- Preparation for the use of this adventure
- Background information for the adventure

Part 1: The Wolf Forest
- Start
- Notes about the forest
- Order of events
- Wandering monster tables and descriptions
- Encounter areas and descriptions

Part 2: The Temple of the Blood Moon
- Start
- Notes about the temple
- Order of events
- Wandering monster tables and descriptions
- Encounter areas and descriptions

Conclusion and follow up

Pre-generated characters

You'll notice that I repeated the "part" section to cover each encounter location. The overall locale changes significantly from the first half of the adventure when the characters are wandering in the forest looking for clues to the second half when they are assaulting the cult's temple. Remember that the basic outline I've provided here is just that, basic. You will undoubtedly need to modify and adjust it to meet the needs of your adventure. As you create the outline, you will inevitably discover things that are missing. Any elements that you identify at this stage make a note of and mark for development. Once you've finished the outline, you will have to dig in and write up all of the remaining material.

The last stage before finishing a product is often the most difficult. You will have to go over any comments made by your play-testers and proofreaders and fix any problems that they have identified. If you haven't done any playtesting or proofreading now is the time to do it before you continue any further. You must fix any existing problems with your narrative, plot, play balance, rewards, and such now before they become embedded into your final document. Once something gets laid out for publication it becomes incredibly time-consuming to go back in and fix problems. With that in mind, add in any supplemental mechanics, maps, and quests now. Build connecting paragraphs or other transitional writing to help the overall flow of your document. Now is the right time to add anything that makes reading your text more accessible for the consumer. Go in and rewrite material that no longer matches the flavor and feel of the adventure anymore. Fixing your work up for publication is an iterative process. It will take time, sometimes as long as the writing and development cycle did in the first place. Any sections that are repetitive, unnecessary or irrelevant should be deleted. A thorough edit of the material often makes the difference between an illegible ramble and a stellar read. There is no set-in-stone method for developing your product. Each development process is unique to the group doing the work. The first time you go through this sort of development cycle a lot of time will be spent in trial and error until you develop a workflow that is comfortable for you. When estimating the production time, you probably ought to budget twice whatever you think it will take. This extra time reflects the trial and error process.

Missing Pieces

A few additional things should be included for your product to be marketable. Make sure that you don't skimp on this section. These last few pieces of work will create the basis for your marketing and presentation material. As such, this material is critical to the success of your final product.

Front cover
Back cover
Page art
Page numbers

Front Cover

The cover is the what everyone will see when they first pick up your product. As such it needs to make a great first impression and catch people's attention. A good cover can make or break your product! The cover should include the following information:

Product title
Author(s)
Company info
RPG rule set(s) the product is compatible with
The character level or overall difficulty level of the adventure
A blurb describing the adventure
Copyright info
Cover art

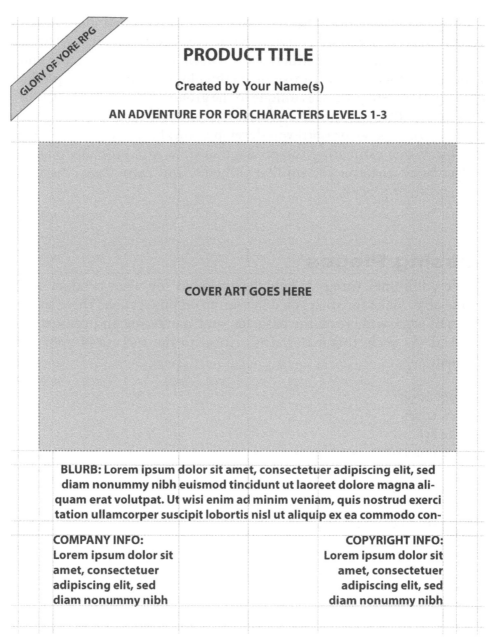

GLORY OF YORE RPG

PRODUCT TITLE

Created by Your Name(s)

AN ADVENTURE FOR FOR CHARACTERS LEVELS 1-3

COVER ART GOES HERE

BLURB: Lorem ipsum dolor sit amet, consectetuer adipiscing elit, sed diam nonummy nibh euismod tincidunt ut laoreet dolore magna aliquam erat volutpat. Ut wisi enim ad minim veniam, quis nostrud exerci tation ullamcorper suscipit lobortis nisl ut aliquip ex ea commodo con-

COMPANY INFO:
Lorem ipsum dolor sit amet, consectetuer adipiscing elit, sed diam nonummy nibh

COPYRIGHT INFO:
Lorem ipsum dolor sit amet, consectetuer adipiscing elit, sed diam nonummy nibh

Cover template (© 2018 Greg Johnson)

I am going to base the design for this particular product on classic *Dungeon & Dragons* modules like *Against the Giants* and *Keep on the Borderlands*. This seems appropriate for a retro-clone set of "Old School Rules" like *Glory of Yore*.

The product title should be something descriptive and evocative. If you don't already have one developed, take the time now to write up a list of words that describe your adventure. Afterward, try combing pairs of descriptors and creating a memorable title for your product.

Some parts such as your name, company info, and compatible rule sets are pretty straightforward. Just make sure that this information is on your cover page and presented legibly. Present your name as: "Created by Your Name." Make sure to include your company information if you have one. The company's name, logo, and website address would probably suffice. If you've been using this book as a guide, then the compatible rules sets section should include the following, "designed for the *Glory of Yore* role-playing game."

The character level for your adventure is another easy one. The appropriate descriptor here is "Beginner" or "Introductory." You can add in "for levels 1–3" as well to define the character level for the adventure. If you used a different game system or designed the game for a different power level, then you will have to use a different set of descriptors to say so. Otherwise, this section should read something like, "An introductory module for levels 1–3."

It is critical that you include proper copyright information for your product if you intend to publish it. The appropriate copyright notice consists of:

1. The symbol© (capital letter C in a circle); the word "Copyright"; or the abbreviation "Copr."
2. The year of first publication. If the work is a derivative work or a compilation incorporating previously published material, the year date of first publication of the derivative work or compilation is sufficient. Examples of derivative works are translations or dramatizations; an example of a compilation is an anthology.
3. The name of the copyright owner, an abbreviation by which the name can be recognized, or a generally known alternative designation of owner.
Example© 2012 Jane Doe
(Circular 3, 2013)

You will also need good artwork. Excellent artwork, maps, diagrams and other visuals can add zest to your product and bring it to life in the reader's imagination. When incorporating artwork into your publication, don't just slap it down in the center of a page. Consider how each piece of artwork works with the content around it. Artwork should always enhance the readability and usability of your adventure otherwise it has no place being there! Use art to break up a large chunk of text, clarify an encounter, or to help visualize a location. You can either create the artwork yourself, hire someone to do it for you, or find images that are out of copyright and thus open to fair use. Creating the artwork yourself is always a safe bet. You will need access to a decent piece of illustration software. If you can afford it, software such as Adobe Photoshop or Corel Painter makes a good choice. Alternatively, both Krita and Gimp are solid performers and free to download and use. Of course, you can always use pencil, paper, ink, and paint and do the artwork the old-fashioned way. The single most important piece of artwork is the cover. It needs to be excellent in quality and capable of grabbing people's attention. An image with a strong composition and vivid colors that accurately evokes the mood of your adventure is what you will need. You will also need at least a few (2–3) half-page pieces of artwork and a similar number (2–4) of spot art pieces. These interior artworks are used to illustrate momentous scenes in your story and fill in blank spots not taken up by the text. Pay careful attention to the image resolution of the pictures you use for publication. The proper resolution for printed material is 300 dpi (dots per inch). This means that a standard sized sheet of paper, that is, an 8.5 × 11 inch sheet, translates to 2550 × 3300 pixels in your imaging software. A horizontal half-page piece of art, say 5 × 7 inches in dimension, will be roughly 2100 × 1500 pixels. Spot art is usually a quarter or fifth of a page and so is correspondingly smaller. When creating your artwork it doesn't hurt to work larger than what is specified here. You can always shrink a piece of artwork to fit. You can't enlarge artwork, though. If you try to make the artwork bigger, you will only blur and pixelate it and end up with something unusable. If you can't draw then you can hire someone to do the artwork for you. You can also try your hand at photography if you are so inclined. The final option is to try and find a suitable piece of artwork whose copyright has expired meaning that you are free to use it. Any work published in the United States before January 1, 1923 should be in the public domain and free to use. It is always best to verify the copyright status of any work before use however since publishing a copyrighted work of art will likely get you sued!

One thing you will have to consider is whether or not to make the interior of your publication in color or not. Color interiors are more engaging but are harder to design and significantly more expensive to produce. If your goal is to sell your product for a profit, then this will mean a significant mark up above and beyond what it costs you to print the product.

Include a short blurb on the front cover describing the contents of the adventure. This blurb is a brief description of the product and its contents that usually runs about 5–7 lines of text. Explicit info about the rule set the product uses, and a little something to pique the interest of potential customers forms the content of the cover blurb.

GLORY OF YORE RPG

Temple of the Blood Moon

by Greg Johnson

AN ADVENTURE FOR FOR CHARACTERS LEVELS 1-3

The Wolf Forest is a dark and ancient place thick and impenetrable in many places. Gnarled and twisted trees cast their shadows upon the ruins of ancient buildings that predate man's arrival in the land. Strange and unnatural beasts stalk the depths of this forest, and only a few hardy souls dare to live on the fringes of this enormous woodland expanse. Can the players solve the mystery of what haunts this grim woodland? Can a brave group of adventurers brave the horrors of the Temple of the Blood Moon?

GREGtheARTIST

Sample cover art: Temple of the blood moon

You will also have to prepare a backcover with another, more in-depth, blurb about your adventure. More artwork can be used here as well as providing space for a nice ISBN (International Standard Book Number) barcode if you plan to have your work printed by a traditional printer (as opposed to an on-demand printer which doesn't strictly need an ISBN tag). Bowker (www.isbn.org) is the agency in the U.S. from which you can purchase a legitimate ISBN. ISBNs are declining in use since print-on-demand services don't strictly require them. If you do opt to include an ISBN, use a free online barcode generator to create the image file of the scannable barcode. Make sure that you do some research on ISBNs before making a final decision if you intend to market your book. Getting something like this wrong when creating a portfolio piece or demo isn't so bad. Getting something wrong when you are investing serious money, on the other hand, is terrible. Always research everything thoroughly before spending your money!

BACK COVER ART GOES HERE

BACK COVER BLURD or WRITE UP: Lorem ipsum dolor sit amet, consectetuer adipiscing elit, sed diam nonummy nibh euismod tincidunt ut laoreet dolore magna aliquam erat volutpat. Ut wisi enim ad minim veniam, quis nostrud exerci tation ullamcorper suscipit lobortis nisl ut aliquip ex ea commodo consequat. Duis autem vel eum iriure dolor in hendrerit in vulputate velit esse molestie consequat, vel illum dolore eu feugiat nulla facilisis at vero eros et accumsan et iusto odio dignissim qui blandit praesent luptatum zzril delenit augue duis dolore te feugait nulla facilisi.
Lorem ipsum dolor sit amet, cons ectetuer adipiscing elit, sed diam nonummy nibh euismod tincidunt ut laoreet dolore magna aliquam erat volutpat. Ut wisi enim ad minim veniam, quis nostrud exerci tation ullamcorper suscipit lobortis nisl ut aliquip ex ea commodo consequat.
Lorem ipsum dolor sit amet, consectetuer adipiscing elit, sed diam nonummy nibh euismod tincidunt ut laoreet dolore magna aliquam erat volutpat. Ut wisi enim ad minim veniam, quis nostrud exerci tation ullamcorper suscipit lobortis nisl ut aliquip ex ea commodo consequat. Duis autem vel eum iriure dolor in hendrerit in vulputate velit esse molestie consequat, vel illum dolore eu feugiat nulla facilisis at vero eros et accumsan et iusto odio dignissim qui blandit praesent luptatum zzril delenit augue duis dolore te feugait nulla facilisi.
Lorem ipsum dolor sit amet, cons ectetuer adipiscing elit, sed diam nonummy nibh euismod tincidunt ut laoreet dolore magna aliquam erat volutpat. Ut wisi enim ad minim veniam, quis nostrud exerci tation

BACK COVER COPYRIGHT, COMPANY, or OTHER INFO: Lorem ipsum dolor sit amet, consectetuer adipiscing elit, sed diam nonummy nibh euismod tincidunt ut laoreet dolore magna aliquam erat volutpat. Ut wisi enim ad minim veniam, quis nostrud exerci tation ullamcorper suscipit lobortis nisl ut aliquip ex ea commodo consequat. Duis autem vel eum iriure dolor in hendrerit in vulputate velit esse molestie consequat, vel illum dolore eu feugiat nulla facilisis at vero eros et accumsan et iusto odio dignissim qui blandit praesent luptatum zzril delenit augue duis dolore te feugait nulla facilisi.

Back cover template

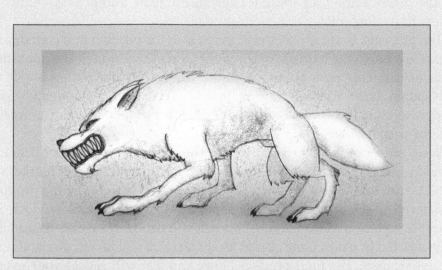

Britain during the dark ages is a grim and unforgiving land. The old Roman civilization has fallen to waves of barbarian invaders from the mainland. Tribes of Angles, Saxons and Jutes have recently displaced the former Romans from the coast. The ancient forests to the west are still the home of the resilient Welsh. Fierce Scottish and Pictish clans live in the northlands. Many petty kingdoms constitute the land of Britain, each ruled by an armored force of knights and a local king. Dark forces prowl the fringes of this chaotic land working towards their evil goals.

If you enjoy this adventure then purchase other products by GregTheArtist and the Genres Game Systems company such as:

Toonzy!: the Cartoon Role-Playing Game
Toonzy!: Do-It-Yourself Drawing Book
Toonzy!: Game of Scones campaign setting
Toonzy!: Supple-Mint expansion
Toonzy!: Fun Pack adventure set
Going Somewhere: the Sci-Fi Parody RPG

- and look for upcoming releases such as:
Atomic Age Adventures: the 1950's RPG
Boy Band of Brothers: the humorous pop music and dance RPG

Sample back cover

You will also have to format and design your publication or hire a freelance book designer to do it for you. You can use professional page layout software like Adobe Indesign or QuarkXPress or just put it all together in a word processor such as Microsoft Word or Libre Office. Whatever path you choose to take, you will need to make sure that the software can export a PDF document. Make it a point to read through some professional modules and take note of how they arrange each product. A well laid out document is one where the reader never has to hunt around for the information they need, is enjoyable to read, and provides intuitive access to its contents.

The title page is usually the very first page in the product and contains the title of the book, the name(s) of the author and illustrator(s), the publisher's information, copyright info, and other necessary information about the publication. Next, you will want to include a table of contents to allow your readers to quickly locate a specific area of your product, and don't forget to add the page numbers!

Your final product needs to reflect the interests of your audience. It should possess the appropriate tone and theme that your target market will expect from this sort of product. Research similar and competing products to determine the proper style and approach for your type of product. For example, a game aimed at young children will probably be easy to read and light-hearted in nature, one geared for wargamers will be wordier and more serious in tone. The final product's look and feel will reflect your overall approach.

Make sure that you proofread your product before publication. Proofreading consists of more than spell checking everything (though you should make sure that you do that of course too). Read through every part of your product, from the first to the last page, and look for problems. Any lengthy written document is bound to possess errors in spelling, punctuation, content, omissions, and other types of mistakes. You are well advised to get as many pairs of eyes checking your work as you can manage. Fresh reads like this will help you spot errors in logic and omissions faster than trying to do so yourself. It helps for you to put the product down and walk away from it for a bit before trying to proofread it yourself. Your mind and eyes will have grown so accustomed to looking at the material that you won't be able to look at it impartially. If you leave it alone for a week or so you can come back to it with a fresh eye, and you will most certainly find a host of errors that you had missed earlier. Pay close attention to the flow, spelling, and grammar of your document when proofreading. Run a spell check on everything and keep a dictionary and thesaurus handy to help you quickly rewrite and problem areas that you find. Remember that a computerized spell check is no substitute for proofreading your document. A spell checker won't necessarily ascertain errors in logic, flow, or the omission of some critical piece of your adventure. Only a good pair of eyes can do that.

Finding grammar mistakes can be difficult. You can find many good books on grammar at your local library or online that can help you. You will also need to make sure that the contents have an orderly and easily understood flow to them. The sentences and paragraphs of your work need to have a natural progression from one topic to another. Keep in mind that what seems logical to you might not make any sense whatsoever to your readers. You need other people helping you at this point. Recruit your friends and family to proofread your work. If you are having trouble with the writing, you can always hire a professional editor to help you with this stage.

Conclusion

We've gone over a brief outline of all of the things you need to do to finalize and bring your project to production ready status. While space doesn't allow us the room to include everything there is to know about page layout, design, and production, you should have enough information to get started and guide you through the process. Preparing a product for publication is all about paying attention to the nitty-gritty details of the process and not skimping on any of the minutiae of your product. Now is the time to check, re-check, and check again everything associated with your product. Take your time. This stage will probably take at least as long as actually writing the product did!

Assignment

Using the outline and examples presented in this chapter, plus plenty of professional publications as a reference, try putting your project into its final form. Use either a page layout or word processing program to format your final draft. Craft both a front and back cover, include a title page, design your maps, and incorporate any illustrations you need throughout the text. Make sure that everything you plan to include in the product is at least 300 dpi (300 dots per inch) resolution. Don't forget to playtest and proofread your product thoroughly before you publish it.

Chapter 23
Publishing

The Final Steps

You've created your masterpiece, and you now need to decide what to do with it. Is it merely a portfolio piece that demonstrates your skill and craft? Do you want to publish it on an Internet forum and freely distribute it as a publicity stunt or to give something to the gaming community? Alternatively, do you want to try and make money off of it? Any of these answers are acceptable, and there can be generous degrees of overlap between them. It is entirely possible to put the module you've written into your portfolio, distribute a free PDF, online and put a print-on-demand (POD) version up for sale on several different websites. Whatever the answers to these questions are, there remain a few final things you still need to address.

More About Copyrighting Your Work

The first thing you must do is copyright your work before publishing it anywhere. Understand that you automatically own the copyright to anything you create by default. However, you will need something substantial to back up your claim if you ever have to prove that you own the copyright to a piece of work. A copyright notice embedded in your picture or document can provide a basic level of documentation for your work, which is why we included a formal copyright notice on the cover and title page.

While putting a copyright notice on your work is a significant first step, you need to take the additional measure of registering your copyright with the government if you are serious about publishing your material. This formal step serves as a legal public record, and holds considerable weight if you are ever involved in a legal copyright suit. In the United States, you can fill out an application online at the United States Copyright Office at www.copyright.gov. There is a basic fee you will need to pay. Additional information about copyright, forms, procedures, and frequently asked questions are on the same website. The good news is that copyright protects your work for your entire lifetime plus an additional 70 years!

Publicity or Profit?

Are you trying to profit off of your work? If you want money, then you're going to want to publish your work in a salable manner. Direct your attention to the following section on self-publishing or finding a publisher for some information on your business options. If you're not after money then are you going for publicity? If good publicity is your bag, then think about posting your adventure as a PDF file to a popular website devoted to tabletop role-playing games like Dragonsfoot.org, Drivethrurpg.com, or the appropriate forum on Reddit or other RPG related websites. If you are giving your module away for free, you can post your work anywhere that will allow it and try and get your work to as broad an audience as possible. If you're not looking for good public relations, you can simply play your module with your friends and put a copy of it in your portfolio as a demonstration of your creative talents.

Self-Publishing or Finding a Publisher

Now that you've secured your copyright, you will need to decide whether you are going to self-publish your work or try and find a publisher for your product. There are pros and cons to both approaches. If you self-publish your work, then you retain clear ownership of it and make more profit on anything you manage to sell. The downside lies in marketing your product. It is quite difficult to sell anything when no one knows who you are! Unless you already have an established fan base, a lot of social media presence, or other avenues to market your product, you probably won't see much in the way of sales unless you focus a tremendous amount of effort on self-promotion or hire someone to run a marketing campaign for your product.

If you decide to go with a publisher, you have to find a publisher willing to distribute and promote your work. Understand that you will most likely lose control of your work since you are in effect selling it to the publisher. Depending upon the terms of the contract you sign, you may not have any say at all in what happens afterward. It can still be worthwhile to work with a publisher since they should have a well-built distribution and marketing network that can get your work to a vast audience. If the publisher doesn't have proper distribution and marketing channels, then there's probably not much reason to deal with them since that's no better than doing it yourself. Understand that if you work with a publisher, then they will be the ones earning the lion's share of the profits, not you. You may or may not collect a small royalty fee per unit sold depending upon your specific contract agreement. If you are working with a well-known publisher, there might be a certain level of name recognition that can be helpful when building up your resume. A lot of the decision regarding whether or not to self-publish boils down to how much control over your work you wish to have and how hard you are willing to work to promote yourself. It is essential to think things through and analyze your options before jumping into this decision.

Creating Your Own Business

Make sure that you are starting a business for the right reasons. You need to have a viable business plan along with a salable product or service and marketing plan. Try attending a local Small Business Administration event and doing some research on running a business. See if your county or city has a local council on small business or has a group that offers advice on starting and running a small business, and attend a few of these events. You will want to do a lot of research on the process of creating a company in your state before you start it.

If you are still firm in your desire to begin a business after you've done your research, then you will need to pick a good name for your business. The name needs to reflect your product, interests, and style while being appealing to your customers. Something easy to spell and remember is best. Sit down with a sheet of paper and write down every word that could be used to describe your product or company, and try to come up with a handful of great names. Then, run your favorite choices past everyone you know and gauge their reactions and get some feedback. Narrow it down to a few candidates that could work as your business name. That was the simple part. The hard part consists of the next two things.

You have to check and make sure that another business in your state hasn't already registered that name. Conduct a corporation search for your specific state or country, and see which names are already registered. Most states have a searchable database of corporate names that have been registered or reserved that you can search through online, but you may have to dig around your state's various government agencies and websites to discover the proper webpage to gain access to this database. Once you've found a business name that's available in your state, you will need to check and see if that name is also available as a web domain (i.e., an internet address). This part can be tricky since people have gone through the dictionary and registered almost every word in it as a web domain already. You can look up available web domain names at any number of different domain name service providers such as GoDaddy.com or BlueHost.com.

It will require no small amount of ingenuity on your part to find a good domain name that also works as a business name. Conduct an Internet search to make sure that whatever you pick it isn't too close to an already established company, or that your company's name is common slang for something, or has some hidden humorous meaning. Choosing a name similar to another company's could land you in legal trouble and isn't worth the risk. Once you've managed to find a company name that is available in your state, has a viable domain name, and isn't too close to another existing company, then you are all set. Now you can reserve the name on your state government's database website and purchase your domain name from a reputable domain name service (e.g., GoDaddy, HostGator, etc.). Check the terms of the domain name service and make sure you are getting a good deal. A domain name is useless without a website to go along with it, so you will also have to purchase a web hosting plan (often times free with the purchase of the domain name) and design a website for your business. Alternatively, you can find an all-in-one domain, hosting, and basic design service like Wix.com, SquareSpace.com or WordPress.com and use that instead.

Unfortunately, I cannot be more precise in the steps you will need to create your business, since each state or country has different laws and methods for doing so there simply isn't room in one book to cover everything you might need. I do implore you to conduct your own research on an appropriate business structure for the specific area in which you are setting up your business. Determine for yourself what if any legal business structure you want or need to form in order to publish your game. I recommend thoughtful research and seeking appropriate legal advice before committing to your plan as there can be both legal and financial repercussions to your decision.

Decide what format you want your adventure to be available in. Are you doing a PDF, e-book, print-on-demand (POD), or a traditional print run? If you are doing a standard print run, you will want to get a proper ISBN for your adventure book from Bowker.com. If you are only making a POD, PDF, or e-book, an ISBN isn't strictly required anymore. POD, PDF, and e-book are popular formats because of the low overhead cost of doing business using them. Amazon.com, Lulu.com, and DriveThruRPG.com all offer various POD and e-book services that you can use. Each website has particular specifications about size, formatting, and other details that you will have to deal with to use their service. Make sure that you get a few proof copies from whichever service you are using to do a final proofread and one last check for any errors in formatting, grammar, and spelling before you put your work on the market. Remember that this product is a reflection of you and your abilities, so you want it to be as professional and polished as possible.

Doing the publicity and marketing for your product is, frankly, every bit as challenging, perhaps even more so, than creating the product in the first place! You will need to learn how to leverage social media sites such as YouTube, Facebook, Twitter, Instagram, and Twitch for potential customers to learn about your product. Try visiting local gaming stores to talk to the owners and see if your product can get a place on the shelf. You'll need to promote grassroots marketing on various forums or consider advertising on Google, Yahoo, or Bing. In my own experience, the marketing of the product is way harder than making the product. To that end, it may behoove you to hire someone to run a marketing campaign for your product or to sell it on a commission basis.

Conclusion

You've now received a broad overview of what it takes to publish your adventure. The material in this chapter is every bit as complicated and laborious, maybe even more so, than producing the module itself. Do not jump into doing these things lightly. If you choose to publish your work or start a business to do so, you will need to do your research and keep track of everything very carefully to avoid making a mess of things. With that said, I found that creating my own business has been very rewarding and enjoyable. Just remember to do your due diligence, thorough research, and always proceed with careful planning and professional advice.

Assignment

Decide what you wish to do with your project now that you have finished developing it. Write up a document (1000–2000 words) describing how you intend to implement these goals and documenting the research that you have done in support of this plan of action.

Chapter 24

Post-mortem

A post-mortem document is a way to list and describe all of the things that went right and wrong with a project. Do a post-mortem so the person and team can learn from the development cycle they've just completed and hopefully do things better the next time around. It is important to realize that a post-mortem is not a review. It is an analysis of the production done by one or more of the team members who produced the game itself. Doing a post-mortem is a great way to analyze your mistakes and successes and learn to avoid the former and replicate the latter in future projects. The result serves as a lessons learned document that the team can leverage in future productions.

Description

It helps to describe the project in full before getting into the good and bad aspects of the project. That way anyone who reads the post-mortem document will have an easier time understanding the nature of the issues described. For example, I can do a write-up of my own role-playing game that some friends and I put out a couple of years ago. Even if you've never seen the game, the description can be used to give you a good idea of what I'm talking about once I dive into the major points of the post-mortem itself.

Post-mortem for *Toonzy! the Cartoon Role-Playing Game*

What happens when a group of friends dare each other to create something, *Toonzy! The Cartoon Role-Playing Game* that's what (available at Amazon.com)! Inspired by our years of playing heavily customized RPGs, we rather off-handedly decided that we actually could do better than some of the games we had been playing. After mulling it over for a couple of weeks, we sat down, outlined the core rules, and began iteratively playtesting and developing the game further. It took us about six months to fully develop and write up the rules and another six months to create the artwork, page layout, and final document. Throw in a couple of months for building a company to publish the game, a website, and setting things up on Amazon and we ended up with our lovely little RPG.

Toonzy! the Cartoon Role Playing Game

We ended up doing a cartoon role-playing game because there weren't many out there. The closest thing was the *Toon* RPG by Steve Jackson games, but that game hasn't been in publication for decades, so there wasn't any real competition. Keeping things as simple as possible and yet still provide a severe test of our game mechanics was another factor. With the extreme over-the-top action and comedic elements involved, we thought doing a cartoon game would serve as the perfect test for our system which we could later turn into a universal rule set which we could use for any number of future games.

What Went Right

In this section list out at least five things that worked well and that you'd try to replicate again if you did a similar project. Try and be as specific and detailed as you can. Being completely honest with yourself and your peers is the only real way you can learn from the experience. Doing this part shouldn't be too hard. It is relatively easy to pat yourself on the back and offer accolades to your colleagues. Make a note of anyone's specific contribution that turned out well or areas of the project that ended up being beautiful or exceptional. Mention any good advice that you received or production methods that helped out. I'll use *Toonzy!* as the example.

1. *Mechanics*: Everyone who played the game loved it. The game captures the flavor and style of the old Saturday morning cartoons that we set out to replicate in the first place. The system is easy to understand, easy to play, and extremely fun. It turns out that playing the game is physically tiring due to everyone laughing so much. After an hour of playing, all of the players are exhausted! We've even had people fall out of their chairs they were laughing so much playing the game. I don't know a better compliment for a game designed to be humorous than that.

2. *Artwork*: Allen Lewonski, who did the lion's share of the artwork for the game, knocked everyone's socks off. His loose, sketchy, yet cartoony style defines the overall feel of the game to a great extent. The artwork turned into a beautiful compliment to the rule set and helped to make the finished game a fantastic book.

3. *Production*: Michael Betancourt, who did the page layout and production work, was a true professional. He brought years of experience as an editor and designer to the project, and it shows in the quality of the final book. The game we made looks better, has fewer mistakes, and a higher degree of polish than practically any other game product I've seen recently because of his stellar efforts.

4. *Teamwork*: The project ran quite smoothly. We did have one member of the team quickly drop out of things for the most part, but aside from that the team worked very well together. This harmony was in large part due to all of those involved being quite good friends

no doubt, but it is a testament to the team that we're all still good friends even after undertaking a significant and complicated project like this. Being friends allowed us to adopt a very organic and loose hierarchy that nevertheless managed to split production tasks into discreet elements we could hand off to the person best fit to do that part of the project.

5. *Award*: The end product was good enough that we got nominated for the 2016 ENnie Award for "Best Free Game" (Whitehead, 2016). Not bad for a game from a completely unknown publisher that received practically no marketing or promotion! We even got an offer to buy out the rights to the game from another publisher. The deal never panned out but the fact the game brought in such interest is very flattering and a sign that we did things on the production end right.

What Went Wrong

In this section, list out at least five things that didn't work or go as planned. These are the things you need to avoid the next time. Again, be as specific and detailed as you can and even more critically, be honest. Honesty is the part that hurts. It can be incredibly difficult to come clean about the problems you had in production. It is quite honestly the toughest thing you will have to do regarding any given process. It is the toughest section since it will help you learn what to avoid in the future. This section can also serve as a guide to those capabilities you need to develop or address more fully the next go-around. Try to analyze each mistake and discern precisely why and how things went wrong. This analysis will help you figure out solutions to each problem. Remember that you should be realistic. Having your first project not turn into a billion-dollar blockbuster doesn't qualify as a realistic expectation. Shoot for the sky but keep your expectations within practical limits. Once again, *Toonzy!* will be my example.

1. *Publicity and marketing*: If there is something we fell terribly short on it was in our publicity and marketing plan. Simply put, we didn't have one. No plan at all besides some vague notions about how to go about it. It turns out that having one game designer, one combination graphic designer/editor, and a great illustrator works well in making the product, but none of us had the foggiest clue whatsoever when it came time to sell the resulting product. All of us handily forgot that companies commonly spend anywhere from 10% to 50% of their budget for a product on marketing it. We could have used a person on the team who was good at marketing and grass-roots advertising. All of our other mistakes pale in comparison to this one. Not having a solid marketing plan was a fundamental mistake and one that will

scupper any future projects as well unless we figure out a solution to this problem. The source of this mistake was, quite basically, our naiveté and inexperience. Based upon our previous professional experience, we really should have had a clue, and the fact we didn't is down to our unfamiliarity with doing this sort of production work for ourselves.

2. *Production schedules for part-timers*: The production took a lot longer than we had initially estimated. It is natural for the first project a team does to experience many setbacks and delays. After all, the team has to figure out how it needs to do each step and, since this is the first time doing it, there will inevitably be mistakes and failures before you find what works. The fact that it took longer than we thought is a simple inevitability of doing things for the first time. Considering how smoothly things worked despite the delays is a real feather in our cap and speaks well to everyone on the team. It was quite difficult for us to balance our full-time jobs, family lives, and a significant production effort as well. In hindsight, I am quite surprised we managed to pull it off. Again the source of this mistake was our inexperience in doing this sort of work.

3. *Contracts amongst friends*: Getting people to sign contracts was something that did not work at all. We tried. I wrote up more than one version of a very generous deal for the team. Everyone was too skittish to put anything into writing. Since the game did not become a raging sales success, the lack of proper contracts among the team members didn't end up mattering much at all. Projects involving significant expenditures can become a festering sore point among even good friends, and we ran that risk without really thinking about it much beforehand. Again, it is indicative of the high quality of people on the team that no one became upset about any of the sometimes trying aspects of the production. That said, on any future serious projects this really should be the first thing that happens, up front, and before anyone invests time into the effort. This one really was our own fault. We all knew better. Everyone involved had worked professionally enough to see that we needed to do this. We simply didn't manage to do it.

4. *Money spent and not seen again*: Closely related to the contracts issue was the amount of cash out of pocket we spent doing the project. Between buying numerous domain names for the endless variations of the company name the group couldn't decide upon, to purchasing pre-press versions of the book along with expedited shipping for error checking, to just the time invested on the project, we put a significant amount of money into getting our product to print and in the store. While *Toonzy!* serves as a great portfolio piece and is quite a fun game, none of us will ever recover the money we sank

into the project barring a miracle. This failing doesn't surprise any of us. We went into the project knowing that profitability was a long shot but it still caught us all a bit by surprise just how much time and money we ended up investing. Maybe I can convince myself to see losing money as a success in this regard? No? Well, at least it wasn't a big surprise. We expected to lose money on this project.

5. *The convention.* The lowest point for team morale was undoubtedly participating in a local fan convention. Unfortunately, we signed up for a con the year it changed convention sites in our town and it wasn't as well attended or organized as years past. In retrospect, we spent too much time and money and got too little foot traffic to warrant a booth in the con's vendor room. We spent an entire weekend in a room full of other vendors with only a few customers coming through. After our great optimism was crushed by the frustrating showing at the convention, we gave up on any further marketing or developing of the game. In hindsight, that was our biggest mistake. The game had great potential for continued development, but after the convention, we had all lost heart, and no one had the will to power through the type of tough, grass-roots marketing campaign the product needed. Picking up development after a lengthy hiatus has proven to be more difficult than any of us ever expected.

The Post-Mortem's Conclusion

Use the conclusion to go over the things you would do again or how you would change those things you wouldn't want to repeat for the better. Try to explain your justifications for your proposals. The conclusion is where you can respond to any criticisms about the project that you have received. Analyze other people's comments for any constructive critiques or valid points. Try to be as detailed and fair as possible in your defense. Include specifics wherever possible. You can use the same section headers I am using, that is, "was it all worth it?," "things to change," "what's next," and "afterword." These sections will let you think about how you can apply the lessons you've learned from this production to your future endeavors and hopefully provide you with some specifics to make judgments. The "was it all worth it?" section is for a general overview of the totality of the process and where you place any big picture items. In the "things to change" portion, list out and describe any specifics you need to change. The "what's next" segment offers you an opportunity to describe how you will apply any lessons learned to any upcoming projects. Lastly, the "afterword" lets you think back upon your project and consider any aspects that you found particularly challenging, rewarding or that need more focus. I'll wrap up my example on *Toonzy!* here.

Was it all Worth it?

Yes. Making *Toonzy!* was an enjoyable experience overall and I am quite proud of the results we managed to get out of it. I'm also pretty impressed that we're all still good friends at the end of it. Putting friendships under this sort of pressure was not one of the goals when we started this process, but it happened nevertheless. If I were to repeat the process, I'd probably be a bit more cautious getting into it if the team involved any other people. Conversely, I know full well that I can trust my comrades who partook in the *Toonzy!* project. If I were to undertake another project with them, I could do so without question as to their commitment. That's a critical thing to know about your team. I have every confidence in their abilities and understand each of our strengths and weaknesses pretty well at this point. Any future work we do I know will proceed a lot more smoothly as a result.

Things to Change

On the other hand, I probably wouldn't do something like this again without a great deal more thought and effort given to how we intend to market and publicize our product. Having a great product that no one knows even exists is the same as not having a product at all. You aren't going to sell anything. Of course, if I am doing something just as a portfolio piece then that's a different proposal altogether.

I'd also try to be more realistic about the production schedule. Knocking out a product as a part-time exercise is no small matter and takes a LOT longer than you initially think. I'd probably double or even quadruple my initial estimate for how long any future projects will take.

If there's any chance of there being large amounts of money involved, then you really ought to insist on writing up a simple contract up front before you start development. Anyone who doesn't sign is summarily off of the project until they sign on. The paperwork will let everyone involved know what they're working towards and for up front and save you a lot of potential legal headaches if the project succeeds.

If I were doing it over again, I'd skip local events entirely and make an effort to go to huge conventions like GenCon in Indianapolis or DragonCon in Atlanta.

What's Next

We've got at least one or two supplements mostly written as well as a campaign setting. If the team can work up enough interest, we might finish these other supplements eventually. Realistically though, the team has gone on a hiatus. We're all too busy pursuing our full-time careers, family matters, and other projects to devote the kind of time we need to produce something more. There are a lot of unfinished projects we've got lying about—at least two or three entire games have been roughed out and partially written up but finding the time to do the artwork and layout has been quite challenging. Additionally, we are still wrestling with the core problem of how to market and publicize our products.

Afterword

The significant challenges and failures were almost universally down to our inexperience in doing this sort of project. There were a considerable number of problems which I have already mentioned and countless others which were too trivial to remember. A game like this is no small undertaking, and we were somewhat glib about it when we first started. A fair number of problems were ones which I am a bit embarrassed to say we didn't think through beforehand while others were to be expected given our circumstances. I am very proud of what we ended up with and would happily show off the game to anyone interested.

Chapter Conclusion

A post-mortem lets you analyze your mistakes and successes in depth and provides you with an opportunity to improve any future projects. Honesty, along with specific details and an in-depth analysis of what worked and what didn't are the hallmarks of a proper post-mortem. Remember to be as professional as possible in your comments since it is entirely possible that other members of your team might read your document and because doing so reflects better upon you as a developer. Don't make the post-mortem a personal attack on a specific team member or group. That isn't a helpful approach and generally speaking, won't yield good results for anybody. Instead, analyze your mistakes and make sure that you don't repeat them.

Assignment

Using this chapter as a guide create a 1–4 page post-mortem for your project. You can use the same headers and format that I used for the example. Remember to be as honest, open, and detailed as you possibly can be. The goal here is to learn whatever lessons you can from your experience and make sure that your next project is even better than this one.

Chapter 25

Turning Your Adventure into a Video Game

The Differences between a TTRPG and a Video Game

If you want to turn the adventure that you've created into a video game you've got more work to do. The first thing that you'll have to grapple with are the differences between a pen-and-paper table-top role-playing game and a video game. In a TTRPG the players are unconstrained. If they want to, the characters can wander off and do something entirely outside the scope of the adventure. Creating that sort of open world for a computer game is a truly enormous effort that only the most prominent and best-funded game companies typically try to tackle. Video games have much narrower options for what a character can do. Simply put, a video game character can't just switch gears and become something else like a TTRPG character can. If you are playing *Doom* your character isn't suddenly able to break into a song and dance routine! Video games are limited by what the developers put into the game. If it isn't programmed into the game, then the players aren't going to be able to do it. While theoretically, a developer could put anything they want into the game, each option or feature added requires time and money. If there's not a reasonable rationale for including it, then they are unlikely to do so. Additionally, video games are always constrained by the technology used to create them. Everything in the video game has to be built for it. All of the environments need to be mapped out, all of the dialog scripted, and every art asset digitally created and then animated. There's no room for improvisation like what you can find in a TTRPG. While it is possible to have procedurally generated content, that isn't a particularly easy solution either. Someone still has to create the algorithms used to make all of the material (though with the advent of Artificial Intelligence programs that might change). This requirement means that if you are going from a TTRPG to a video game, you will have to make many adjustments and build everything that the video game will require. Unlike in a TTRPG, in a video game, you can't leave any sections of the adventure open to interpretation.

Making a Video Game

There are only a few realistic options if you want to make your idea into a video game. You can create the video game yourself, or you can use the adventure you've written, and hopefully published, to help you get a job in the video game industry. Creating it yourself takes a LOT of time and effort. Fortunately, there are websites like KickStarter.com around through which can fund the development process. Even so, doing up a video game on your own is a daunting process fraught with risks, though the rewards for those who succeed can be great. A far easier alternative is to use your adventure as a portfolio piece to help you get a game development job. You can then propose an idea to your company after you've established a reputation for yourself.

Doing it Yourself

If you are serious about making the game yourself, then you've got a great deal of work to do. Frequently the designer writes up all of the specifics the game will need in what is known as a Game Design Document, which can be quite a challenge in and of itself (Freeman, 1997; Kelling, 2014; Ryan, 1999a). A Game Design Document, or GDD, is an in-depth write up of the entire game that includes everything the game needs to get built (Freeman, 1997; Ryan, 1999a). It includes concept art, level design, game mechanics, minimum system specifications, user interface designs, plus a whole lot more. Making a full-blown GDD is a HUGE undertaking and not something to undertake unless you know that the game is going to get built. Instead of spending the next few months writing up a GDD, you'd be far better off creating what is called a Game Pitch. A Game Pitch can be used to get crowdfunding on sites like Kickstarter, Indiegogo, and Figure, or even to put your idea to other potential investors (Davis, 2010). You're going to need money and time to work up a proper game which means either funding it yourself, working on it part-time, crowdfunding, or finding investors.

How to Create a Game Pitch for a Video Game

No matter which funding approach you decide to use, you will no doubt need to work up a game pitch. The good news about creating a polished game pitch is that you've already done a lot of the work. The TTRPG adventure you've written can serve as a quite functional basis for a new video game pitch. You'll need to write up a video game concept document, create a presentation, and then either pitch your game to a developer, crowdfund it, or work it up yourself. If you intend to work on developing the game yourself, then the goal is to identify what the game will need to acquire funding, recruit teammates, and get produced. If you are pitching this to a developer or crowdfunding it then you have to convince your audience to invest money into your idea. To be convincing, you need to provide details about your proposal and a lot of WOW factor too (Davis, 2010; Greene, 2017; Nichiporchik, 2015). The first step is figuring out the details of your video game proposal which involves creating a video game concept document.

The Video Game Concept Document

A video game concept document is a brief overview of your game that includes many specifics about your game idea. The report consists of more than just the details about the game itself but also such things as how the game will get monetized, marketed, as well as any competing products, and much, much, more. The video game concept document serves to establish the outlines of what your game will consist of as well as the various financial arguments used to justify the game's production (Powers, 2014; Ryan, 1999c; Schell, 2008, 382–387; Sellers, 2018, 193–212). In some measure, it is a similar document to the one you wrote up at the beginning of the book for your adventure idea while in others it involves a lot of new research and work. To help you get started on your own video game concept document, you can fill out the outline and questionnaire included below.

VIDEO GAME CONCEPT DOCUMENT

Project Name

A pretty simple question but the name needs to be something catchy, appropriate to the genre, have an available website address, and not be too close to an existing video game or similar product. For branding purposes, the name needs to be unique enough that you can own the word in the minds of your players.

Owner: Your Name Goes Here

Don't leave this one out. Establishing ownership is important.

Briefly Describe the Overall Game Concept

In a few sentences, write out about what the game is about. You can develop this information based upon your elevator and comparison pitches. A short paragraph ought to suffice.

Provide a Short Overview of the Story

Write up a summary of the game's plot, narrative, and overall storyline. Indeed, this is just a general overview of how you expect the game to play out most of the time. Most games have relatively linear structures but if your product includes multiple different endings or other options be sure to mention them here. Make sure that you clearly state what the central conflict of the game is. The other details about the game can change later on, but the core conflict is what drives the story for the whole game and should remain constant unless you intend on rewriting everything.

List the Key Selling Points of the Game

Write up a brief description of any features that will be unique selling points for your game. These features might include an intricate plot, superb characters, new technical features, or anything else that might appeal to your target audience. When developing this part of the video game concept document keep in mind the so-called rule of thirds: one third of your proposal should be new and original to it, one third should be material that will already be familiar to the player, and the final third should offer a novel twist or variation on what the player expects (Bratt, 2016). Keeping the rule of thirds in mind write up the selling points for your proposal. Be aware that everything you are proposing will have to be created and that doing so will cost the developer money. In particular, introducing new technical or mechanical features will require significant money, and you will need strong justifications to warrant their development.

What is the Game's Genre?

If you are basing your proposal off of the adventure which you have already written up, then the answer to this question will be "Fantasy" or one of the subcategories thereof such as comic fantasy, dark fantasy, heroic fantasy, strange mystery, or some such descriptor. It all depends on the exact flavor of the game you are pitching but if you aren't sure then "fantasy" should cover most things.

What Role Does the Player Serve in the Game?

Is the player the principal protagonist or one of a group of protagonists? Maybe they're the villain (or one of a group of villains) of the story. Perhaps they think they're the hero up until a dramatic reveal at the end of the story. Whatever part the player assumes in the game should be defined in this section (Sellers, 2018, 206–209).

What are the Player's Goal(s) and Motivation(s)?

The character, and through the character the player, needs a goal. The best goals are one that the character, and player, can be passionate about. The more connected the player is to the character's goal the more likely they are to want to finish the game and buy game stuff such as in-game purchases and other merchandise. Strong goals will help create a compelling storyline. After all, the conflict in a story stems from the player, or players, being thwarted in the attainment of the goal. The antagonist will be whoever stands in the way of their goal. This section is where you illuminate the objective and through that goal show who the antagonist is. Clarifying the player's motivations will also help you identify your target audience (Adams, 2008).

Who is the Principal Antagonist in the Game?

Detail out the primary antagonist and their background as well as how they relate to the player's goal. Describe what reason the antagonist has for opposing the player. The better the villain, the better the story will be. A powerful villain gives the hero(es) a chance to shine.

How Does the Player Win, or Lose, the Game?

Define how the player wins the game in this section. Does the player succeed by achieving their primary goal or is there some other measure by which the player can win? The method of completing the game can be an important distinction if it forms part of a series—you don't want the player achieving their ultimate goal in part one of a series. Then there'd be no reason to play the sequels! The flip side of that coin is how the player can lose the game or even if that is possible at all. Many games just let the player go back to a saved point and try again. However you decide to handle winning and losing in the game write it up here.

Describe the Core Game Mechanic(s) for this Game

This section is where you write up any new mechanics the game will use plus the game mechanics you will use for things like character advancement, combat, magic, skills, equipment, and any other abilities present in the game (Taylor, 2018). If you are using an existing game engine such as the Unreal or Unity game engines, then quite a bit of the fundamental game mechanics are already well defined and don't need to be further elaborated. Even so, this section can amount to quite a bit of information if you start detailing out everything, so it is best to work up only the central features. You leverage things like the "D20 System Resource Document" from Wizards of the Coast under the Open Game License to help you build up a meaningful set of game mechanics that you can legally use for the game in much the same way you did when writing the adventure (Tweet et al., 2000–2003).

Describe the Gameplay Experience

Provide an outline of how the game narrative and plot will unfold and how this relates to what the player experiences. How does the game start? How is the player introduced to the main character and the central conflict of the game? What sort of experience are you providing to the player? You don't need to drone on at length here, just be succinct and to the point.

Define the Visual Style of the Game

Put any concept art, sketches, or reference images that relate to your game concept in this section. You are trying to define the overall look of your game in this section. If you use any pictures or artwork that aren't your own, then be sure to cite your sources and provide proper credit to the artists who made the images. Game companies are VERY sensitive about the adequate attribution of artwork and look dimly upon anyone who steals artwork or doesn't provide credit to the original artist.

What is the Audio Style of the Game?

Include samples or snippets of dialog, music, and audio effects that define the general sound and style of your game here (Sellers, 2018, 209–210; Taylor, 2018). Just like with the artwork make sure that you provide proper attribution of where you got the work from (try using either the MLA or Chicago style documentation for a works cited page). Once again, companies feel strongly about correctly attributing the material to their authors.

Describe the UI (User Interface) for the Game

Include some simple UI mock-ups, UI flow charts, menu styles, and even a mock-up of the in-game HUD (Heads-Up-Display) if you can (Taylor, 2018). Leave this section out if you don't have the skills to mock these elements up.

Describe the Different Game Levels

If the game consists of different levels or places, then it is a good idea to write up a brief yet thorough description of these areas. Include any salient terrain features a well as any other elements that are key to the gameplay. Providing a few maps or illustrations of the level is an excellent idea to give the reader a good feel for what you are proposing.

What Similar Products Have Already Been Released or Announced?

Answering this tricky question is crucial. You will need to research games that are similar to what you are proposing and take careful note of who their audience was and what their market performance was. If there are too many games like the one you are offering, then the market is flooded, and there probably isn't room for another similar title unless you include something innovative to differentiate your product from the competition. On the flip side. if there aren't at least a couple of existing titles close to what you are pitching a big company won't touch the idea. Breaking new ground is a risky proposition and companies tend to be cautious in their investments. Businesses try to arrange to the highest degree possible a guaranteed return on any money that they invest in a project. This careful approach is the reason why you see so many remakes of existing IP (intellectual property, a vital buzzword to remember) coming out of Hollywood. The thinking goes something like this; many people used to like show "X" back in the day. If we make a new movie based off of that show, then people who loved it will be sure to see it thus covering the production cost of the film. Any kids or friends of the original viewers will likely go too and if we can market the product to new markets such as China or a younger demographic we (i.e. the studio) can make a tremendous amount of money. The result is that you end up with remakes of a ton of old shows rather than anything new and original. The same thought process applies to games. *Mario, Pokemon, Call of Duty, Grand Theft Auto, Final Fantasy, Assassin's Creed, Resident Evil, Halo, Doom*, and *Tomb Raider* are all examples of long-running franchises based off of one original idea and then morphed into any number of games, sequels, and spin-offs. If you want to break new ground in games, then you might be looking at doing an indie title and not something at a big studio. Figuring out where your game idea falls along the spectrum from proven approaches to entirely new and unique is the point of filling out this specific section of the game concept document. It can help you figure out to whom you should target your game pitch.

Who is the Target Market?

Whatever company you manage to sell your idea to is going to have to spend considerable money on marketing the game to its potential audience (Sellers, 2018, 200–204). Defining the target market is one of the most crucial in the whole process of pitching a game idea. In order for your game to be produced, you'll have to identify the target audience and provide a lot of good reasons for them to want to buy your game. A straightforward approach to figuring out your target audience is to look through the list of similar games you put down as your competitors. Your target audience is probably the same people as your competitors (Carroll, 2017; Sailer, 2016).

What Makes this Game Different from the Competition?

Talk about the things in your game that will make your target market want to buy your game over any competitors' products (Sellers, 2018, 204–205). Hark back to the "Rule of Thirds" and recall that approximately one-third of your game ought to be fresh and innovative, one-third familiar with a twist on it, and the last third similar to other games the player is already familiar with (Bratt, 2016). Compare your game to any similar games you've listed as your competitors and make sure that your game meets the rule-of-thirds criterion for fresh, familiar, and different. Since the paradigm includes everything from storyline and characters to the user interface and technical accessories you have ample play room. Whatever solution you arrive at, make sure that it will help the game sell, since making money from the game is the ultimate goal for any company looking to produce it.

What Technical Innovations Does this Game Require?

Technical roadblocks are giant red flags for any potential investors. Technological innovation requires a LOT of risky development work which might not pay off and this sort of risk makes it very unlikely an investor will want to put money into your project. On the other hand, if you've already successfully done the development work for the game, then this might make them more likely to invest.

What are the Game's Hardware?

If your game requires any accessories or additional hardware to run, make sure that you note it here. Having a needed accessory can either work for you or against you depending on the company you're presenting to and whether or not you're tying the game into an existing product that a company is striving to push. A company might quite like a game that is leveraging or promoting a product they're rolling out whereas they'd probably take a dim view on a game that uses their competitor's hardware.

What is the Expected Date of Completion?

This question can be a tough nut to crack if you don't already have a lot of development experience in your pocket. If it is a visually intensive and realistic game, then you can safely put down 4–5 years. Less time is required if you are using stylized graphics. At a minimum, you're still talking a minimum of 2 years no matter what.

How can this Game be Monetized, that is, Direct Sales, Micro-Transactions, Toys, Accessories, and any Other Potential Revenue Streams?

A critical component to any company's decision-making process is how they will be able to leverage your game to make even more money. If your game can turn into a movie, TV show, book, comic series, and toy line, then this will help convince a company to invest in your product. The potential for sequels and spin-off games is also a factor here. You will have to decide what money making processes your game is going to leverage. Are you using micro-transactions, direct sales, or some other money making method for your game (Freeman, 1997; Rose, 2013; Sellers, 2018, 210–211)? The more revenue streams you can potentially demonstrate the better your chances of getting a company to bite.

Try to answer each question in the video game concept document with at least 3–5 sentences each. Doing so will force you to include enough details to make your paper instructive. This document will serve as the informational basis of your presentation. A printed copy can make an informative handout during any demonstration you make whereas a PDF version might help people on Kickstarter decide your game proposal is worthwhile enough to fund. Handing the members of your audience a copy of your video game concept document plus a copy of your adventure and letting them peruse through these while you make a slick presentation will undoubtedly serve to impress them.

Creating the Presentation

You've got your adventure, and you've got your video game design document, now it is time to use these to build a presentation pitch. First off, leverage the artwork, maps, and encounters you've already written for your adventure to provide content and visuals for your presentation (Ryan, 1999a). Try to add some WOW to your delivery by adding in extra artwork, sound, and animation wherever you can (Gameshubadmin, 2017). Create the presentation as a video, PowerPoint slide show, or an PDF. You can use the video game concept document as the source for your talking points and fill in the details with info from your adventure. Make sure you practice until you get to where the presentation flows smoothly so you can do it without any hiccups. During the pitch, you have to explain your game idea, provide the main selling points to your product, and then reinforce these points repeatedly throughout your presentation (Davis, 2010, 2). The goal is to be memorable and to make a good impression (Strom, 2015). If you are doing this presentation for Kickstarter or another crowdfunding site, then you will need to record it as a video and upload it. Make sure you have lots of great graphics and sound on your video to impress your audience.

Don't ever say bad or negative things about your product during your pitch. Keep everything upbeat and with a positive spin. Don't use any negative terminology such as can't, won't, not, or no. You always need to promote the best elements in your game plus any good selling points that you can think off (Davis, 2010, 1).

Focus on your game's best features and leave minor details out of the picture. If it isn't essential to your game, then you drop it from the presentation (Davis, 2010, 2). Stick to your main features and best-selling points (Davis, 2010, 2; Tunnell, 2007). One significant aspect of the game you will need to talk about is the gameplay of your proposal (Strom, 2015). If you can have a playable demo ready to show, then your presentation will be all the more potent for it (Gameshubadmin, 2017; Tunnell, 2007). Nothing beats being able to demonstrate the product!

Limit the scope of your game to what you (and your team) are capable of (Tunnell, 2007). No one is going to drop a million dollars into your lap if he or she doesn't think you can pull off making the game. You'll likely need a proven track record before any amount of funding happens. Develop that record by making smaller games which are more limited in scope and scale first.

Know your budget and costs beforehand. You need to know how much is required to pay your artists, programmers, managers, and other staff to get the game made (Tunnell, 2007). You will need to be able to say how much it will cost to include each element present in the game and have a solid grip on the finances you are going to need if you want people to take you seriously.

All in all, you need to have your act together to make a compelling pitch that is going to win over your audience and either get you a lot of funding or investment!

What You Can Do with a Game Pitch

Now that you have your presentation, game concept doc, and playable adventure to serve as your game pitch, you can try to get funding for your game. Funding can come from a wide variety of sources and enable you to live while you develop the title yourself, pay your friends to help out, or even let you start a company and hire workers. The game industry is so huge it pays to go digging around for new sources of funding since these are always opening up in sometimes unexpected places. Typically though, you get funding by either acquiring a partner, crowdfunding, finding investors, or obtaining a grant (Perry, 2018).

Partners

Game Pitches can be used to sell your idea to a game company (Gameshubadmin, 2017; Perry, 2018; Tunnell, 2007). Potential partners typically request an official pitch meeting or remote video conference for you to present your game idea to the company execs. Your game pitch will form the core of this presentation, and you can use the adventure you've written as supplemental material. Depending on how much you are bringing to the table the developer will take a share of the profits while assuming a proportional amount of the development cost (Sloper, 2010b; Tunnell, 2007). Realize that these game companies get bombarded with fans pitching random ideas at them all of the time, so if you want to go this route, you need to have your act together and have an extremely impressive and professional pitch. You will need to have a playable demo, video footage, or some animation as well as plenty of great artwork done to get a bunch of professionals to take you seriously (Edge Staff, 2015; Sloper, 2010b; Tunnell, 2007). Make sure your team can project an air of experience and is ready to work (Gameshubadmin, 2017; Perry, 2018). It helps to have a contact within the company beforehand, so you aren't trying to fight your way through a flood of people striving to get someone's attention. Practically speaking, all of this means that some of the people on your team need to have shipped at least one game previously. Otherwise, you can have a tough time convincing a big company to take you seriously. Even if you have everything done correctly, it is still an incredibly difficult job to get a big company to invest in your game (Gameshubadmin, 2017; Sloper, 2010b).

Crowdfunding

You can use your game pitch as a marketing tool to get funding on Kickstarter, Fig, Patreon, or another crowdfunding websites. Crowdfunding sites are a great way to get some initial capital for small start-ups who haven't shipped a title yet (Gameshubadmin, 2017; Perry, 2018). Being successful on these sites is by no means easy. It helps to have a relationship with several web personalities who can help promote your game as well as maintaining a consistently entertaining web presence yourself. Even if you have everything going for, the internet is notoriously fickle and creating a successful marketing campaign of this sort is very time consuming. At best, you probably aren't going to be able to pull in more than twenty thousand dollars, which isn't enough to fund much of a game (Edge Staff, 2015; Perry, 2018). That said, this is still a decent way to get started, but be careful what you promise, and do your research before you get started!

Investors

Investors are anyone else who might be willing to offer you money to finish your product. They can be anyone from your parents or other family members all the way up to various flavors of professional investors (Gameshubadmin, 2017; Perry, 2018). The details will vary enormously depending on with whom you are dealing. Your family might be fairly forgiving with their money while a group of venture capitalists will most certainly not be. An investment is a type of loan, not a gift.

Other Sources

Depending on the product, you might be able to find other sources of money to support your development work. Government grants, bank loans, or companies outside of the game industry are all potential sources of capital (Gameshubadmin, 2017; Perry, 2018). Be creative when looking for non-traditional sources of funding, you never know who might be interested in investing in a potentially lucrative market like video games.

No matter where you get the money for development from always be acutely aware of the terms of any contract or agreement you enter into and consequences of failure if you want to go down this path. Game development is a risky affair that involves an enormous amount of work, management, marketing, and more. Don't get yourself into a terrible financial or legal situation if you can't afford to do so.

Conclusion

The truth is taking your adventure and turning it into a video game is a significant commitment on your part no matter what approach your take. Unless you are an industry professional, a big video game publisher probably won't consider your idea, but this doesn't mean that you can't secure other sources of funding and do it yourself (Sloper, 2010b). If you're not in a position to take financial risks or devote enough time to it, then you can use your adventure as a resume point. The module, in and of itself, shows that you can do level design, characterization, dialog, story, plot, narrative, encounter design, and a host of other critical skills that are central to any successful game designer. It is a significant accomplishment to have created an adventure and maybe even having published it. If you have followed through with everything in this book then you should have the following things in hand:

- A finished table-top role-playing game product for your portfolio.
- Hopefully, you have managed to publish your adventure through Amazon, DriveThruRPG, or even just on an online venue like DragonsFoot.org.
- You've written up a Video Game Concept Document.
- You might have also built a Game Pitch presentation.

Even better you've accomplished the following things:

- You've gained experience with a lot of tough design issues including storytelling, narrative, plot, encounter design, game balancing, level design, and a raft of other game design and development issues and techniques.
- You have honed your writing, art, and layout skills.
- You've even improved your presentation and salesmanship abilities as well.

Make sure you submit your product to the ENnie Awards (www.ennie-awards.com). If you get nominated or win, it will serve as a real mark of distinction on your resume!

Farewell and good luck with your gaming!

Greg Johnson

Appendix

Worksheets

Video Game Concept Document

Project Name:

Owner: Your name goes here

Briefly describe the overall game concept.

Provide a short overview of the story.

What are the key selling points of the game?

What is the game's genre?

What role does the player serve in the game?

What are the player's goal(s) and motivation(s)?

Who is the principal antagonist in the game?

How does the player win or lose the game?

Describe the core game mechanic(s) for this game.

Describe the gameplay experience.

Define the visual style of the game.

Describe the audio style of the game?

Describe the UI (user interface) for the game.

Describe the different game levels.

What similar products have already been released or announced?

Who is the target market?

What makes this game different from the competition?

What technical innovations does this game require?

What are the game's hardware requirements and does the game require any accessories?

What is the expected date of completion?

How can this game be monetized, that is, direct sales, micro-transactions, toys, accessories, and any other potential revenue streams?

Resources

Dice conventions and other definitions can be found in the introductory chapters of each of the table-top role-playing games. This book is compatible with such as *Glory of Yore, Labyrinth Lord, Spells & Wizardry, Castles & Crusades, OSRIC, OD&D,* the first and second editions of *AD&D,* and the Holmes/Moldvay/Mentzer versions of *Basic D&D.*

Table-Top Role Playing Game Systems

Advanced Dungeons & Dragons 1st edition
Basic Dungeons & Dragons
Dungeons & Dragons 3.5 edition
Dungeons & Dragons 5th edition
Call of Cthulhu
Dogs in the Vineyard
Gamma World 1st or 2nd edition
GURPS
Paranoia
Runequest 2nd edition
Shadowrun
Star Wars D6
Toonzy! the Cartoon Role-Playing Game
Traveller
Vampire the Masquerade

Table-Top Role Playing Game Modules

The module and Dungeon adventure lists hereafter are derived from Mona's "The 30 Greatest D&D Adventures of All Time" article in Dungeon magazine 116 and Morrus's "15 Best D&D Modules of All Time" on ENworld.org. The focus is on *D&D* flavored games because that matches the material in this book. There are some wonderful adventures for non-D&D books out there such as *Queen Euphoria* for the *Shadowrun* system, *Masks of Nyarlathotep* for the *Call of Cthulhu* RPG, or some of the *Paranoia* RPG material if you want to explore other systems.

- Low-level Modules (levels 1–3)
  - *B2 Keep on the Borderlands*
  - *B4 The Lost City*
  - *L1 The Secret of Bone Hill*
  - *L2 The Assassin's Knot*
  - *N1 Against the Cult of the Reptile God*
  - *T1-4 The Temple of Elemental Evil*
  - *U1 The Sinister Secret of Saltmarsh*
  - *The Forge of Fury*
- Mid-level Modules (levels 4-7)
  - *A1-4 Scourge of the Slave Lords*
  - *C1 The Hidden Shrine of Tamoachan*
  - *C2 The Ghost Tower of Inverness*
  - *I1 Dwellers of the Forbidden City*
  - *I6 Ravenloft*
  - *WG4 Forgotten Temple of Tharizdun*
  - *X1 Isle of Dread*
  - *X2 Castle Amber*
  - *Dead Gods*
  - *The Gates of Firestorm Peak*
- High-level Modules (levels 8–14)
  - *GDQ1-7 Queen of Spiders*
  - *S1 Tomb of Horrors*
  - *S2 White Plume Mountain*
  - *S3 Expedition to the Barrier Peaks*
  - *S4 Lost Caverns of Tsojcanth*
  - *WGR6 City of Skulls*
  - *City of the Spider Queen*
  - *Dragon Mountain*
  - *For Duty and Deity*
  - *Return to the Temple of Elemental Evil*
- Epic-level Modules (levels 14+)
  - *A Paladin in Hell*

- *Labyrinth of Madness*
- *Return to the Tomb of Horrors*
- *The Bloodstone Pass Saga*
- *The Dancing Hut of Baba Yaga*

Dungeon Magazine Adventure Articles

"*Into the Fire*" by Grant & David Boucher, Dungeon 1, September/October, Fall 1986.

"*Seige of Kratys Freehold*" by Ted James, Thomas Zuvlch, Dungeon 33, January/February 1992.

"*The Mud Sorcerer's Tomb*" by Mike Shel, Dungeon 37, September/October 1992.

"*The Lady of the Mists*" by Peter Aberg, Dungeon 42, July/August 1993.

"*Kingdom of the Ghouls*" by Wolfgang Baur, Dungeon 70, September/October 1998.

"*Eye of Myrkul*" by Eric L. Boyd, Dungeon 73, March/April 1999.

"*The Forgotten Man*" by Steve Devaney, Dungeon 75, July/August 1999.

"*The Harrowing*" by Monte Cook, Dungeon 84, January/February 2001.

"*Life's Bazaar*" by Christopher Perkins, Dungeon 97, March/April 2003.

"*The Lich-Queen's Beloved*" by Christopher Perkins, Dungeon 100, July 2003.

Further Non-Fiction Reading

Campbell, J. *The Hero with a Thousand Faces.*

Capwell, T. *The Real Fighting Stuff: Arms and Armour at Glasgow Museums.*

Cotterell, A. *Chariot: From Chariot to Tank, the Astounding Rise and Fall of the World's First War Machine.*

Dougherty, M.J. *The Medieval Warrior: Weapons, Technology, and Fighting Techniques, AD 1000–1500.*

Edelstein, L. *Writer's Guide to Character Traits.*

Durant, W. and Ariel. *The Age of Faith.*

Durant, W. and Ariel. *The Renaissance.*

Frazer, J.G. *The Golden Bough.*

Gies, J. and Frances. *Life in a Medieval Castle.*

Gies, J. and Frances. *Life in a Medieval City.*

Herodotus. *The Histories.*

Quiggin, A. H. *A Survey of Primitive Money.*

Sturluson, S. *The Prose Edda.*

Trout, P. *Deadly Powers: Animal Predators and the Mythic Imagination.*

Further Fiction Reading

Anderson, Poul *Three Hearts and Three Lions, The Broken Sword.*

Anonymous. *The Epic of Gilgamesh.*

Anthony, Piers *A Spell for Chameleon, The Source of Magic, Castle Roogna.*
Aristotle. *The Poetics.*
Barker, M. A. R. *The Man of Gold, Flamesong, and others.*
Baum, L. F. *The Wonderful Wizard of Oz, and others.*
Burroughs, E. R. *A Princess of Mars, At the Earth's Core, Tarzan of the Apes, and others.*
Carroll, L. *Alice's Adventures in Wonderland, Through the Looking Glass.*
Chambers, R. W. *The King in Yellow.*
Cherryh, C. J. *Gate of Ivrel, Well of Shiuan, Fires of Azeroth, Exile's Gate.*
Cook, G. *The Black Company series, Garrett P.I. series, and others.*
de Camp, L. S. *The Goblin Tower, The Clocks of Iraz, The Unbeheaded King.*
Dunsany, L. *The King of Elfland's Daughter, The Gods of Pegāna.*
Eddison, E. R. *The Worm Ouroboros.*
Feist, R. *The Riftwar Cycle, and others.*
Goodkind, T. *The Sword of Truth, and others.*
Grimm, J. and Wilhelm. *Grimms' Fairy Tales.*
Guest, C. *The Mabinogion.*
Haggard, H. R. *King Solomon's Mines, She.*
Homer. *The Illiad.*
Homer. *The Odyssey.*
Howard, R. E. *Conan The Barbarian, Solomon Kane, Kull, and others.*
Jordan, R. *The Wheel of Time.*
King, S. *The Dark Tower Series.*
Kurtz, K. *Deryni Rising, and others.*
Lackey, M. *Arrows of the Queen, Exile's Honor, Winds of Fate, and others.*
L'Engle, M. *A Wrinkle in Time.*
Le Guin, U. *A Wizard of Earthsea, and others.*
Lee, T. *The Birthgrave.*
Leiber, F. *Fafhrd and the Gray Mouser, and others.*
Lewis, C. S. *The Lion, The Witch, and the Wardrobe, and others.*
Lovecraft, H. P. *The Rats in the Walls, The Call of Cthulhu, At the Mountains of Madness, and others.*
Malory, T. *Le Morte d'Arthur.*
McCaffrey, A. *Dragonriders of Pern, and others.*
McKillip, P. A. *The Riddle-Master of Hed, Heir of Sea and Fire, Harpist in the Wind.*
Moorcock, M. *The Elric Saga, Hawkmoon, Glorianna, and others.*
Moore, C. L. *Jirel of Joiry, and others.*
Mundy, T. *Tros of Samothrace.*
Norton, A. *Witch World series, and others.*
Offutt, A. *Shadowspawn, The Iron Lords, Shadows Out of Hell, The Lady of the Snowmist.*
Pratchett, T. *Reaper Man, The Color of Magic, The Light Fantastic, and others.*
Saberhagen, F. *Book of Swords, and others.*
Shakespeare, W. *The Complete Works of William Shakespeare.*
Smith, C. A. *The Black Diamonds, The Coming of the White Worm, The Dark Eidolon, and others.*
Tolkien, J. R. R. *The Hobbit, The Lord Of The Rings, The Silmarillion.*
Vance, J. *Tales of a Dying Earth, and others.*
Verne, J. *Journey To The Center Of The Earth, Twenty Thousand Leagues Under the Sea.*
Watt-E., L. *The Lords of Dus Series.*

Weis, M. and Hickman, T. *The Dragonlance Chronicles.*
Wellman, M. W. *Worse Things Waiting, and others.*
Wells, H. G. *The Time Machine.*
White, T. H. *The Once And Future King.*
Wolfe, G. *The Shadow of the Torturer, The Claw of the Conciliator, The Sword of the Lictor, The Citadel of the Autarch, The Urth of the New Sun.*
Zelazny, R. *The Amber Chronicles, and others.*

Films

The Lost World (1925)
Tarzan the Ape Man (1932)
King Kong (1933)
The Adventures of Robin Hood (1938)
The Wizard of Oz (1939)
The Thief of Bagdad (1940)
Seven Samurai (1954)
The Seventh Seal (1957)
The 7th Voyage of Sinbad (1958)
Spartacus (1960)
Jason and the Argonauts (1963)
Willy Wonka & the Chocolate Factory (1971)
Fantastic Planet (1973)
The Three Musketeers (1973)
The Four Musketeers (1974)
Zardoz (1974)
The Land That Time Forgot (1975)
Monty Python and the Holy Grail (1975)
Wizards (1977)
The Hobbit (1977)
Superman (1978)
Flash Gordon (1980)
Time Bandits (1981)
Excalibur (1981)
Dragonslayer (1981)
Clash of the Titans (1981)
The Sword and the Sorcerer (1982)
The Dark Crystal (1982)
The Beastmaster (1982)
Conan the Barbarian (1982)
Krull (1983)
Ghostbusters (1984)
Red Sonja (1985)

Ladyhawke (1985)
Highlander (1986)
Big Trouble in Little China (1986)
The Princess Bride (1987)
Evil Dead II (1987)
Willow (1988)
The Adventures of Baron Munchausen (1988)
Erik the Viking (1989)
Delicatessen (1991)
Army of Darkness (1992)
The City of Lost Children (1995)
The Mummy (1999)
The 13th Warrior (1999)
Gladiator (2000)
The Lord of the Rings: The Fellowship of the Ring (2001)
The Lord of the Rings: The Two Towers (2002)
The Lord of the Rings: The Return of the King (2003)
Hellboy (2004)
The Brothers Grimm (2005)
Pan's Labyrinth (2006)
300 (2006)
John Carter (2012)
Mad Max: Fury Road (2015)

Websites

A good site to buy lots of RPG products. drivethrurpg.com.

An online language construction kit. www.zompist.com/kit.html.

A repository of lots of AD&D resources from the early days of the interweb www.textfiles.com/rpg/.

A source for many strange tables and ideas. elfmaidsandoctopi.blogspot.com.

A wonderful source of old books, films, and websites. archive.org.

Foldup Paper Models for gaming with miniatures. archive.wizards.com/default.asp?x=dnd/fpm/archive.

Home to a world of legal and free ebooks. www.gutenberg.org.

How to build your own fantasy world. www.world-builders.org.

How to use Google to beef up your RPG experience. www.nerdsourced.com/use-google-to-buff-your-rpgs/.

Morrus' Unofficial Tabletop RPG News and forum website. www.enworld.org.

The all devouring pop-culture wiki. tvtropes.org.

The home page for the "Glory of Yore RPG." www.madmutantgames.com.

The internet sacred text archive. A good site for source material for creating your own religions and cultures. www.sacred-texts.com.

The website for the current version of the D&D game. dnd.wizards.com.

References

@mikemearls. "*5e lifetime PHB sales > 3, 3.5, 4 lifetime #WOTCstaff.*" Twitter, August 12, 2016, 4:27 p.m., twitter.com/mikemearls/status/764241988128419840.

"*5E: How to reward players without piles of magic items?*" Reddit, July 2016, www.reddit.com/r/DnD/comments/4uvhoe/5e_how_to_reward_players_without_piles_of_magic/. Web. Accessed May 28, 2017.

Achberger, S. B. et al. "*How do Can I Come up with Fantasy Names and Places?*" Quora, April 2017, www.quora.com/How-do-can-I-come-up-with-fantasy-names-and-places. Web. Accessed August 6, 2018.

Achterman, D. "*The Craft of Game Systems: General Guidelines.*" Gamasutra. UBM Technologies, November 18, 2011, www.gamasutra.com/view/news/128271/The_Craft_of_Game_Systems_General_G. Web. Accessed August 23, 2016.

Adams, E. W. *The High Concept Document.* Ernest W. Adams, 2008, www.csc.kth.se/utbildning/kth/kurser/DH2640/grip08/HighConceptTemplate-Inl4.pdf. Web. Accessed August 1, 2018.

Adducci, R. "*D&D Adventurers League Marketing Resources.*" D&D Adventurers League. Wizards of the Coast, April 10, 2015, dndadventurersleague.org/marketing-resources/. Web. Accessed August 30, 2016.

Amirault, A. "*12 Famous People Who Play D&D.*" Tribality, May 12, 2015, www.tribality.com/2015/05/12/12-famous-people-play-dd/. Web. Accessed August 30, 2016.

Anderson, T. "*The History of Zork.*" Wayback Machine. New York Times, 1985, web.archive.org/web/20060427000213/http://www.csd.uwo.ca/Infocom/Articles/NZT/zorkhist.html. Web. Accessed September 2, 2016.

Anthony, M. "*Answer Is…The Riddle!.*" Dragon 175, November 1991: 91–94.

Appelcline, S. *"A Brief History of Game #1: Wizards of the Coast: 1990-Present."* RPG.net. Skotos Tech, Inc., 2006.

Aristotle. *Poetics*. Translated by S. H. Butcher, Web Atomics, 1994–2000, classics.mit.edu/Aristotle/poetics.mb.txt. Web. Accessed December 31, 2016.

ARK Survival Evolved Wiki. *"Crafting."* GamePedia. Curse Inc., August 8, 2016, ark.gamepedia.com/Crafting. Web. Accessed August 25, 2016. www.rpg.net/columns/briefhistory/briefhistory1.phtml. Web. Accessed August 30, 2016.

"Authentic Names." Regia Anglorum, 2004, regia.org/members/names.php. Web. Accessed August 6, 2018.

Bartle, R. *Designing Virtual Worlds*. New Riders, 2003.

Bartle, R. *"Early MUD History."* R. Bartle, 1990a, mud.co.uk/richard/mudhist.htm. Web. Accessed September 3, 2016.

Bartle, R. *"Hearts, Clubs, Diamonds, Spades: Players Who Suit MUDs."* R. Bartle, 1996, mud.co.uk/richard/hcds.htm. Web. Accessed September 25, 2016.

Bartle, R. *"MUD History, Who Invented MUD's, How MUD's Were Invented."* LivingInternet.com, November 15, 1990b, www.livinginternet.com/d/di_major.htm. Web. Accessed August 23, 2016.

Bartle, R. *"Reviews - UK."* Bartle, 1999, mud.co.uk/richard/imucg4.htm. Web. Accessed August 23, 2016.

Barton, M. *"The History of Computer Role-Playing Games Part III: The Platinum and Modern Ages (1994–2004)."* Gamasutra. UBM Technologies, April 11, 2007, www.gamasutra.com/view/feature/129994/the_history_of_computer_.php?print=1. Web. Accessed August 28, 2016.

Barton, M. and Loguidice, B. *"A History of Gaming Platforms: Atari 2600 Video Computer System/VCS."* Gamasutra. UBM Technologies, October 19, 2013, www.gamasutra.com/view/feature/131956/a_history_of_gaming_platforms_.php. Web. Accessed August 28, 2016.

Barwood, H. and Falstein, N. *The 400 Project Rule List*. Finite Arts. Hal Barwood, March 18, 2006, www.finitearts.com/Storage/400_Project_Master_Rule_List_032306.zip. Accessed May 2, 2017.

Beatty, K. J. *Human Leopards*. Hugh Rees, Ltd., 1915.

Beedle, M. et al. *Principles behind the Agile Manifesto*. Wayback Machine. Agile Alliance, 2001, web.archive.org/web/20100614043008/http://www.agilemanifesto.org/principles.html. Web. Accessed August 28, 2016.

Blizzard Entertainment. *"Games."* Blizzard Entertainment, 2016, us.blizzard.com/en-us/games/. Web. Accessed August 28, 2016.

Blizzard Entertainment. *"World of Warcraft."* Blizzard Entertainment, 2004, Microsoft Windows. Video Game.

Bond, C. *"7 Historical Parallels to Game of Thrones."* Mental Floss, Inc., May 9, 2014. mentalfloss.com/article/56558/7-historical-parallels-game-thrones. Web. Accessed July 18, 2018.

Bowery, J. *"Spasim (1974) The First First-Person-Shooter 3D Multiplayer Networked Game."* J. Bowery, 2001, web.archive.org/web/20010410145350/http://www.geocities.com/jim_bowery/spasim.html. Web. Accessed September 2, 2016.

Boyer, B. and Cifaldi, F. *"The Gamasutra Quantum Leap Awards: Role-Playing Games."* Gamasutra. UBM Technologies, October 6, 2006, www.gamasutra.com/view/feature/1809/the_gamasutra_quantum_leap_awards_.php?print=1. Web. Accessed August 28, 2016.

Brathwaite, B. and Schreiber, I. Challenges for Game Designers. Charles River Media, August 2008.

Bratt, C. "*25 years of Civilization: We talk with Sid Meier.*" Eurogamer. Gamer Network, October 2016, www.eurogamer.net/articles/2016-10-19-25-years-of-civilization-we-talk-with-sid-meier. Web. Accessed July 7, 2018.

Brown, E. and Cairns, P. "*A Grounded Investigation of Game Immersion.*" *CHI '04 Extended Abstracts on Human Factors in Computing Systems*, April 24–29, 2004, 1297–1300.

Brown, T. B. and Denning, T. *Dark Sun Boxed Set.* TSR, Inc., 1991.

Buzan, T. "*Mind Mapping.*" Tony Buzan, 2011, web.archive.org/web/20160318012000/http://www.tonybuzan.com/about/mind-mapping/. Web. Accessed October 31, 2016.

Campbell, J. *The Hero with a Thousand Faces.*" Pantheon Books, 1949.

Carroll, J. "*How to Research Your next Game's Target Audience for Free.*" Gamasutra. UBM Technologies, March 13, 2017. www.gamasutra.com/blogs/JustinCarroll/20170313/258979/How_to_Research_Your_next_Games_Target_Audience_for_Free.php. Web. Accessed July 7, 2018.

Castronova, E. *Synthetic Worlds: The Business and Culture of Online Games.* University of Chicago Press, 2006, 10, 291.

Chaosium. "*About Us.*" Chaosium, Inc., n.d. www.chaosium.com/about-chaosium/. Web. Accessed August 30, 2016.

Chaosium. *Basic Roleplaying.* Chaosium, Inc. www.chaosium.com/basic-roleplaying/. Web. Accessed August 25, 2016.

Chaosium. "*Call of Cthulhu.*" Chaosium, Inc. www.chaosium.com/on-call-of-cthulhu/. Web. Accessed August 25, 2016.

Chua, C. "*25 Useful Brainstorming Techniques.*" Personal Excellence, 2016, personal-excellence.co/blog/brainstorming-techniques/. Web. Accessed October 31, 2016.

Church, T. "*Gamasutra: Thomas Church's Blog - The Basics of MMO Story Writing.*" Gamasutra. UBM Technologies, December 15, 2012, www.gamasutra.com/blogs/ThomasChurch/20121215/183609/The_Basics_of_MMO_Story. Web. Accessed August 23, 2016.

Circular 3. U.S. Copyright Office, February 2013, www.copyright.gov/circs/circ03.pdf. Web. Accessed July 22, 2017.

Cline, C. M. "*The 7-Sentence NPC.*" Dragon 184, August 1992, pp. 22–24.

Colley, S. "*Stories from the Maze War 30 Year Retrospective.*" DigiBarn Computer Museum, 1998, www.digibarn.com/history/04-VCF7-MazeWar/stories/colley.html. Web. Accessed August 28, 2016.

Cook, D. "*Loops and Arcs.*" Lostgarden. N.p., April 29, 2012, www.lostgarden.com/2012/04/loops-and-arcs.html. Web. Accessed August 24, 2016.

Cook, D. *Planescape.* TSR, Inc., 1994.

Cook, M. "*Dungeoncraft: Dungeon Adventures, Part 2: The Map.*" Dragon 310, August 2003b, 92–95.

Cook, M. "*Dungeoncraft: Dungeon Adventures, Part 3: The Inhabitans.*" Dragon 311, September 2003c, v96–99.

Cook, M. "*Dungeoncraft: Dungeon Adventures, Part 4: The Weird Stuff.*" Dragon 312, October 2003d, 94–96.

Cook, M. "*Dungeoncraft: Characterization, Part 1: Bringing Your Characters To Life.*" Dragon 320, June 2004a, 104–106.

Cook, M. "*Dungeoncraft: Characterization, Part 2: One DM, One Millions Characters.*" Dragon 321, July 2004b, 92–95.

Cook, M. *"Dungeoncraft: Designing Wilderness Adventures: Into The Wild."* Dragon 317, March 2004c, pp. 96–98.

Costikyan, G. *"I Have No Words & I Must Design."* Interactive Fantasy: The Journal of Role-Playing and Story-Making Systems (2), Hogshead Publishing, 1994, London, UK.

Costikyan, G. et al. *Paranoia*. West End Games, 1984.

Cousineau, P. *The Hero's Journey: Joseph Campbell on His Life and Work*. Harper & Row, 1990.

Craddock, D. L. *Dungeon Hacks: How NetHack, Angband, and Other Roguelikes Changed the Course of Video Games*. Press Start Press, 2015.

Cross, K. *"What Tabletop Games Can Teach Video Games about 'Wandering.'"* Gamasutra. UBM Technologies, December 14, 2015a, www.gamasutra.com/view/news/261293/ What_tabletop_games_can_teach_video_games_about_w. Web. Accessed August 23, 2016.

Cross, K. *"Q&A: Wickerman Explores What Tabletop Games Can Teach Video Game Devs."* Gamasutra. UBM Technologies, October 15, 2015b, www.gamasutra.com/view/ news/257234/QA_Wickerman_explores_what_tabletop_games_can_teach_video_ game_devs.php. Web. Accessed August 23, 2016.

Cyber Creations Inc. *"MMORPG Games - All MMO Games."* mmORPG.com. Cyber Creations Inc., 2002, www.mmorpg.com/gamelist.cfm/show/all/All-Games.html. Web. Accessed August 26, 2016.

Dancey, R. S. *"Adventure Game Industry Market Research Summary (RPGs) V1.0."* Wizards of the Coast. 2000, www.seankreynolds.com/rpgfiles/gaming/WotCMarket ResearchSummary.html. Web. Accessed September 18, 2016.

Davis, C. *"How To Pitch Your Project To Publishers."* Gamasutra. UBM Technologies, November 10, 2010, www.gamasutra.com/view/feature/134571/how_to_pitch_your_ project_to_.php?print=1. Web. Accessed November 7, 2016.

Dee, J. and Herman, J. *Villains & Vigilantes*. Fantasy Games Unlimited, 1979.

Demachy, T. *"Extreme Game Development: Right on Time, Every Time."* Gamasutra. UBM Technologies, July 16, 2003, www.gamasutra.com/view/feature/131236/extreme_ game_development_right_on_.php. Web. Accessed August 28, 2016.

Dent, L. *"The Lester Dent Pulp Master Fiction Plot."* Paper Dragon Productions, May 1, 2013, www.paper-dragon.com/1939/dent.html. Web. Accessed January 18, 2017.

Department of the Army. *TC 5–31 Viet Cong Boobytraps, Mines, and Mine Warfare Techniques*. U.S. Army, May 1967.

DeVarque, A. R. *"Literary Sources of D&D."* Wayback Machine. DeVarque, 2009, web. archive.org/web/20091027151422/http://geocities.com/rgfdfaq/sources.html. Web. October 27, 2009. Accessed August 26, 2016.

deYoung, M. *"One Face of the Devil: The Satanic Ritual Abuse Moral Crusade and the Law."* Behavioral Sciences & the Law 12(4), 1994, 389–407. doi: 10.1002/bsl.2370120408. Web.

Donovan, D. *For Duty & Deity*. TSR, Inc., 1998.

Dreyer, B. *"Going Agile - The 7 Simple Stages of Why and How to Get it Done (I'm not saying easy)."* Gamasutra. UBM Technologies, April 4, 2013, www.gamasutra.com/blogs/ BrianDreyer/20130408/190077/Going_Agile__The_7_Simple_Stages_of_Why_and_ How_to_Get_it_Done_Im_not_saying_easy.php. Web. Accessed August 28, 2016.

Dunn, J. *"Bullets & Bombs: The history of first-person shooters."* GamesRadar+. Future Publishing Limited, 2008, www.gamesradar.com/bullets-bombs-history-first-person-shooters/. Web. Accessed September 5, 2016.

Dunnell, B. "*Dungeon Mastery: Great Rewards.*" Dragon 267, January 2000, pp. 84–86.

Edge Staff. "*How to pitch your game to publishers.*" Games Radar. Future Publishing Limited, February 23, 2015, www.gamesradar.com/how-pitch-your-game-publishers/. Web. Accessed July 7, 2018.

Emmerich, R., director. *Stargate.* Metro-Goldwyn-Mayer, et al., 1994.

Emsley, C. et al. "*London History - Currency, Coinage and the Cost of Living.*" Old Bailey Proceedings Online, version 7.0, May 23, 2017, www.oldbaileyonline.org/static/Coinage.jsp#coinage, Web. Accessed May 23, 2017.

Ewalt, D. M. *Of Dice And Men.* Scribner, 2013.

Finch, M. *Swords & Wizardry.* Fantasy Flight Games, 2008.

Flash Gordon. Directed by Mike Hodges, performances by Melody Anderson, Sam J. Jones, Max von Sydow, and Topol, Starling Films, 1980.

Forster, E. M. *Aspects of the Novel.* Mariner Books, 1956.

Fowler, M. and Highsmith, J. *The Agile Manifesto.* Agile Alliance, 2001.

Freeman, T. "*Creating A Great Design Document.*" Gamasutra. UBM Technologies, September 12, 1997, www.gamasutra.com/view/feature/131632/creating_a_great_design_document.php. Web. Accessed July 31, 2018.

Furness, William Henry III. "*Stone Money of Uap.*" 1903, String Figures, by Caroline Furness Jayne, Charles Scribner's Sons, 1906, opposite p. 160. commons.wikimedia.org/wiki/File:Stone_Money_of_Uap,_1903,_Jayne,_String_Figures,_p.160.jpg. Web. Accessed August 9, 2018.

Gameshubadmin. "*How To Fund Your Indie Game.*" The Games Hub, April 10, 2017, thegameshub.com/fund-indie-game/. Web. Accessed July 7, 2018.

Gamespot. "*Metroid.*" Wayback Machine. CBS Interactive Inc., 2013, web.archive.org/web/20131003050311/www.gamespot.com/gamespot/features/video/hist_metroid/p2_01.html. Web. Accessed September 2, 2016.

Gard, T. "*Action Adventure Level Design: Kung Fu Zombie Killer.*" Gamasutra. UBM Technologies, May 7, 2010, www.gamasutra.com/view/feature/4413/action_adventure_level_design_.php. Web. Accessed August 29, 2016.

Gazzard, A. "*Unlocking the Gameworld: The Rewards of Space and Time in Videogames.*" Games Studies 11(1), February 2011, gamestudies.org/1101/articles/gazzard_alison. Web. Accessed July 22, 2018.

Gemperlein, J. and Scheinman, T. "*An Interview with Nolan Bushnell.*" Wayback Machine. The Tech Museum of Innovation, 2000, web.archive.org/web/20000823135348/www.thetech.org/revolutionaries/bushnell/i_a.html. Web. Accessed September 2, 2016.

Gerstmann, J. "*The Legend of Zelda Review.*" Game Spot. CBS Interactive Inc., November 22, 2006, www.gamespot.com/reviews/the-legend-of-zelda-review/1900-6162256/. Web. Accessed September 2, 2016.

Glancey, P. *The Complete History of Computer and Video Games.* Emap Images, 1996.

Granato, L. "*Boons and Benefits.*" Dragon 217, May 1995, 10–16.

Greene, J. "*How to Pitch Your Game 101.*" Gamasutra. UBM Technologies, October 11, 2017, gamasutra.com/blogs/JasmineGreene/20171011/307342/How_to_Pitch_Your_Game_101.php. Web. Accessed July 31, 2018.

Greenwood, E. "*What Has He Got In His Pocketses, Anyway?*" Dragon 164, n.d., 80–82.

Gruden, M. "*Some Renaissance & Baroque Examples of Religious Symbolism in Art.*" Faculty/Staff home pages, Virginia Commonwealth University, n.d., www.people.vcu.edu/~djbromle/art-symbolism/student-projects-2001/Religious-Symbolism-renaissance-gruden.html. Web. Accessed May 21, 2017.

Guss, M. "*The Secrets of Successful Dungeon Building*." Dragon 227, March 1996, pp. 8–13.

Gygax, G. *Dungeon Masters Guide*. TSR, 1979a.

Gygax, G. *The Keep on the Borderlands*. TSR, Inc., 1979b.

Gygax, G. *Players Handbook*. TSR, 1978a.

Gygax, G. *Dungeon Module S1 Tomb of Horrors*. TSR Hobbies, Inc., 1978b.

Gygax, G. *Dungeon Module G 1–2-3 Against the Giants*. TSR Hobbies, Inc., 1981.

Gygax, G. and Arneson, D. *Dungeons & Dragons*. 1st ed. Vol. 1. Tactical Studies Rules, 1974. 3 vols.

Gygax, G. and Arneson, D. *Dungeons & Dragons Fantasy Adventure Game Basic Rulebook*, edited by Moldvay, T., TSR, 1981.

Haas, B. "*Some Notes On How You Do It*." Ben Haas, 1975, jamesreasoner.blogspot.com/2012/02/how-to-write-pulp-western-ben-haas.html. Web. Accessed August 4, 2018.

Hallford, N. and J. Hallford. *Swords and Circuitry: A Designer's Guide to Computer Role Playing Games*. Premier Press Incorporated, 2001.

Hammack, A. *Dungeon Module C2 The Ghost Tower of Inverness*. TSR Hobbies, Inc., 1980.

Harris, J. "*Gamasutra - Game Design Essentials: 20 RPGs*." Gamasutra. UBM Technologies, July 2, 2009, www.gamasutra.com/view/feature/4066/game_design_essentials_20_rpgs.php?print=1. Web. Accessed August 23, 2016.

Hartzog, S. "*Branching Narrative*." Stephen Hartzog, 2003, www.nukes.org/ds4/assign/branching.html. Web. Accessed July 19, 2018.

Hausman, C. "*Write Like a Pro: Ten Techniques for Getting Your Point Across at Work (and in Life)*." Praeger March 28, 2016.

Hedlund, J. "*Character Worksheet*." Blog. Jody Hedlund, 2010, jodyhedlund.blogspot.com/p/character-worksheet.html. Web. Accessed April 17, 2017.

Hiwiller, Z. "*What Is Systems Design? (02)*." Zack Hiwiller. Hiwiller.com, January 12, 2011, www.hiwiller.com/2011/01/11/what-is-systems-design. Web. Accessed August 23, 2016.

How to Write for the Press. London, Horace Cox, 1899.

Huizinga, J. *Homo Ludens*. Routledge & Kegan Paul Ltd., 1949.

Humphrey, B. "*Something Completely Different*." Dragon 179, March 1992, 21–24.

Humphries, M. "*World of Warcraft peaked at 12 million players, World of Tanks just passed 75 million*." Geek.com. Matthew Humphries, December 16, 2013, www.geek.com/games/world-of-warcraft-peaked-at-12-million-players-world-of-tanks-just-passed-75-million-1579885/. Web. Accessed November 13, 2018.

Hunicke, R. et al. "MDA: A Formal Approach to Game Design and Game Research." *In Proceedings of the Challenges in Games AI Workshop, Nineteenth National Conference of Artificial Intelligence*. 2004, 1–5.

Hunter, W. "*Player 1 Stage 1: Bits From the Primordial Ooze*." emuunlim. William Hunter, 2000a, www.emuunlim.com/doteaters/play1sta1.htm. Web. Accessed September 2, 2016.

Hunter, W. "*Player 1 Stage 2: Atari Rising*." emuunlim. William Hunter, 2000b, www.emuunlim.com/doteaters/play1sta2.htm. Web. Accessed September 2, 2016.

Hunter, W. "*Player 3 Stage 6: The Great Videogame Crash*." emuunlim. William Hunter, 2000c, www.emuunlim.com/doteaters/play3sta6.htm. Web. Accessed September 2, 2016.

Hunter, W. "*Player 4 Stage 1: The Productivity Eaters*." emuunlim. William Hunter, 2000d, www.emuunlim.com/doteaters/play4sta1.htm. Web. Accessed September 2, 2016.

Indvik, L. "*The Fascinating History of Online Role-Playing Games*." Mashable.com, November 14, 2012, mashable.com/2012/11/14/mmorpgs-history/#99SBLLEqNuqK. Web. Accessed August 23, 2016.

Irvine, I. *"60 Ways To Create and Heighten Conflict."* Ian Irvine, 2016. www.ian-irvine.com/on-writing/60-ways-to-create-conflict/. Web. Accessed July 15, 2015.

Iwatani, T. et al. *Pac-Man.* Namco, 1980. Video game.

Janes, J. *Fundamentals of Humor.* TSM Artists Inc., 2014.

Jackson, S. *Generic Universal RolePlaying System.* Steve Jackson Games, 1986.

Jerz, D. G. *"Somewhere Nearby Is Colossal Cave: Examining Will Crowther's Original 'Adventure' in Code and in Kentucky."* Digital Humanities Quarterly 1(2), 2007: n. pag. www.digitalhumanities.org/dhq/vol/001/2/000009/000009.html. Web. Accessed September 2, 2016.

Jon, A. A. "The Development of MMORPG Culture and The Guild." *Australian Folklore: A Yearly Journal of Folklore Studies 25,* 2010, 97–112. www.researchgate.net/publication/283281457_The_Development_of_MMORPG_Culture_and_The_Guild. Web. Accessed August 22, 2016.

Jones, N. T. *"The Orr Group Industry Report: Q1 2015."* Roll 20 Blog. The Orr Group, LLC. April 15, 2015, blog.roll20.net/post/116828584295/the-orr-group-industry-report-q1-2015. Web. Accessed August 30, 2016.

Jury, A. *"The History, Current State of OGL Publishing, Pathfinder, and 'd20'."* A. Jury, March 28, 2015, adamjury.com/2015/the-history-current-state-of-ogl-publishing-pathfinder-and-d20/. Web. Accessed September 8, 2016.

Juul, J. "A Clash between Game and Narrative." *First International SKIKT Conference on Digital Arts and Culture,* SKIKT, November 1998, Bergen, Norway. Paper.

Keith, C. *"Agile Game Development With Scrum: Teams."* Gamasutra. UBM Technologies, August 26, 2010a, www.gamasutra.com/view/feature/134412/agile_game_development_with_scrum_.php. Web. Accessed August 28, 2016.

Keith, C. *"The State of Agile in the Game Industry."* Gamasutra. UBM Technologies, March 4, 2010b, www.gamasutra.com/view/feature/132683/the_state_of_agile_in_the_game_.php. Web. Accessed August 28, 2016.

Kelling, A. *"Writing a GDD your team can actually use."* Gamasutra. UBM Technologies, October 6, 2014, www.gamasutra.com/blogs/AbbyFriesen/20141006/227048/Writing_a_GDD_your_team_can_actually_use.php. Web. Accessed July 31, 2018.

Kent, S. *"Electronic Nation."* Videotopia. Steven L. Kent, 1997. www.videotopia.com/edit2.htm. Web. Accessed September 2, 2016.

Kim, J. *"Free RPG List: open-license."* DarkShire.net. J. Kim, 2015a. web.archive.org/web/20161007154237/http://www.darkshire.net:80/jhkim/rpg/freerpgs/bykeyword/open-license.html. Web. Accessed September 8, 2016.

Kim, J. *"RPG Company List."* Darkshire.net. J. Kim, April 14, 2016, web.archive.org/web/20160922062714/http://www.darkshire.net:80/jhkim/rpg/freerpgs/fulllist.html. Web. Accessed August 30, 2016.

Kim, J. *"What Is a Role-Playing Game?"* Darkshire.net. J. Kim, April 10, 2009, web.archive.org/web/20161110074433/http://www.darkshire.net:80/jhkim/rpg/whatis. Web. Accessed August 23, 2016.

Kim, J. *"Mobile Game Design: Iteration vs. Planning, MVP = Dangerous!."* Gamasutra. UBM Technologies, February 24, 2015b, www.gamasutra.com/blogs/JosephKim/20150224/237157/Mobile_Game_Design_Iteration_vs_Planning_MVP__Dangerous.php. Web. Accessed August 28, 2016.

Kupersmith, K. *"Agile is a Fad."* BAtimes.com. July 4, 2011, www.batimes.com/kupe-kupersmith/agile-is-a-fad.html. Web. Accessed August 28, 2016.

Lawrence, D. M. *"Telengard."* Aquest.com. Daniel M. Lawrence, n.d., www.aquest.com/telen.htm. Web. Accessed September 2, 2016.

Lee, J. *"Game Reward Systems."* Learning Theories, January 15, 2016, www.learning-theories.com/game-reward-systems.html. Web. Accessed May 20, 2017.

Lievano, G. *"Story Driven vs. Gameplay Driven Game Design."* Gamasutra. UBM Technologies, May 27, 2010, www.gamasutra.com/blogs/GabrielLievano/20100527/87415/Story_Driven_vs_Gameplay_Driven_Game_Design.php. Web. Accessed January 31, 2016.

Lindsay, C. *"August 2016 D&D Survey."* Hasbro, Inc., 2016, dnd.wizards.com/articles/features/august-2016-dd-survey. Web. Accessed September 18, 2016.

Linnell, J. D. C. et al. *The fear of wolves: A review of wolf attacks on humans.* NINA: Norsk institutt for naturforskning, 2002.

Livingstone, I. *Dicing with Dragons.* Plume Books, 1983.

LoPresti, M. *"Assassin's Creed: The Failed Hashshashin Simulator and its Aftermath."* Gamasutra. UBM Technologies, December 17, 2010. www.gamasutra.com/blogs/MatthewLoPresti/20101217/88494/Assassins_Creed_The_Failed_Hashshashin_Simulator_and_its_Aftermath.php. Web. Accessed July 15, 2018.

Lovecraft, H. P. *"Notes on Writing Weird Fiction."* Donovan K. Loucks, 2009, www.hplovecraft.com/writings/texts/essays/nwwf.aspx. Web. Accessed September 17, 2016.

Lovejoy, B. *"8 Supposedly Cursed Gems."* Mental Floss. Mental Floss, Inc., 2016. mentalfloss.com/article/68465/8-supposedly-cursed-gems. Web. Accessed May 28, 2017.

Lucas, G., director. *Star Wars Episode IV: A New Hope.* Twentieth Century Fox, 1977.

Lucas, G., director. *Star Wars Episode V: The Empire Strikes Back.* Twentieth Century Fox, 1980.

Ludgate, S. *"Virtual Economic Theory: How MMOs Really Work."* Gamasutra. UBM Technologies, November 16, 2010, www.gamasutra.com/view/feature/134576/virtual_economic_theory_how_mmos_.php?print=1. Web. Accessed August 26, 2016.

MacDonald, G. et al. *Champions.* Hero Games, 1981.

Machin, C. *"A Brief History of the MMO."* CGMagazine, 2001, www.cgmagonline.com/2015/11/12/a-brief-history-of-the-mmo/. Web. Accessed September 5, 2016.

Mandryka, A. *"Fun and uncertainty."* Game Whispering, Inc., July 12, 2012, gamewhispering.com/fun-and-uncertainty/. Web. Accessed July 2, 2017.

Marshall, S. *OSRIC.* S. Marshall, 2008.

Matuszek, D. *"Design Patterns and Refactoring."* University of Pennsylvania, 2003, www.cis.upenn.edu/~matuszek/cit591-2003/Lectures/49-design-patterns.ppt. Power point presentation. Accessed August 28, 2016.

McChristian, J. A. *Mines and booby traps used by the Viet Cong in South Vietnam.* U.S. Army, November 1965. PDF.

McGuire, R. *"Paper Burns: Game Design with Agile Methodologies."* Gamasutra. UBM Technologies, June 28, 2006, www.gamasutra.com/view/feature/131151/paper_burns_game_design_with_.php. Web. Accessed August 28, 2016.

McIntosh, B. et al. *"Nonlinear Narrative in Games: Theory and Practice."* Game Career guide, August 17, 2010, www.gamecareerguide.com/features/882/nonlinear_narrative_in_games_.php?print=1. Web. Accessed August 11, 2018.

McRoberts, B. et al. *"PC Gen."* pcgen.org. PC Gen, 2016, pcgen.org/about/. Web. Accessed August 30, 2016.

Memory Alpha. *"Vulcan."* FANDOM, 2018, memory-alpha.wikia.com/wiki/Vulcan. Web. Accessed August 6, 2018.

Meulle, V. *"Agile, a Practical Point of View."* Gamasutra. UBM Technologies, July 7, 2014, www.gamasutra.com/blogs/VincentMeulle/20140702/220083/Agile_a_practical_point_of_view.php. Web. Accessed August 28, 2016.

Miller, P. *"Top 10 Pitfalls Using Scrum Methodology for Video Game Development."* Gamasutra. UBM Technologies, July 15, 2008, www.gamasutra.com/view/feature/132121/top_10_pitfalls_using_scrum_.php. Web. Accessed August 28, 2016.

Miller, Pace, J. *"The Art of Fantasy Names."* Pace J. Miller, March 1, 2009, pacejmiller.wordpress.com/2009/03/01/the-art-of-fantasy-names/. Web. Accessed August 6, 2018.

Mona, E. et al. *"The 30 Greatest D&D Adventures of All Time."* Dungeon 116, November 2004: 69–81.

Moorcock, M. *"How to Write a Novel in 3 Days."* Ghostwoods, May 2010, www.ghostwoods.com/2010/05/how-to-write-a-book-in-three-days-1210/. Web. Accessed March 12, 2017.

Morrison, B. *"Meaningful Choice in Games: Practical Guide & Case Studies."* Gamasutra. UBM Technologies, November 19, 2013, www.gamasutra.com/blogs/BriceMorrison/20131119/204733/Meaningful_Choice_in_Games_Practical_Guide__Case_Studies.php. Web. Accessed December 31, 2016.

Morrissey, R. *"15 Best D&D Modules of All Time."* Morrus's Unofficial Tabletop RPG News, January 5, 2015, www.enworld.org/forum/content.php?2206-The-15-Best-Official-D-D-Modules-Of-All-Time. Web. Accessed August 5, 2018.

Murray, J. H. *Hamlet on the Holodeck.* The Free Press, 2017.

Nakamura, J. and Csikszentmihalyi, M. "Flow theory and research." *Oxford Handbook of Positive Psychology*, edited by C. R. Snyder and S. Lopez, Oxford University Press, 2009, 195–206.

Neidlinger, J. *"4 Simple Brainstorming Techniques That Will Help You Write Killer Content."* CoSchedule Blog. Coschedule, 2015, coschedule.com/blog/brainstorming-techniques/. Web. Accessed October 31, 2016.

News Team. *"The History of…First Person Shooters."* TacticalGaming.net News, February 14, 2014, www.tacticalgaming.net/hq/news/2014/the-history-first-person-shooters. Web. Accessed September 5, 2016.

Nichiporchik, A. *"How to Pitch Your Game."* Gamasutra. UBM Technologies, September 17, 2015, www.gamasutra.com/blogs/AlexNichiporchik/20150917/253886/How_To_Pitch_Your_Game.php. Web. Accessed July 31, 2018.

Niles, D. *Dungeon Module N1 Against the Cult of the Reptile God.* TSR Hobbies, Inc., 1982.

Norvelle, A. *Glory of Yore.* Mad Mutant Games, 2016.

Nutt, C. *"AGDC: Bateman Reveals the 'Temperament Theory'."* Gamasutra. UBM Technologies, September 12, 2007, www.gamasutra.com/view/news/106421/AGDC_Bateman_Reveals_The_Temperament_Theory.php. Web. Accessed July 19, 2018.

Nutt, C. *"The Elegance of Metroid: Yoshio Sakamoto Speaks."* Gamasutra. UBM Technologies, April 23, 2010, www.gamasutra.com/view/feature/4333/the_elegance_of_metroid_yoshio_.php. Web. Accessed August 28, 2016.

Ohannessian, K. *"Dungeons & Dragons Next' Creators Look to Simplicity, Open Development to Regain Lost Gamers."* Fast Company & Inc. Mansueto Ventures, LLC, 2012, www.fastcocreate.com/1679620/dungeons-dragons-next-creators-look-to-simplicity-open-development-to-regain-lost-gamers. Web. Accessed August 30, 2016.

Olchawska, M. *Pitching e-Book.* Magda Olchawska, 2015. PDF.

Olivetti, J. *"The Game Archaeologist and the Ultima Prize: The History."* Engadget. Aol Tech, 2010, www.engadget.com/2010/05/04/the-game-archaeologist-and-the-ultima-prize-the-history/. Web. Accessed September 5, 2016.

Parlett, D. *The Oxford History of Board Games.* Oxford University Press, 1999.

Parr, T. *"Extreme Programming."* CS601/CS342: Object-Oriented Software Development. University of San Francisco, January 21, 2009, www.cs.usfca.edu/~parrt/course/601/lectures/xp.html. Web. Accessed August 28, 2016.

Passuello, L. "*What is Mind Mapping? (and How to Get Started Immediately)*." Litemind. Luciano Passuello, 2016, litemind.com/what-is-mind-mapping/. Web. Accessed October 31, 2016.

Pepe, F. "*Amnesiac Heroes: Why Are We Abandoning Gaming History?*" Gamasutra. UBM Technologies, January 9, 2014, www.gamasutra.com/blogs/FelipePepe/20141009/227370/Amnesiac_Heroes_Why_are_we_abandoning_gaming_history.php. Web. Accessed August 23, 2016.

Perrin, C. "*The Open Game License: A Case Study in Open Source Markets*." TechRepublic. CBS Interactive, July 14, 2011, www.techrepublic.com/blog/linux-and-open-source/the-open-game-license-a-case-study-in-open-source-markets/. Web. Accessed August 30, 2016.

Perrin, S. and Turney, R. *Runequest*. Chaosium, 1978.

Perry, W. "*How Learning Games Get Funded*." Gamasutra. UBM Technologies, April 30, 2018, www.gamasutra.com/blogs/WickPerry/20180430/317216/How_Learning_Games_Get_Funded.php. Web. Accessed July 7, 2018.

Petersen, S. *Call of Cthulhu*. Chaosium, 1981.

Peterson, J. "*The Ambush at Sheridan Springs How Gary Gygax Lost Control of Dungeons & Dragons*." Medium.com. A Medium Corporation, July 28, 2014, medium.com/@increment/the-ambush-at-sheridan-springs-3a29d07f6836. Web. Accessed August 30, 2016.

Phillips, C. J. et al. "Videogame Reward Types." *In Proceedings of the First International Conference on Gameful Design, Research and Applications*. University of Waterloo, October 2–4, 2013, Ontario, eprints.qut.edu.au/65011/. Web. Accessed May 20, 2017.

Pitts, R. "*Fallout: The Game That Almost Never Was*." Polygon. Vox Media, March 8, 2012, www.polygon.com/gaming/2012/3/8/2855595/fallout-gdc-black-isle-interplay-obsidian-bethesda. Web. Accessed September 5, 2016.

Powers, M. "*A Game Concept*." Gamasutra. UBM Technologies, April 21, 2014, www.gamasutra.com/blogs/MattPowers/20140421/214272/A_Game_Concept.php. Web. Accessed July 31, 2018.

Pratchett, T. *The Discworld Companion*. Victor Gollancz, 1994.

Proctor, D. *Labyrinth Lord*. Goblinoid Games, 2010.

Quiggin, A. H. *A Survey of Primitive Money*. Methuen & Co. Ltd., 1949.

Radoff, J. "History of Social Games." Wayback Machine. Radoff.com, April 23, 2012, web.archive.org/web/20120423074120/http://radoff.com/blog/2010/05/24/history-social-games/. Web. Accessed August 23, 2016.

Rantaeskola, S. "*The Myth of Agile Empowerment*." Gamasutra. UBM Technologies, October 23, 2013, www.gamasutra.com/blogs/SamuelRantaeskola/20131023/202975/The_Myth_of_Agile_Empowerment.php. Web. Accessed August 28, 2016.

Raush, A. "*Magic & Memories: The Complete History of Dungeons & Dragons - Part I*." Gamespy. IGN Entertainment, August 16, 2004a, pc.gamespy.com/articles/538/538262p1.html. Web. Accessed August 30, 2016.

Raush, A. "*Magic & Memories: The Complete History of Dungeons & Dragons - Part II*." Gamespy. IGN Entertainment, August 26, 2004b, pc.gamespy.com/articles/539/539197p1.html. Web. Accessed August 30, 2016.

Raush, A. "*Magic & Memories: The Complete History of Dungeons & Dragons - Part III*." Gamespy. IGN Entertainment, August 17, 2004c, pc.gamespy.com/articles/539/539628p3.html. Web. Accessed August 30, 2016.

Raush, A. "*Magic & Memories: The Complete History of Dungeons & Dragons - Part IV*." Gamespy. IGN Entertainment, August 18, 2004d, pc.gamespy.com/articles/539/539972p1.html. Web. Accessed August 30, 2016.

Raush, A. "*Magic & Memories: The Complete History of Dungeons & Dragons - Part V.*" Gamespy. IGN Entertainment, August 19, 2004e, pc.gamespy.com/articles/540/540509p1.html. Web. Accessed August 30, 2016.

Raush, A. and Lopez, M. "*A History of D&D Video Games - Part II.*" Gamespy. IGN Entertainment, August 16, 2004f, pc.gamespy.com/articles/539/539300p1.html. Web. Accessed September 5, 2016.

Realmshelp. "*Feats Finder.*" Realmshelp.net, 2016, www.realmshelps.net/charbuild/feat-search.shtml. Web. Accessed August 30, 2016.

Reeve, C. "*Exploring Interactive Narrative – Traditional Storytelling.*" Carlton Reeve, October 14, 2010a, playwithlearning.com/2010/10/14/exploring-interactive-narrative-part-1-of-6. Web. Accessed July 17, 2018.

Reeve, C. "*Exploring Interactive Narrative – Branching.*" Carlton Reeve, October 21, 2010b, playwithlearning.com/2010/10/21/exploring-interactive-narrative-part-2. Web. Accessed July 17, 2018.

Reeve, C. "*Exploring Interactive Narrative – Parallel Paths.*" Carlton Reeve, October 28, 2010c, playwithlearning.com/2010/10/28/exploring-interactive-narrative-part-3. Web. Accessed July 17, 2018.

Reeve, C. "*Exploring Interactive Narrative – Non-linear.*" Carlton Reeve, November 2, 2010d, playwithlearning.com/2010/11/02/exploring-interactive-narrative-non-linear. Web. Accessed July 17, 2018.

Reeve, C. "*Exploring Interactive Narrative – Dynamic.*" Carlton Reeve, November 10, 2010e, playwithlearning.com/2010/11/10/exploring-interactive-narrative-dynamic. Web. Accessed July 17, 2018.

Rein-Hagen, M. *Vampire: The Masquerade.* White Wolf Publishing, 1991.

Reynolds, S.K. "*Breakdown of RPG Players.*" seankreynolds.com, November 29, 2005, www.seankreynolds.com/rpgfiles/gaming/BreakdownOfRPGPlayers.html. Web. Accessed May 21, 2017.

Rogers, S. *Level Up!: The Guide to Great Video Game Design.* Chichester, John Wiley & Sons, Ltd., 2010.

Rose, M. "*Understanding the Realities of Video Game Monetization.*" Gamasutra. UBM Technologies, November 22, 2013, www.gamasutra.com/view/news/205412/Understanding_the_realities_of_video_game_monetization.php. Web. Accessed August 1, 2018.

Rosewater, M. *Ten Things Every Game Needs, Part 1 & Part 2.* Making Magic. Wizards of the Coast LLC, December 19, 2011, magic.wizards.com/en/articles/archive/making-magic/ten-things-every-game-needs-part-1-part-2-2011-12-19. Web. Accessed April 7, 2017.

Rosner, E. "*Brainstorming Techniques That Will Make You a Creative Genius.*" Bloominari. San Diego Digital Marketing & Creative Agency, 2014, www.bloominari.com/blog/brainstorming-techniques-that-will-make-you-a-creative-genius. Web. Accessed October 31, 2016.

Rossney, R. "*Metaworlds.*" Wired. Conde Nast, June 1, 1996, www.wired.com/1996/06/avatar-2/?pg=3. Web. Accessed September 6, 2016.

Rourensu. "*How Do You Come Up with Names for People/Places in Fantasy Writing?*" Reddit, Inc., 2017, www.reddit.com/r/fantasywriters/comments/5dicip/how_do_you_come_up_with_names_for_peopleplaces_in/. Web. Accessed August 6, 2018.

Rubin, K. *Overview of the Scrum Framework.* Scrum Alliance, 2018, www.scrumalliance.org/ScrumRedesignDEVSite/media/ScrumAllianceMedia/Files%20and%20PDFs/Agile%20Resources/S_OverviewofScrumFrame_1.pdf. Web. Accessed July 14, 2018.

Rundle, M. "*HG Wells' 'Little Wars': How an Icon of Sci-Fi Invented Modern War Games 100 Years Ago.*" Huffpost Tech United Kingdom, March 9, 2013, www.huffingtonpost.co.uk/2013/04/09/hg-wells-little-wars-how-_n_3044934.html. Web. Accessed August 29, 2016.

Ryan, T. "*Beginning Level Design, Part 1.*" Gamasutra. UBM Technologies, April 16, 1999a, www.gamasutra.com/view/feature/131736/beginning_level_design_part_1.php. Web. Accessed July 2, 2017.

Ryan, T. "*Beginning Level Design Part 2: Rules to Design by and Parting Advice.*" Gamasutra. UBM Technologies, April 23, 1999b, www.gamasutra.com/view/feature/131739/beginning_level_design_part_2_.php. Web. Accessed July 2, 2017.

Ryan, T. "*The Anatomy of a Design Document, Part 1: Documentation Guidelines for the Game Concept and Proposal.*" Gamasutra. UBM Technologies, October 19, 1999c, www.gamasutra.com/view/feature/3384/the_anatomy_of_a_design_document_.php Web. Accessed July 31, 2018.

Ryan, T. "*The Anatomy of a Design Document, Part 2: Documentation Guidelines for the Functional and Technical Specifications.*" Gamasutra. UBM Technologies, December 17, 1999d, www.gamasutra.com/view/feature/131818/the_anatomy_of_a_design_document_.php. Web. Accessed July 31, 2018.

Sailer, B. "*How to Find Your Target Audience and Create the Best Content That Connects.*" CoSchedule, August 1, 2016, coschedule.com/blog/how-to-find-your-target-audience/. Web. Accessed July 2, 2017.

Salen, K. and Zimmerman, E. *Rules of Play: Game Design Fundamentals.* MIT Press, 2004.

Saltzman, M. and Bleszinski, C. "*Secrets of the Sages: Level Design.*" Gamasutra. UBM Technologies, July 23, 1999, www.gamasutra.com/view/feature/131767/secrets_of_the_sages_level_design.php?page=6. Web. Accessed May 10, 2017.

Sandars, N. K. *The Epic of Gilgamesh.* Harmondsworth: Penguin, 1972.

Sanders, A. "*Early English Currency, Roman Numerals for Dates and Currency, and Tally Sticks.*" Goucher College, 2014, faculty.goucher.edu/eng240/early_english_currency.htm. Web. Accessed May 23, 2017.

Schreiber, I. "*Level 10: Nonlinear Storytelling.*" Ian Schreiber, July 30, 2009, gamedesignconcepts.wordpress.com/2009/07/30/level-10-nonlinear-storytelling/. Web. Accessed July 16, 2018.

Schell, J. *The Art of Game Design: A Book of Lenses.* Morgan Kaufmann Publishers, 2008.

Scholar, The Lazy. "*How to Create a Character Profile.*" The Internet Writing Journal, Writers Write, Inc., June 1998, www.writerswrite.com/journal/jun98/how-to-create-a-character-profile-6986. Web. Accessed April 17, 2017.

Schroeder, D. "*Planning Creative Treasures.*" The Dragon III(5), October 1978: 13.

Scott, M. "*A Monument to the Player: Preserving a Landscape of Socio-Cultural Capital in the Transitional MMORPG.*" New Review of Hypermedia & Multimedia 18.4, 2012: 295–320. www.tandfonline.com/doi/abs/10.1080/13614568.2012.746743. Web. Accessed August 23, 2016.

Scott, R., director. *Gladiator.* Red Wagon Entertainment, Scott Free Productions, 2000.

Selinker, M. "*Logic Missiles.*" Dragon 282, April 2001: 34–41.

Selinker, M. "*Powerword: Baffle.*" Dragon, 271, May 2000: pp. 6–35.

Sellers, M. *Advanced Game Design: A Systems Approach.* Pearson Education, Inc., 2018.

Shapiro, D. "*A Brief History of Gaming.*" The Game Journal. D. Shapiro, March 2004, www.thegamesjournal.com/articles/BriefHistory.shtml. Web. Accessed September 6, 2016.

Sicart, M. "*Defining Game Mechanics.*" The International Journal of Computer Game Research 8.2, 2008: gamestudies.org/0802/articles/sicart. Web. Accessed August 22, 2016.

Siembieda, K. *Palladium Fantasy Role-Playing Game.* Palladium Books, Inc., 1983.

Siembieda, K. *Rifts.* Palladium Books, 1990.

SirotaSOFT. "*The History of Rebus.*" SirotaSOFT, 2014, rebus1.com/en/index.php?item=history_of_rebus. Web. Accessed May 9, 2017.

Sloper, T. "*Frequently Asked Question #2: Sample outline for a Game Design Document.*" Sloperama Productions, July 2010a, www.sloperama.com/advice/specs.htm. Web. Accessed August 1, 2018.

Sloper, T. "*Game Design 101.*" Sloperama Productions, July 2010b, www.sloperama.com/advice/idea.htm. Web. Accessed August 1, 2018.

Smith, A. "*1TL200: A Magnavox Odyssey.*" They Create Worlds. A. Smith, January 22, 2014a, videogamehistorian.wordpress.com/2015/11/16/1tl200-a-magnavox-odyssey/. Web. Accessed September 2, 2016.

Smith, A. "*One, Two, Three, Four I Declare a Space War.*" They Create Worlds. A. Smith, January 22, 2014b, videogamehistorian.wordpress.com/2014/08/07/one-two-three-four-i-declare-a-space-war/. Web. Accessed September 2, 2016.

Smith, A. "*The Priesthood at Play: Computer Games in the 1950s.*" They Create Worlds. A. Smith, January 22, 2014c, videogamehistorian.wordpress.com/2014/01/22/the-priesthood-at-play-computer-games-in-the-1950s/. Web. Accessed September 2, 2016.

Smith, A. et al. "*SHADES - What the Computer Magazines USED to Say.*" Games World, 2003, games.world.co.uk/shades/inshades/history/Mags.htm. Web. Accessed September 5, 2016.

Smith, H. "*Player Character Concepts.*" Gamasutra. UBM Technologies, November 8, 1999, www.gamasutra.com/view/feature/131798/player_character_concepts.php. Web. Accessed August 3, 2018.

Sponias, C. "*How to Keep a Dream Journal - Free Psychotherapy in Your Own Dreams.*" Journal for You! Deborah Watson-Novacek, 2012, journalforyou.com/how-to-keep-a-dream-journal-free-psychotherapy-in-your-own-dreams/. Web. Accessed October 31, 2016.

SSI. *Pool of Radiance.* Strategic Simulations, Inc., 1988, MS-DOS. Video Game.

St. Andre, K. and Steve, P. *Stormbringer.* Chaosium, Inc., 1981.

Stackpole, M. "*The Pulling Report.*" Rpgstudies.net. M. Stackpole, 1990, www.rpgstudies.net/stackpole/pulling_report.html. Web. Accessed August 30, 2016.

Stafford, G. and Willis, L. *Basic Role-Playing.* Chaoisum, 1980.

Stevens, L. "*Paizo Publishing's 10th Anniversary Retrospective - Year 0 (2002).*" Paizo Blog, Paizo, February 9, 2012, paizo.com/paizo/blog/v5748dyo5ld43?Paizo-Publishings-10th-Anniversary. Web. Accessed August 30, 2016.

Stewart, W. "*Summary MUD History.*" LivingInternet, W. Stewart, 2000, www.livinginternet.com/d/di_major.htm. Web. Accessed September 5, 2016.

Stormfront Studios. *Neverwinter Nights.* Strategic Simulations, Inc., 1991. MS-DOS. Video Game.

Stout, M. "*Learning from the Masters: Level Design in the Legend of Zelda.*" Gamasutra. UBM Technologies, January 3, 2012, www.gamasutra.com/view/feature/134949/learning_from_the_masters_level_.php. Web. Accessed July 2, 2017.

Strom, D. "*How to Pitch Your Game to Publishers.*" Gamasutra. UBM Technologies, August 21, 2015, www.gamasutra.com/blogs/DanielStrm/20150821/251906/How_to_Pitch_Your_Game_to_Publishers.php. Web. Accessed July 7, 2018.

Studio Wildcard. Instinct Games, Efecto Studios and Virtual Basement *Ark: Survival Evolved*. Studio Wildcard, 2016. Microsoft Windows.

Sullivan, G. *How to Win at Video Games*. Scholastic Book Services, 1982.

Superplay Magazine. "*Miyamoto Interview*." Wayback Machine. A. Robinson/C. Johnson, April 23, 2003, web.archive.org/web/20060907074051/http://www.miyamotoshrine.com/theman/interviews/230403.shtml. Web. Accessed September 2, 2016.

Sutherland, J. "*What Every Game Developer Needs to Know about Story*." Gamasutra. UBM Technologies, July 27, 2005, www.gamasutra.com/view/feature/130770/what_every_game_developer_needs_to_.php. Web. Accessed July 15, 2018.

Sutherland, J. and Schwaber, K. "*The Scrum Guide*." Scrum.Org and Scrum Inc., 2016, www.scrumguides.org/scrum-guide.html. Web. Accessed August 28, 2016.

Tassi, P. "'*World of Warcraft' Still A $1B Powerhouse*." Forbes, July 19, 2014, www.forbes.com/sites/insertcoin/2014/07/19/world-of-warcraft-still-a-1b-powerhouse-even-as-subscription-mmos-decline/#5d0ce8c07725. Web. Accessed August 22, 2016.

Taylor, C. "*Design Document for: Name of Game*." RunawayStudios.com, 2018, www.runawaystudios.com/articles/ctaylordesigntemplate.docx. Web. Accessed July 31, 2018.

Taylor, D. "*Ten Principles of Good Level Design (Part 1)*." Gamasutra. UBM Technologies, September 29, 2013, www.gamasutra.com/blogs/DanTaylor/20130929/196791/Ten_Principles_of_Good_Level_Design_Part_1.php. Web. Accessed July 2, 2017.

Tedman, R. A. and Tedman, D. K. *Evolution of Teaching and Learning Paradigms in Intelligent Environment*. Springer, 2007.

Tennant, G. *SIX SIGMA: SPC and TQM in Manufacturing and Services*. Gower Publishing, 2001. ISBN: 0-566-08374-4.

Thoman, P. "*2014: The First Year of the CRPG Renaissance*." PCgamer, December 31, 2014, www.pcgamer.com/2014-the-first-year-of-the-crpg-renaissance/. Web. Accessed August 23, 2016.

Thompson, J. "*The Tunnels*." Vietnam Veterans Association of Australia (Victorian Branch Inc.), 2002. web.archive.org/web/20021124033225/http://home.vicnet.net.au:80/~vvaaeduc/content/Cu%20Chi%20Aust%20Story.html. Web. Accessed October 23, 2018.

Timmons, D. H. "*How to Create a Color Mood Board*." About Inc., 2016, www.thespruce.com/how-to-create-a-color-mood-board-797789. Web. Accessed August 28, 2016.

Tolkien, J. R. R. "*The Hobbit*." George Allen & Unwin, 1937.

Tolkien, J. R. R. "*The Lord of the Rings*." George Allen & Unwin, 1968.

Tresca, M. J. "*The Evolution of Fantasy Role-Playing Games*." McFarland, 2010.

Troika Games. *The Temple of Elemental Evil*. Atari, 2003. Microsoft Windows. Video Game.

Trout, P. A. *Deadly Powers*. Prometheus Books, 2011.

Tunnell, J. "*How to Pitch Your Game*." Jeff Tunnell, September 5, 2007, makeitbigingames.com/2007/09/how-to-pitch-your-game/. Web. Accessed July 7, 2018.

TV Tropes. "*Tabletop Game/Gamma World*." TV Tropes, n.d. tvtropes.org/pmwiki/pmwiki.php/TabletopGame/GammaWorld. Web. Accessed August 30, 2016.

TV Tropes. "*Vancian Magic - TV Tropes*." TV Tropes, n.d. tvtropes.org/pmwiki/pmwiki.php/Main/VancianMagic. Web. Accessed August 24, 2016.

Tweet, J. et al. "*System Reference Document*." Wizards of the Coast, Inc., 2000–2003, www.wizards.com/default.asp?x=d20/article/srd35. Web. Accessed June 12, 2018.

Van Eck, R. *Gaming and Cognition: Theories and Practice from the Learning Sciences*. IGI Global, 2010.

Varney, A. "*Retro-Clones*." The Escapist. Defy Media LLC, August 27, 2009, www.escapistmagazine.com/articles/view/tabletop/columns/days-of-high-adventure/6415-Retro-clones. Web. Accessed August 30, 2016.

Vego, M. *"German War Gaming."* Naval War College Review 65(4), Autumn 2012: Naval War College Press, 2012, Newport, RI.

Velde, F. *"Canting Arms."* Heraldica. Francois Velde, March 1997, www.heraldica.org/topics/canting.htm. Web. Accessed May 9, 2017.

Venis, L. *Inside the Room: Writing TV with the Pros at UCLA Extension Writers' Program.* Penguin Publishing Group, 2013.

Vogel, C. *The Writer's Journey: Mythic Structure for Writers.* Michael Wiese Productions, 2007.

Wargaming. *"About World of Tanks."* World of Tanks.com, Wargaming, 2016a, worldoftanks.com/en/content/guide/general/. Web. Accessed August 25, 2016.

Wargaming. *"Achievements."* Wargaming.net Wiki. Wargaming, 2016b, wiki.wargaming.net/en/Achievements. Web. Accessed May 28, 2017.

Wargaming. *"Battle Mechanics."* Wargaming.net Wiki. Wargaming, 2016c, wiki.wargaming.net/en/Battle_Mechanics. Web. Accessed August 25, 2016.

Wawro, A. *"20 Years Later, David Brevik Shares the Story of Making Diablo."* Gamasutra. UBM Technologies, March 18, 2016. www.gamasutra.com/view/news/268507/20_years_later_David_Brevik_shares_the_story_of_making_Diablo.php. Web. Accessed August 28, 2016.

Weis, M. et al. *Dragonlance Campaign Setting.* Wizards of the Coast, 2003.

Weisman, J. et al. *Shadowrun.* FASA Corporation, 1990.

Whitehead, C. *"2016 ENnie Award Winners."* ENnies, 2016, www.ennie-awards.com/blog/about-us/2014-ennie-awards-nominees/2015-ennie-award-winners/2016-ennie-award-winners/. Web. Accessed July 29, 2018.

Wichman, Glenn. *"A Brief History of 'Rogue'."* Wayback Machine. Glenn R. Wichman, 1997, web.archive.org/web/20050829080411/http://www.wichman.org/roguehistory.html. Web. Accessed September 2, 2016.

Williams, S. *"Treasures More Real."* Dragon 168, April 1991: 79–82.

Winninger, R. *"Dungeoncraft."* Dragon 262, August 1999b: 18–20.

Winninger, R. *"Dungeoncraft."* Dragon 263, September 1999c: 18–20.

Winninger, R. *"Dungeoncraft."* Dragon 264, October 1999d: 16–20.

Winninger, R. *"Dungeoncraft."* Dragon 265, November 1999e: 16–20.

Winter, D. *"Noughts and Crosses - The Oldest Graphical Computer Game."* pong-story. David Winter, July 8, 2013, www.pong-story.com/1952.htm. Web. Accessed September 2, 2016.

Wintjes, J. *"Europe's Earliest Kriegsspiel? Book Seven of Reinhard Graf zu Solms' Kriegsregierung and the 'Prehistory' of Professional War Gaming."* Researchgate.net, 2015, www.researchgate.net/publication/283461658_Europe's_Earliest_Kriegsspiel_Book_Seven_of_Reinhard_Graf_zu_Solms'_Kriegsregierung_and_the_'Prehistory'_of_Professional_War_Gaming. Web. Accessed January 22, 2017.

Wizards of the Coast. *"Systems Reference Document (SRD)."* Wizards of the Coast, LLC. Hasbro, 2016, dnd.wizards.com/articles/features/systems-reference-document-srd. Web. Accessed September 8, 2016.

Wizards RPG Team. *Dungeons & Dragons 3.5 Dungeon Master's Guide.* Wizards of the Coast, 2003.

Wizards RPG Team. *Dungeons & Dragons 3.5 Player's Handbook.* Wizards of the Coast, 2012.

WoWpedia. *"Ice Lance."* GamePedia. Curse Inc., August 16, 2016, wow.gamepedia.com/Ice_Lance. Web. Accessed August 25, 2016.

WoWwiki. *"Skill."* WoWwiki. Fandom Games Community, n.d., wowwiki.wikia.com/wiki/Skill. Web. Accessed August 26, 2016.

Wyatt, P. *"24 Pro Tips for Creating Inspirational Mood Boards."* Creative Bloq. Future Publishing Limited Quay House, January 27, 2014, www.creativebloq.com/graphic-design/mood-boards-812470. Web. Accessed April 30, 2017.

Zimmerman, E. *"How I Teach Game Design. (Lesson 1: The Game Design Process)."* Gamasutra. UBM Technologies, October 19, 2013, www.gamasutra.com/blogs/EricZimmerman/20131019/202710/How_I_Teach_Game_Design_Lesson_1_The_Game_Design_Process.php. Web. Accessed August 28, 2016.

Zucker-Scharff, A. *"Branching Narrative Schema and Similar Narrative Structures."* Aram Zucker-Scharff, March 2, 2011, hacktext.com/2011/03/branching-narrative-schema-and-similar-narrative-structures-834/. Web. Accessed July 19, 2018.

Index

9 780367 137885